Huaihua International Inland Port

Modern China Series

Huaihua International Inland Port

Shu Xiaohui
Hou Tengteng
Tian Guang

North American Business Press

Huaihua International Inland Port

ISBN: 978-1-948915-34-2

North American Business Press
Atlanta, Georgia
Miami, Florida
New York, New York
Toronto, Canada

FIRST PRINTING, 2024

About Modern China Series

As one of the oldest civilized regions globally, China has emerged as a "new world" because it embraces its essence and heritage and links them to viable economic strategies. In the last 25 years, China has made tremendous strides. The country and its people have every right to take pride in these accomplishments. Many Chinese leaders and intellectuals anticipate continuing growth with these successes. Furthermore, China's plans and strategies are often based on this premise.

The U.S. has tremendous interest in the Chinese economy and business environment. China has emerged as a global superpower, and scholars and business people in the U.S. are keenly interested in learning how this will affect them and do business with China. In response to growing interest from international and Asian scholars, North American Business Press is pleased to announce our Modern China Series (MCS) books. It is the first book series about modern China in the U.S., garnering tremendous interest in the U.S. and worldwide. With our first book reaching stores in September 2011, this initiative develops relationships between NABP and Chinese scholars. They desire to promote their academic and applied business writings to the rest of the world.

We have had an overwhelming demand for the Modern China Series from authors who would like to publish in the series and people who would like to read the books. The books have been viewed by thousands of people from the U.S. and the rest of the world. There are currently ten books published in the series, and we have a couple of dozen books that we are considering for the series.

We have published books on several areas revolving around the Chinese business environment. We have a few that focus on the best practices in marketing in China; some are compared to "best practices" in doing business in China, and a few are on the outlook of the Chinese economy. The market for the Modern China Series is enormous. There are tens of thousands of scholars who are keenly interested in the continued growth of the Chinese economy and the implications that it will have on the business world. Even more significant are the millions of business people interested in the impact that China will continue to have on the global economy. It is difficult to pinpoint the exact demand for the series, but it Is enormous.

We have big plans to grow the Modern China Series. It can be one of the most significant economic/business series ever produced. We are very selective with the books we will add to the collection, but we encourage scholars who think they have unique and exciting perspectives on China to submit their book manuscripts. From the readers' perspective, we are committed to producing high-quality books regularly, so readers should expect a steady stream of insightful books to come out for many years.

This initiative is headed by Dr. Robert Tian, a renowned researcher and academic. He spearheads our efforts to partner with foreign authors and administer the day-to-day operations of this series. Dr. Tian, the Vice-President of North American Business Press and Editor of this series, spends much of his time in Beijing, Shanghai, and other Chinese cities, focusing on developing and managing our interests with authors and universities. Below is the list of the books we have published:

Enterprise Strategy: New Horizon, authored by Zhang Xiuyu

Governance of Private Enterprises in Modern China, authored by Zhong Qin

The Art of War and Enterprise Strategy Management, authored by Fu Shouzhi

Marketing Issues in Modern China, edited by Robert Guang Tian et al.

The Footprints of the Academician, authored by Fu Zhouzhi

Marketing and Economics in Modern China (I) edited by Xiaoguang Qi et al.

Marketing and Economics in Modern China (II) edited by Wang Tianjin et al.

An Islamic Heritage in China, authored by Ma Zhanming

China Environmental Anthropology authored by Wang Tianjin, Tian Guang, and Ma Jianfu

Can China Rule the New World? Authored by Tian Guang and Chen Gang

Critiques on Pan-marketization authored by Li Cunlin, Liu Hongfei, and Tian Guang
Economic and Business Anthropology in China, edited by Xiaoguang Qi and Tian Guang
China-Mongolia Economic Corridor authored by Eerdun Taoketao, Zhang Zhe, Wang Gang, and Wei Lisi
Anthropology of Chinese Foodways authored by Tian Guang and Chen Gang
Urbanization of Rural China, authored by Li Taohong
Child Rearing in Rural China by Jiang Youchun and Yang Yunyi
Belt and Road vs. China and World by Tian Guang and Chen Gang
Modernization of China by Tian Guang, Luo Kanglong and Chen Qian
Abnormal School Behaviors: China vs. South Korea by Yu Yanyan
China in Xi Jinping Era by Shu Xiaohui, Li Yangkuo and Tian Guang
Shi Zhengyi and Chinese Ethnological Economics by Tian Guang and Zhong Ni
Decoding Entrepreneurial Vision by Fan Xiaoping
Huaihua International Inland Port by Shu Xiaohui, Hou Tengteng and Tian Guang

Table of Contents

Preface

In the current globalized economic landscape, the construction and development of international inland ports are significant for promoting regional economic growth and strengthening international trade cooperation. Our book entitled *Huaihua International Inland Port* focuses on the development strategy, competitiveness, spillover effects, impact on China-Laos trade, and residents' housing demand due to the development of the Huaihua International Inland Port. It gives readers a comprehensive and three-dimensional perspective on the development and associated effects.

As an essential node of the new land-sea corridor in western China, the construction and development of the Huaihua International Inland Port not only concerns the economic prosperity of the Huaihua region but also strongly promotes the development of an open economy in inland China. Our book aims to provide valuable references for relevant policymakers, business managers, and academic researchers through a detailed study of the inland port to promote sustainable development and further enhance its function and role in the regional economy and international trade.

Our book first analyzes the existing research and development strategies of Huaihua International Inland Port, re-evaluates its strategic positioning, explores new strategic directions on the Chinese and international stages, and puts forward some constructive suggestions. Subsequently, by constructing an indicator system for the competitiveness of international inland ports, using the combination of subjective and objective weighting method and grey relational TOPSIS method, empirical analysis and ranking were conducted on the competitiveness of 182 major international inland ports in China, providing a reference basis for improving the competitiveness of inland ports. In addition, the SARIMA time series analysis model was also used to analyze the spillover effects of the inland port on the regional and surrounding economies based on the general public budget revenue of local governments in Huaihua International Inland Port Economic

Development Zone, Hecheng District, and Zhijiang Dong Autonomous County.

At the same time, our book examines the strategic role and functions of Huaihua International Inland Port in China-Laos trade from a new perspective. It explores its current development status and potential. It provides new ideas for promoting bilateral economic and trade cooperation between China and Laos. Moreover, through the study of the housing market in the Huaihua area, the impact of the inland port on the housing demand of residents was analyzed, providing a basis for the local government and related industries to make rational decisions. In addition, our book explores the necessity and feasibility of building a comprehensive regulatory center in Huaihua. It proposes corresponding suggestions to provide more extensive support for the development of Huaihua International Inland Port.

We believe that our book has essential theoretical and practical significance for a deeper understanding of the development laws of international inland ports, promoting the construction of Huaihua International Inland Port construction, and promoting regional economic development. We hope this book can provide readers with valuable information and inspiration and jointly promote research and development in international inland ports.

Acknowledgment

When this book is finally presented to the public, we are filled with emotions and gratitude. The completion of this book owes to the assistance of many scholars and colleagues, such as Lv Lu, Xiao Sidi, and Li Yangkuo, teachers from the School of Business, Huaihua University. They have offered a great deal of inspiration for the writing of this book, and here we express our appreciation to them. We are indebted to Ms. Ashley Young, who aided us in translating a large quantity of the text from Chinese to English. We are grateful for the support from the Hunan Provincial Social Science Foundation's Western Project, "Research on Hunan's Joint Construction of the Western Land Sea New Corridor." Project No. 23YBX004. Finally, we thank the editorial team of North America Business for their encouragement and dedicated work.

Foreword

New Perceptions on Strategic Positioning of Huaihua International Inland Port

Tianjin Wang

Minzu University of China

International inland ports are a unique concept in international economic development. Located at the intersection of railroads and highways in the inland economic centers, they are the ports of commerce open to the outside world following the relevant international transport regulations, treaties, practices and domestic regulations. They are stations facilitating cargo handling, transportation, storage, distribution, and the distribution of related international freight documents. They have facilities and equipment such as parking lanes, cargo inspection, loading and unloading platforms, warehouse yards, sorting plants, office buildings, and production and living facilities. Moreover, they can handle documents, inspect goods, load and unload, and store and distribute them for international freight transportation. From the history of international economic and social development, constructing the international port is essential for inland cities to seek economic growth. It can build an open pattern for inland areas with massive channels, platforms and hubs. With the strong support of the central government and Hunan government departments at all levels, Huaihua City, Hunan Province, has stepped up the construction of the international inland port and deeply integrated it with China's Belt and Road Initiative and related projects. The economic achievements of the international inland port have already been manifested. However, it is necessary to accelerate the pace of construction and contribute more to promoting the economic and social development of China's central and western inland regions.

New Path in the Economic Development of Contemporary Countries

The construction of inland ports is relatively new in contemporary countries' economic development. Many related problems need to be solved by Chinese and foreign experts. The concept of inland ports has been interpreted in many ways. Munford (1980) examined the inadequacy of container handling equipment and available space at the Port of Buenos Aires, Argentina. He proposed a program to develop new container berths at the port with participation from the private sector. The concept of inland port projects emerged for the first time. It is mainly defined as building terminals in the hinterland area to alleviate the transportation pressure of the coastal port corridor and share the freight pressure of the area where the port is located. Since the emergence of inland port projects, scholars worldwide have varied definitions of inland ports. The United Nations Conference on Trade and Development (UNCTAD) defined an inland port as a place inland fulfilling original port functions in 1982 (Cullinane and Wilmsmeier, 2011).

More scholars have conducted related research as inland port construction continues to develop overseas. Walter and Poist (2003), professors at Iowa State University, evaluated the establishment of an inland port in central Iowa. They argue that the inland port concept was introduced to provide facilities and information, enabling shippers and carriers to handle exports and imports better. Roso, Woxenius and Lumsden (2009), research fellows at Chalmers University of Technology in Gothenburg, Sweden, concluded that the construction of inland ports could relieve some congestion in seaport towns and provide improved logistical solutions for shippers in the port hinterland. Inland ports in North America and Europe have been in place for over 20 years. However, scholars have summarized the concepts from actual projects, which are still confined to shippers and carriers and some congestion in seaport cities. In recent years, inland port construction has been generally sluggish, mainly affected by the anti-globalization forces in Europe and North America.

In 2008, China's central government approved the construction of Xi'an International Trade & Logistics Park, the first inland trade port established in China. People in China have been yearning and struggling to build inland ports using the Chinese style. In August 2019, China's National Development and Reform Commission issued the Framework Plan for New Land and Marine Routes for Western Regions. In this document, Huaihua City in Hunan Province was positioned as an essential node city on the main channel linking Chongqing, Huaihua, Liuzhou and Beibu Gulf (the National Development and Reform Commission, 2019). CPC Huaihua Municipal Committee and Huaihua MunicipalPeople's Government decided to promote the construction of Huaihua International Inland Port as a strategic project. The people of Huaihua City work together to speed up the project. On January 6, 2022, Huaihua International Inland Port launched the first international freight train of the China-Laos Railway (Huaihua-Vientiane). It was the first international line from Hunan Province to the Association of Southeast Asian Nations (ASEAN) countries. This train carried goods such as sweet oranges from Mayang, small agricultural machines from Shuangfeng County, and small excavators from SANY HEAVY INDUSTRY CO., LTD., traveling about 2,098 kilometers (Chen, 2022). These products are well-marketed for their high quality and low prices. Mayang Miao Autonomous County of Huaihua City produces sweet oranges with distinctive colors and flavors and abundant juice. In November 2022, sweet oranges planted in the county amounted to 19,000 hectares, ranking first in China in terms of area and output, with a brand value of RMB 2.25 billion (Wang, 2023). As a result, Mayang County was praised as"the capital of sweet oranges in China." In May 2022, the Hunan Provincial People's Government issued the"Implementation Plan on Deeply Integrating into the Belt and Road and Supporting the Construction of Huaihua International Inland Port." The plan elevates the construction of Huaihua International Inland Port to a provincial strategy.

Inspiring Achievements

People worldwide can see a bright future in the concept and actual construction of inland ports and their achievements. Inland ports have been recognized and practiced by more and more countries. Despite the short duration of the Huaihua International Inland Port, its achievements have been very encouraging. When something new grows, it is bound to have many shortcomings. Therefore, it is meaningful to implement the following solutions.

Building an Intelligent Platform for Inland Port Operations

The modern logistics industry is a typical energy-consuming industry with high carbon emissions. China introduced the national strategic goals of carbon dioxide peaking and carbon neutrality in 2020. Inland ports must implement this national strategy to build a new development pattern. China is firmly committed to a green, low-carbon, high-quality development path that prioritizes ecological civilization. It will ensure that the carbon dioxide peaking and carbon neutrality goals are achieved as planned (Central Committee of the Communist Party of China and the State Council, 2021). We must utilize new models, technologies, and systems to build an intelligent inland port by eliminating the traditional approach to infrastructure.

It is necessary to elaborate and effectively implement the Internet+ action plan, laying the foundation for using mobile Internet, cloud computing, big data, and IoT in the future. We can only plan well in advance, build two platforms online and offline, and merge them into an open and efficient synergy. In this way, we can create a perfect scene of production and life in the Internet era for the people in the Wuling Mountain area, where Huaihua City is located. It should widely absorb social capital for intelligent development and improve the existing infrastructure of the inland port. High-tech applications such as self-service customs clearance, advanced machine inspection and intelligent identification should be introduced step by step. Moreover, we must integrate the informatization facilities of Huaihua City and build a comprehensive platform for intelligent ports by applying big data technology. We will continue to enhance cooperation with Chinese and foreign logistics networks at sea, land and air ports, pursue higher economies of scale and strategic mutual benefits, and ultimately realize the highest goal of global intermodal transportation and joint development.

Building an International Inland Port and Promoting Traditional Tea Culture

The construction of Huaihua International Inland Port should parallel the inheritance and promotion of the traditions of the Tujia and Miao ethnic groups. The distinctive cultural characteristics of ethnic minorities in Xiangxi Prefecture are tea planting and sales. Many people's life practices are related to tea. By 2020, the area of tea plantations in the prefecture reached 50,000 hectares, ranking first in Hunan province. In 2020, the prefecture's tea production was 13,500 tons, and the comprehensive output value of tea exceeded RMB 5.7 billion (Pu, 2021). Guzhang County has produced Mao Jian tea since the Tang Dynasty. The tea leaves are plump and thick, have a tender texture, and have white hair, and they are of excellent quality. It used to be a tribute to the imperial palace since ancient times. In contemporary times, they are exported to Japan, the United States, and Europe. In 1990, the market price of Guzhang Maojian Tea was as high as 700 U.S. dollars per kilogram in the London market (Xiang, 1992). Currently, the area of tea plantations in Guzhang County is 11,700 hectares.

The green and organic tea plantations have reached 3,000 hectares, and the green and organic rate has reached 25.7%, ranking among the top in China. With the innovative development of the tea industry, Guzhang County was awarded the honor of "The National Demonstration County of Organic Product Certification and the first"Hometown of Chinese Organic Te" in Hunan Province (Lin, Lin and Zhang, 2020). In 2012, after the evaluation and examination by the Trademark Office of the State Administration for Industry and Commerce, Guzhang Maojian Tea was approved to become China's Famous Trademark for the 1st Batch of Local Public Brands in Hunan's and China's Tea Sector (Wu, 2012). Lu Yu (733-804 AD) of the Tang Dynasty is honored as the founder of tea culture. In 780 AD, Lu Yu wrote The Classic of Tea, the world's first meta-dictionary of tea culture. He believed it best to drink tea because of its cold properties. Drinking tea in silence and looking into ourselves helps us to become intelligent and diligent and to develop good habits of self-discipline and frugality. Tea has been deeply integrated into the lives of Chinese people and has become an important carrier of Chinese culture. Utilizing the brand effect of Guzhang Maojian Tea can promote tourism with tea, develop the tea industry with tourism, and promote the reciprocal activities of tea and tourism. We can organize tea ceremonies, tea tastings, and other events to enhance the attraction and influence of tea culture and attract more visitors.

To develop the charm of tea culture, we need to recognize the shortcomings of tea production in western Hunan. The leading enterprises or co-operatives in organic tea production in Guzhang County have weak comprehensive strength and low management levels, affecting tea planting and sales (Lin, Lin and Zhang, 2020). One of the business models of the organic tea industry in the county is based on the cooperation between the company (tea factory), the base and the farmers. The construction of Huaihua International Inland Port involves the creation of a base from the management system that can fuel the operation of the tea industry. It can sign contracts to purchase organic tea leaves for export, thus establishing strict regulatory rules. Also, farmers occasionally attend lectures on modern production management theories to improve their literacy. In ancient times, tea traveled through the Tea Horse Road to the Central and Southern Peninsula. Guzhang Maojian Tea is being exported to Europe and Africa by leveraging Huaihua International InlandPort's strength in the 21st Century Maritime Silk Road.

Learning from the Sister Provinces and Cities and Overseas Cases

The construction of Huaihua International Inland Port started late and accumulated little experience. Therefore, learning from other regions should be a must. Xi'an is one of China's first inland trade ports. In 2014, the Chinese government approved the establishment of the Xi'an National Aviation City Experimental Zone. Xi'an has become a three-dimensional international open city with rail, sea and air transportation connections (Jia, 2017). Chang'an, the starting point of China's ancient Silk Road, is now open to the outside world on an even larger scale. TheChang'ann" China-EU liner has been regularized to run 16 central lines, covering 45 countries and regions along the Belt and Road. Reform and opening up have substantially increased Xi'an's economic strength, greatly enhancing its support for Shaanxi province and other regions. From 2018 to 2020, the contribution of the Xi'an International Inland Port's Logistics Subsystem to its hinterland composite system was significantly higher than that of the hinterland city's economic subsystem. In 2020, it surpassed that of the hinterland cities (Wang, 2022). Xi'an has established an information-sharing platform linking the inland port and the airport with functions of information convergence, data sharing, cargo tracking and financial services (Wang, 2018). With much experience constructing Xi'an International Inland Port, Huaihua should learn more and make innovations to move forward.

At the same time, Huaihua still needs to learn from the successful experiences of other countries. Langen (2007), a professor at Erasmus University Rotterdam, the Netherlands, studied the port competition and selection in the imports and exports of goods in Austria's five seaports. He proposed the concepts of "monopoly hinterland and contestable hinterland" arising from the construction of new port hinterlands by people competing for market shares to exchange goods. For exports, western Hunan teas, such as Guzhang Maojian Tea, must compete internally and not be confined to how they are passed down.

Nguyen at the Maritime University in Haiphong, Vietnam, and Thai at the University of Economics Ho Chi Minh City et al. (2021) argued for a multi-criteria and multi-stakeholder approach to assessing the role of inland ports. They developed a hierarchy of evaluation criteria that involved three primary stakeholder groups: inland port users, seaport participants, and the community. They emphasized the primary role of inland port users in driving the port's success. Huaihua International Inland Port should actively connect with various regional industries and develop in synergy to realize the construction goal.

Building a Modernized International Inland Port According to Local Conditions

Huaihua International Inland Port is a large-scale project with many modern elements. In particular, the initial capital construction involves plots of land and buildings. Therefore, it must be adapted to the local conditions and emphasize scientific planning. Seguí and Puig et al. (2016), research fellows at the Universitat Politècnica de Catalunya in Barcelona, Spain, studied 27 inland ports of the European Union (EU). These ports are different in size, business situation and geographic location. The port requires detailed and varied policies and regulations to implement green initiatives and close supervision to ensure they are strictly regulated. In this way, the inland port can improve its environmental performance.

The scientific planning of international inland port construction is crucial. Planning technical routes according to the actual situation for land, water, materials, energy conservation, and environmental protection is necessary. We must analyze comprehensive information on buildable land, select construction materials, and apply mathematical models to determine diverse resource-saving strategies. Logistics and transportation routes should be optimized, and environmental protection measures should be strengthened to maximize benefits with minimal investment.

The international inland port must strive to promote the economic development of Huaihua and serve the development of local undertakings by integrating links and sharing the dividends of reform and opening up. Farmers benefit from the increased volume of exported agricultural products, which helps develop inland port logistics. Agricultural products, like sweet oranges and other fresh fruits, are sold seasonally, demanding time-limited transportation and sales. For this reason, the relevant departments must create a cross-border e-commerce industrial park and vigorously introduce cross-border e-commerce strategic partners. It can promote breakthroughs in online and offline experience sales of cross-border e-commerce for rural agricultural products.

Enhancing the Awareness of the Strategic Positioning

As mentioned above, in the deepening process of globalization, the international inland port, as a critical platform for opening up inland areas, is crucial to promoting regional economic development and strengthening international economic and trade cooperation. Huaihua International Inland Port carries the expectations and dreams of Huaihua and even the whole Hunan region for opening up and rising. It is also important in China's international vision and high-level strategic layout.

The construction and development of Huaihua International Inland Port is a significant initiative of the people of Huaihua to respond positively to China's Belt and Road initiative and Western Development Strategy. Since the construction of the inland port started, Huaihua

Municipal People's Government has worked closely around the goal of building a cargo consolidation center for Central and Western China to ASEAN and an important channel and node for Hunan to dock with RCEP. It has pushed forward the construction and development of the inland port. In this process, the people of Huaihua deeply realize that the development of the port needs the port personnel's efforts, as well as the support and cooperation from all parties.

The book written by Dr. Shu Xiaohui et al. provides a rare opportunity for the people of all ethnic groups in Huaihua. Moreover, the relevant government departments of Huaihua City can systematically summarize the experiences and achievements of inland port development, deeply analyze the existing problems and challenges, and explore future development. By reading the book, we can see that the authors have conducted a comprehensive and in-depth study on Huaihua International Inland Port. They analyze its strategic positioning, competitiveness, spillover effect, impact on China-Laos trade, and the port's effect on residents' housing demand. Besides, they explore the development of the port in depth and put forward many targeted suggestions and countermeasures. These research results offer essential guidance for further clarifying the development idea and optimizing the development strategy of Huaihua International Inland Port.

It should be noted that the authors have proposed the creation of the Huaihua International Inland Port Special Zone as a strategic initiative. In the initial stages of reform and opening up, China planned and developed the special economic zones of Shenzhen, Zhuhai, Shantou and Xiamen, with preferential measures such as tariff reductions and exemptions. The Chinese government created a favorable investment environment, encouraged foreign investment, and introduced advanced technology and scientific management methods, thus promoting China's overall economic development. The Huaihua International Inland Port Special Economic Zone's development is feasible today and an indispensable option at this stage. Tax exemptions and appropriate subsidies can create a favorable environment for the export of technology, capital, commodities, and management. It can encourage inland manufacturers to go abroad, expand the international market, and improve the international competitive advantage of enterprises. Moreover, it can accelerate the development of the economy of the international inland port special zone. Then, it can revitalize China's inland areas for the comprehensive and high-speed development of the national economy.

Since its construction, Huaihua International Inland Port has made remarkable achievements. Its infrastructure has been constantly improved, and logistics and transportation capabilities have been substantially enhanced. It has increased its trade exchanges with regions in China and abroad, significantly enhancing its driving force for the regional economy. These achievements cannot be separated from the hard work of all the people who have contributed to developing the inland port. However, we realize that we must raise our awareness of the strategic position of the Huaihua International Inland Port. We should reconsider it from China's national economic development.

In the future, we expect Huaihua International Inland Port to become highly influential and competitive. It will become an important hub connecting the inland and international markets, injecting new vitality into the economic development of Huaihua and providing solid support for the opening up of Hunan. It will make further breakthroughs and improvements in logistics and transportation, industrial development, international trade, economic impetus, and urban development. At the same time, Huaihua International Inland Port will also trigger significant spillover effects. Firstly, it will vigorously drive the economic development of the neighboring regions and promote in-depth inter-regional cooperation and exchanges. Secondly, it will actively promote industrial upgrading and innovation and comprehensively enhance the industrial competitiveness of the whole region. Thirdly, it will create more jobs and improve people's income and quality of life. Finally, it will further strengthen the close ties with the international market and significantly enhance the status and influence of China's inland areas in the international economy. We believe that with the joint efforts of all parties, Huaihua International Inland Port will play a more critical role in international economic and trade cooperation and promote the leapfrog development of China's inland economy.

Finally, I would like to express my sincere gratitude to the authors for their hard work and in-depth research, as well as to all those who have contributed to the development of the Huaihua International Inland Port. We will work together to improve the awareness of Huaihua International Inland Port's strategic position and contribute to creating a better future for the port.

Chapter 1
New Strategy for Huaihua International Inland Port Development

This chapter analyzes the existing Huaihua International Inland Port studies and regional economic development. On this basis, its strategic positioning is redefined, and its impact on the economic growth of China and the world is analyzed. Furthermore, it explores the port's main challenges under the Belt and Road Initiative and proposes sustainable and healthy development strategies. In the era of globalization, the importance of international trade and logistics has become increasingly prominent. As the world's second-largest economy, China's solid internal logistics infrastructure and well-developed transportation systems are vital to maintaining and expanding its economic vitality. Huaihua International Inland Port is integral to China's Western Development Strategy and has become an essential hub connecting Western China with international markets. The port profoundly impacts the economic vitality of Huaihua and surrounding areas, promoting employment and improving residents' living standards. However, it also faces many challenges in its development. It needs to improve operational efficiency, efficiently coordinate various modes of transportation, attract more industries, and balance economic development and environmental protection. Based on the in-depth analysis indicates the strategic orientations and recommendations for the future development of the port. At the same time, it is expected to provide a reference for other regional economic development projects.

Introduction

This chapter analyzes the existing Huaihua International Inland Port studies and regional economic development. On this basis, its strategic positioning is redefined, and its impact on the economic growth of China and the world is analyzed. Furthermore, it explores the port's main challenges and proposes setting it up as China's first international inland port special zone to ensure long-term sustainable development. In recent years, China's inland ports have shown some variations in their development paths depending on their geographic location, influenced by different institutional and regulatory frameworks. While the central government has an established regulatory framework for dealing with related matters, local-level decision-making is controlled by municipal bodies. It provides ample space for officials to interpret central governance intentions. At the same time, the absence of well-defined policy guidelines poses many challenges to inland ports (Beresford et al., 2012).

In today's globalization, international trade and logistics are increasingly important. As the world's second-largest economy, China has an internal logistics infrastructure and transportation system critical to maintaining and expanding its economic vitality. Huaihua International Inland Port, an integral part of China's Western Development Strategy, has become a key hub connecting West China to international markets. In addition, with the advancement of the Belt and Road Initiative and the entry into force of the Regional Comprehensive Economic Partnership (RCEP), Huaihua International Inland Port has become even more strategically relevant.

In recent years, China has witnessed a boom in the construction of inland ports to adapt to the development trend of economic globalization. Remarkable results have been achieved in such international inland ports as Xi'an, Chongqing, Urumqi, and Huaihua. These ports have formed the strategic layout of the New International Land-Sea Trade Corridor in Western China. They have expanded the scope of import and export of products from the neighboring regions and driven the rapid economic development of the affected regions. Huaihua is located in the center of the border areas of Hunan, Hubei, Chongqing, Guizhou, and Guangxi. The unique geographic location makes Huaihua a bridgehead for Central China to enter South Asia through Southwest China.

At the same time, it is also an influential node city in China's Belt and Road Initiative, connecting Europe and Asia in the north and ASEAN in the south. The construction and development of Huaihua International Inland Port has promoted the rapid social and economic development of Huaihua. Its spillover effect has dramatically driven the economic development of the neighboring regions. In addition, Huaihua is a node city for the freight trains between China and Europe, China and ASEAN, and China and Central Asia. Huaihua is also the starting point of the China-Thailand freight trains and the first city in central China for the two-way operations of the China-Laos and China-Vietnam freight trains. Developing the port's economy can fully transform Huaihua into China's transportation hub to Europe and ASEAN. By exploring the relationship between inland ports and regional economic development, Liu et al. (2021) found that inland ports positively correlate with trade volume. Compared with the cities without inland ports, the trade volume of cities with inland ports will increase by 0.099 times. Thus, inland ports are crucial to the regional economy.

Regarding China's macroeconomic development strategies, the completed Huaihua International Inland Port is one of the critical nodes for implementing the Belt and Road strategy. After several years of development and initial operation, the port has increasingly demonstrated its important strategic position, attracting many investment enterprises and introducing cooperative projects. The port has become a strategic base for foreign economic and trade cooperation in Central and Western China. It has long exceeded its strategic position as a critical economic development project in Hunan Province. Therefore, it must be elevated to a new position as a vital project in the macroeconomic development strategy of Central China and China.

In August 2019, China's National Development and Reform Commission (NDRC) identified the New International Land-Sea Trade Corridor in Western China as a national strategy in the Master Plan of the New International Land-Sea Trade Corridor. The plan identifies Huaihua as a vital node city on the eastern route of the main channel of the corridor. From China's macroeconomic development perspective, the port is a vivid practice of implementing Chinese leaders' strategic thinking of building a new development pattern and creating a high ground for inland reform and opening up. It is the most critical node project for building the New International Land-Sea Trade Corridor in Western China and connecting the Belt and Road. Furthermore, it is a successful model of experience as a national-level international inland port. It can provide a strategic reference for building and developing other international inland ports in China. It is of great practical significance and high operational feasibility for China's long-term stable macroeconomic development.

As mentioned earlier, Huaihua is located in the southwestern Hunan Province, at the center of the border areas of Hunan, Hubei, Chongqing, Guizhou and Guangxi. The geographical advantage makes it an important hub linking the south to the north and the east to the west. The electrification of the second additional line of the Chongqing-Huaihua Railway and the Huaihua-Liuzhou section of the Jiaozuo-Liuzhou Railway has been completed. Subsequently, the Huaihua International Inland Port opened a cargo corridor for the Chengdu-Chongqing urban agglomeration and ports in southern China. Connectivity between ports can significantly stimulate regional economic growth in the long run. Port infrastructure expansion is a potential channel to realize the stimulating effect (Li et al., 2023).

With Huaihua International Inland Port, the transportation condition of the area has been improved, and it also brings new opportunities for the economic development of Huaihua and the surrounding areas. Hou et al. (2023) conducted an empirical study on the economic spillover effect of the development of Huaihua International Inland Port. The results show that the construction and development of the port will inevitably produce positive economic spillover effects on the neighboring areas. In the strategic layout of Hunan Province, Huaihua International Inland Port is positioned as a strategic gateway city to the New International Land-Sea Trade Corridor in Western China. The port serves the logistics needs of the region and serves as a platform for international trade and cultural exchange. Its construction and development align with China's strategic goal of promoting regional economic integration and globalization. It is intended to link western China with Southeast Asia and the broader international market by building an efficient logistics network.

Huaihua International Inland Port has a far-reaching impact on the local and national economy. It boosts Huaihua's and its neighboring regions' economic development, improves enterprises' competitiveness, creates more jobs and improves residents' living standards. Its construction and development enable Huaihua to attract more investments from China and abroad and advance high-tech industries and high-value-added services. However, it also faces many challenges. Specifically, it needs to enhance its operational efficiency, link multiple modes of transportation, attract more industries, and strike a balance with environmental protection. These challenges must be addressed through scientific planning, innovative management and forward-looking strategic decisions. This chapter aims to indicate the strategic direction and propose specific strategies for developing Huaihua International Inland Port under its new strategic positioning. At the same time, it can also provide a reference for other similar regional economic development projects.

Current Development Status and Strategies

Development Status

Since its establishment, Huaihua International Inland Port has become an essential logistics and transportation hub for Hunan Province and Southwest China. The port's current status can be described from the perspectives of infrastructure development, operational efficiency, industrial accumulation, and its role in the regional economy. The infrastructure development of Huaihua International Inland Port is the core of its development. The port owns Huaihuaxi Railway Station, a national railroad marshaling yard. It is one of the nine railroad marshaling yards approved by China State Railway Group Co., Ltd. Huaihuaxi Railway Station is an essential node for railroad cargo transportation and a center for cargo distribution. The railroad network of Huaihua International Inland Port has been greatly strengthened with the completion of the electrification of the Huaihua-Liuzhou section of the Jiaozuo-Liuzhou Railway and the construction of the second additional line of the Chongqing-Huaihua Railway. It strongly supports the New International Land-Sea Trade Corridor in Western China. In addition, the port's highway network is also well developed by connecting several highways, forming an efficient land transportation system. Adolf and Jose (2013) argue that constructing inland ports can improve transportation efficiency and stimulate economic development in inland areas by reducing tariffs on road and rail freight. As a result, transportation costs can be reduced, and foreign trade can be promoted.

Huaihua International Inland Port has excelled in operational efficiency, successfully realizing the rapid development of multimodal transportation. It is well-equipped and has achieved remarkable results in improving customs clearance efficiency and simplifying administrative procedures. Implementing the one-stop service and single-window customs clearance model has significantly shortened the customs clearance time for goods and enhanced logistics efficiency. At the same time, it actively promotes e-commerce and informationization and utilizes advanced information technology to manage logistics and freight forwarding operations, ensuring efficient and transparent operations.

The development of Huaihua International Inland Port has led to the clustering of industries in the surrounding areas, especially in the manufacturing and agricultural products processing industries. The port has several specialized logistics and industrial parks, attracting many enterprises from China and other countries to invest and set up factories there. These enterprises enjoy convenient logistics services and benefit from the various supporting services provided by the port, such as warehousing, processing and distribution. In addition, it boosts the export of local agricultural products, such as tea and bamboo. These products can be sold to various markets in China and globally through the port's platform. By investigating the inland port industry in North India, Adolf and Ismail (2011) found that establishing distribution centers in specific locations is crucial to the regional economic development of developing economies. It can effectively integrate the related industries of the regional economy and accelerate the development of the regional economy.

Huaihua International Inland Port plays a crucial role in promoting regional economic development. As a vital node of the New International Land-Sea Trade Corridor in Western China, it is a necessary logistics and transportation hub and an essential platform for regional economic integration. Its construction and development have produced some positive economic spillover effects on the neighboring regions. It significantly promotes the economic integration of Hunan province and even Southwest China and enhances the region's economic competitiveness (Hou et al., 2023). The port strengthens the connection between Huaihua and markets in China and abroad, especially with the ASEAN market, providing local enterprises with broader market space and more business opportunities. The current state of the port is multifaceted. It has made remarkable achievements in infrastructure development and operational efficiency.

Moreover, it has accelerated the urbanization of the Huaihua region by facilitating industrial agglomeration and promoting regional economic development. Xiao (2023) suggests that building international inland ports can drive the overall development of local economies and societies. It can also encourage population concentration and accelerate the urbanization of inland areas. With the continuous improvement of the port's functions and the in-depth implementation of relevant policies, it is expected to play a more critical role in the future, becoming an essential impetus for local economy and regional integration.

Current Development Strategies

Huaihua International Inland Port's existing strategies focus on the following aspects. Firstly, it strengthens infrastructure development. With Huaihuaxi Railway Station as the core, the railroad network is improved. Meanwhile, it develops the highway network to form an efficient land transportation system. Secondly, it enhances operational efficiency and realizes the rapid development of multimodal transportation. One-stop service and single-window customs clearance mode improve customs clearance efficiency and promote e-commerce and informationization to ensure efficient and transparent operation. Thirdly, it promotes industrial agglomeration and drives the development of manufacturing and agro-processing industries in the neighboring areas. It attracts enterprises to invest and build factories and utilizes supporting services to expand markets. Finally, it reinforces regional economic integration, facilitates economic integration, improves regional competitiveness, and strengthens links with markets in China and abroad (Girish and Adolf, 2019).

However, Huaihua International Inland Port's established strategies are subject to many limitations. The most common factors affecting the development of the port are infrastructure, land use, environment and regulations. State-of-the-art intermodal terminals must be integrated into a complex system, where infrastructure must be in place (Roso, 2008). The port may be under pressure to continue to invest in construction, as large-scale infrastructure development and maintenance require substantial financial support. Railroad and road networks may have capacity bottlenecks or need to be upgraded in response to growing freight demand. All of these require large amounts of capital. Local government support alone is a drop in the bucket.

Regarding operational efficiency improvement, the one-stop service and single window clearance model may have problems such as poor coordination or technical failures in actual operation, affecting stability and efficiency. Informatization construction may face challenges such as data security and system compatibility (Chang et al., 2015). These probable problems must be addressed by professionals, such as highly qualified software and hardware development engineers and experienced operators.

Regarding industrial agglomeration, the port relies excessively on specific industries, with a higher risk of having a homogenous industrial structure. After attracting enterprises, it may suffer from insufficient synergies among enterprises. It may experience fierce competition with other regions regarding regional economic development, and maintaining its advantages is a great challenge. Past studies have also shown that the sustainability of inland ports has become one of the critical issues in future research on inland ports (Miraj et al., 2021). Dependence on a single ASEAN market may also affect Huaihua International Inland Port when the international economic situation changes.

Strategic Positioning

Huaihua's Strategic Status

As one of China's critical regional economic centers, Huaihua's strategic position has been significantly enhanced in recent years. Especially with the deepening of the Belt and Road Initiative and the entry into force of the Regional Comprehensive Economic Partnership (RCEP), Huaihua's geographic and economic advantages have been further magnified. As mentioned above, Huaihua is located at the intersection of Hunan, Hubei, Chongqing, Guizhou and Guangxi. Moreover, it is an essential hub connecting these regions, making it a strategic corridor linking the south to the north and the east to the west. Promoting the New International Land-Sea Trade Corridor in Western China is crucial.

First, Huaihua is one of China's national logistics hubs. As a national railroad station, Huaihuaxi Railway Station, together with the electrification of the second additional line of the Chongqing-Huaihua Railway and the Huaihua-Liuzhou section of Jiaozuo-Liuzhou Railway, constitutes the pattern of "Two Lines and One Station." It strengthens the connection between Huaihua and the Chengdu-Chongqing urban agglomeration and opens up a significant freight transportation channel for its connection to the southern seaports. Implementing these railroad construction projects has dramatically increased Huaihua's freight throughput capacity.

Moreover, they have opened the way for Huaihua's international trade in the Belt and Road Initiative and its deep integration into the New International Land-Sea Trade Corridor in Western China. Second, Huaihua's international cooperation under the Belt and Road Initiative has also increased. Taking advantage of its unique geographic location, Huaihua has actively connected to the ASEAN market by building the Huaihua International Inland Port. It facilitates trade with ASEAN countries in agricultural products, electronic information, apparel and garments. In addition, Huaihua International Inland Port provides numerous logistics and warehousing facilities for the region. It has further improved the related infrastructure and introduced new technologies. All these measures have enormously strengthened the development of Huaihua's open economy.

Huaihua is also strategically positioned as a critical node of China's southbound corridor. With the entry into force of the RCEP, Huaihua has served as a bridge to promote trade between China and ASEAN countries. Huaihua International Inland Port is a logistics transit hub and platform for converging information, capital and technology flow. It provides vigorous support for regional economic integration. The strategic position of Huaihua lies in its geographic centrality and role as a critical platform for regional economic development and international cooperation. In the national strategic layout, Huaihua is vital in connecting markets in China and abroad and facilitating regional economic integration. Huaihua's strategic position will be further reinforced as the port's construction progresses, the transportation infrastructure is further improved, and international cooperation deepens. Huaihua's role in China and the international economic arena will also be more prominent.

Strategic Positioning in Hunan Province

Huaihua International Inland Port was first proposed as a strategic project for the economic development of Hunan Province. It is strategically positioned in Hunan Province as an important hub for regional economic growth, a vital node of the New International Land-Sea Trade Corridor in Western China, and an essential platform for international trade. It is a comprehensive and multi-layered regional development project. With implementing of the Belt and Road Initiative and RCEP, Huaihua International Inland Port's strategic significance has become increasingly prominent. It has become a new high ground for Central and Western China to open up to the outside world and a new growth pole for economic development.

Huaihua is the strategic gateway city of Hunan Province to the New International Land-Sea Trade Corridor in Western China. Huaihua International Inland Port is intended to accelerate regional economic integration by optimizing the transportation and logistics network. It functions as a distribution center for goods and a key node for promoting local industrial upgrading and economic restructuring. The construction and development of the port enable Huaihua to attract more investments from China and abroad and facilitate the development of high-tech and high-value-added industries. Moreover, it will help to enhance the economic strength and competitiveness of the entire Hunan Province.

Huaihua International Inland Port is strategically positioned in Hunan Province as an integral part of Huaihua as a national comprehensive transportation hub. The port effectively reduces logistics costs and improves logistics efficiency by upgrading the multimodal transportation capacity of railroads, highways and waterways. In particular, implementing the "Two Lines and One Station" project has made Huaihua a freight transportation channel connecting the Yangtze River Economic Belt and the Pearl River Delta Economic Belt. Furthermore, it enhances the connectivity between major cities in Hunan Province and Chinese and international markets.

Huaihua International Inland Port has become a platform for developing emerging industries. Given the port's logistic advantages and policy support, Huaihua can attract and cultivate emerging industries such as electronic information, biotechnology, and new materials. These industries will bring new economic growth points to Huaihua and the whole Hunan Province. In addition, the port also provides a broader market for local agricultural products such as tea and bamboo products. Through modern trade methods such as e-commerce, it will introduce local specialty products to regional and international markets.

In conclusion, Huaihua International Inland Port is vital to Hunan Province's development strategies. It is a crucial driver for local economic development and an essential platform for regional economic integration and comprehensive opening. With the continuous improvement of the port's functions and the in-depth implementation of relevant policies, it is expected to play an even more critical role.

Strategic Positioning in Central China

As mentioned earlier, Huaihua International Inland Port is located in Huaihua, southwestern Hunan Province, and has a favorable geographical position. The port has become a crucial transportation and logistics hub in central China by connecting the east to the west and the south to the north. In the context of building the New International Land-Sea Trade Corridor in Western China, the port enhances intra-regional logistics capabilities and promotes economic integration and regional cooperation. The integration of these functions significantly elevates the port's strategic positioning in Central China. Located at the junction of Hunan with Guizhou, Chongqing, Guangxi and Hubei, it has become a significant transportation hub connecting Southwest China with Central and South China.

Due to the electrification of the Chongqing-Huaihua Railway and Jiaozuo-Liuzhou Railway and the construction of the Huaihuaxi Marshalling Yard, Huaihua has become a key node for the logistics transshipment from Central China to West and South China. Because of this, Huaihua International Inland Port occupies a central position in Central China's economic circle and logistics network. It is significant in promoting the coordinated development of the regional economy and the efficient allocation of resources. According to Adolf et al. (2013), the construction of inland ports has eased the congestion of the seaport and significantly improved the efficiency of regional resource allocation.

Huaihua International Inland Port is also strategically positioned to promote the economic development of Central China. It offers a robust economic growth point and a platform for industrial upgrading for neighboring provinces and cities. By improving the quality and efficiency of logistics services, the port has attracted many manufacturing and processing enterprises and boosted high-tech and modern service industries. In addition, its international trade function opens up Chinese and global markets, especially the ASEAN market, for local products. It strengthens the position of Central China in supply chains in China and globally. The port has also demonstrated the importance of its strategic positioning in terms of environmental protection and sustainability. The port has integrated green logistics and low-carbon technologies into its operation and management, striving to realize a win-win result for economic benefits and environmental protection. Its green development strategy aligns with China's requirements for advancing ecological progress. It also enhances the region's sustainability and sets a model for the green development trend in Central China and the rest of the country.

Huaihua International Inland Port is also strategically positioned as a platform for international cooperation. The port is an integral part of the Belt and Road Initiative. The port facilitates international trade between China and other countries through its advanced logistics and transportation facilities. It actively contributes to further developing the China-ASEAN Free Trade Area (CAFTA). Nguyen and Notteboom (2016) argue that vigorously increasing investment in the inland port industry can promote the region's economic development and influence during foreign cooperation. The development of Huaihua International Inland Port enhances Central China's international influence and competitiveness. It also provides a new impetus and platform for opening up the regional economy and international cooperation.

In conclusion, the port has a well-defined and vital strategic position in Central China. It acts as a transportation and logistics hub, promotes regional economic development, serves as a platform for international cooperation, and serves as a model for green and sustainable development. These roles have shaped the port's strategic position in Central China and the country. As the port's functions continue to improve and deepen, its influence in the future regional economic landscape is expected to increase.

Position in China's National Strategy

The construction of Huaihua International Inland Port fulfills local development needs and is an integral part of China's national strategy. The Belt and Road Initiative is essential to China's plan to utilize international resources and accelerate national development. Under the Belt and Road Initiative, Huaihua International Inland Port, as the open door of Hunan Province, has the unique location advantage of connecting the east to the west, the north to the south, and the rivers to the sea. It has strengthened China's economic ties with ASEAN and South Asia and has become a practical platform for promoting the upgraded version of the CAFTA. Because of this, the port can play a more significant role in regional economic cooperation and build a more open internationalized economic operation mechanism through the land-sea linkage.

The new strategic position of Huaihua International Inland Port is becoming increasingly prominent under the framework of China's Western Development Strategy and Belt and Road Initiative. Huaihua is a national logistics hub and an important node city of Western China's New International Land-Sea Trade Corridor. Huaihua International Inland Port serves regional development and aims to connect western China with Southeast Asia and the broader international market. It is an inland component within the seaport system and has become crucial in shaping its container performance and competitive strategy. Similarly, due to intermodal logistics and distribution networks, integrating inland freight distribution systems is essential for an efficient containerized seaport system (Jeevan et al., 2019).

Huaihua International Inland Port is a vital node of Western China's New International Land-Sea Trade Corridor. It strategically connects western China with the Beibu Gulf of Guangxi, southern China and ASEAN countries. The corridor is an integral part of China's Belt and Road Initiative. It aims to accelerate the pace of opening up and economic development of West China by enhancing the land-sea intermodal transportation capacity. Its operation can effectively reduce logistics costs, improve cargo transportation efficiency, and create more direct access to the sea for inland provinces. It is of great significance to promote China's Western Development Strategy.

Huaihua is strategically positioned in China's transportation network as a critical comprehensive transportation hub due to Huaihua's predominant geological location and transportation development. Huaihua's transportation network covers railroads, highways, waterways and airways. Railroad transportation especially occupies an essential position in China's national railroad network. Huaihuaxi Railway Station, as a national railroad marshaling yard, is a vital hub connecting Central China with South and Southwest China. Huaihua's railroad network serves the local economy and is an essential part of China's national southbound corridor, facilitating the transportation of goods across the country.

Huaihua International Inland Port is also strategically positioned as an open platform for international trade. Syahchari et al. (2021) argued that through the construction and operation of inland ports, the region can further attract domestic and foreign investment and promote the clustering of high-tech and high-value-added industries. The Huaihua International Inland Port strengthens links with other areas of China. It also facilitates international trade and cultural exchanges by enhancing direct connections to international markets such as ASEAN. The construction of this platform helps the products and services of Huaihua and its neighboring areas to go global and enhance their international competitiveness.

Huaihua International Inland Port also plays a significant role in supporting regional economic integration. The port strengthens the economic ties between Hunan, Hubei, Chongqing, Guizhou and Guangxi through effective logistics and supply chain management. It promotes the optimized allocation of regional economic resources and industrial upgrading. It enhances the comprehensive competitiveness of local industries and provides practical support and service platforms for regional economic integration. Huaihua International Inland Port is strategically positioned as a regional transportation hub and economic center in China, a national open platform and an important node for international trade. Its development can efficiently promote the integration and development of China's domestic and international trade and advance the in-depth implementation of China's Western Development Strategy and Belt and Road Strategy.

New Ideas for Development Strategy

In the current era, exploring Huaihua International Inland Port's development strategy requires innovative thinking and strategic perspectives. It is crucial to Huaihua's development and will significantly affect the economy of the surrounding areas. By tapping the potential and advantages of the port and continuously enhancing its functions and influence, it can promote higher-quality and more sustainable development and provide a new impetus for regional economic growth.

Increasing Policy Support to Build the Inland Port Special Zone

Huaihua has specific geographic advantages and development potential. The idea of making it the first international inland port special zone in China is significantly innovative and forward-looking. Moreover, it is highly likely to be highly regarded and favored by the Hunan Province and Huaihua City governments. From an academic perspective, analogous to the development of Shenzhen, Zhuhai, Shantou and other special zones, one of the critical factors for their impressive achievements is the strong support of national policies related to their independent development. To achieve the goal of building an international inland port special zone, Huaihua urgently needs all-round policy support from the Chinese government.

The Chinese government can formulate targeted industrial policies, guide the rational allocation of resources, and promote the accumulation and development of related industries. The Ministry of Finance can apply flexible fiscal policies to secure sufficient funds for infrastructure development and scientific and technological innovation in Huaihua. The Chinese government can stimulate the enthusiasm and vitality of the port's market players by introducing preferential tax policies for the Huaihua region. The government can enhance trade facilitation and expand the space of international markets through efficient trade policies.

With the solid support of national policies, Huaihua will fully unleash its inherent potential. Driven by innovation and led by opening up, Huaihua can gradually build up a complete system of the international inland port special zone, thus promoting the rapid development, transformation and upgrading of the regional economy.

Therefore, it can set a new model and benchmark for the open development of China's inland areas. This process requires the local government's active efforts, national strategic layout and policy inclination. Only through the synergy of the two can this development vision of significant significance be accomplished.

Consolidating the Asian Markets

While consolidating the Southeast Asian market, Huaihua International Inland Port must shift its attention to the more complicated South Asian market and the promising West Asian market. In doing so, it will enjoy the benefits of the following three aspects:

Firstly, it can address the risk of over-dependence on specific industries and the risk of a unitary industrial structure. It can obtain market information through an in-depth understanding of the needs and trends of the South and West Asian markets by conducting market research and participating in international exhibitions. It can adjust its product and service strategies in response to market demand. Thus, it can further expand its product range according to the demands of South and West Asian markets and meet the needs of different customers. On the one hand, the port can strengthen the cooperation with local enterprises and jointly develop products suitable for the local market. On the other hand, it also solves the problem of Huaihua being overly dependent on specific industries.

Secondly, the port must take a differentiated route to avoid fierce competition with other regions and maintain its advantages. At present, the neighboring areas of Huaihua are also in full swing in building international inland ports, causing fierce competition for Huaihua International Inland Port. However, the adjacent regions focus on the Southeast Asian market and pay little attention to the South and West Asian markets. Therefore, South Asia and West Asia markets are blue ocean markets for the region. Huaihua International Inland Port has a first-mover advantage in entering this market, which is conducive to accelerating the formation of a moat against competitors.

Finally, avoiding dependence on a single ASEAN market prevents the Huaihua International Inland Port from being significantly affected by changes in the international economic situation. Currently, the international situation is volatile, and China's relationship with Southeast

Asian countries is not stable. Reducing dependence on a single market helps enhance the port's business stability and risk resistance, expanding the scope of trade and gaining more business opportunities and room for growth.

Cross-regional Strategic Cooperation with Hainan Province

Increased maritime freight traffic leads to increased inland freight traffic, which in turn affects the ability of the intermodal transportation system to accommodate the growth of international trade. Inland ports are also developed to support seaport operations and the overall operation of the intermodal transportation system (Bask et al., 2014). Through cooperation with Hainan Province, especially the Yangpu Economic Development Zone, Huaihua International Inland Port can further strengthen its role as a critical node in Western China's New International Land-Sea Trade Corridor. Based on this, it can give new impetus to local economic development. The cooperation covers many aspects, such as information exchange, investment cooperation, industrial linkage and deep logistics cooperation, aiming at realizing regional economic synergy, mutual benefit and win-win results.

First, information exchange is the foundation of cross-regional cooperation. The strategic collaboration between Huaihua City and Yangpu Economic Development Zone should emphasize the importance of information sharing. First, information exchange is the foundation of cross-regional cooperation. The strategic collaboration between Huaihua City and Yangpu Economic Development Zone should emphasize the importance of information sharing. It enhances the transparency and mobility of information and increases the competitiveness of the two places in the local and international markets.

In particular, the Yangpu Economic Development Zone has actively integrated into construction of the Single-Window New International Land-Sea Trade Corridor in Western China. Because of this, Huaihua can make better use of this platform to enhance the overall effectiveness of the corridor economy. Second, in terms of investment promotion, the cooperation between Huaihua and Hainan Province can be further deepened. Both sides jointly promote investment promotion and inspection activities and establish a joint investment mechanism. Such collaboration enables resource sharing and complementary advantages and attracts more investors to follow the industrial development of the two places through joint promotion. The two places can establish a regional cooperation mechanism for investment promotion primarily through regular communication between chambers of commerce and civil organizations. Thus, it can ensure the introduction of high-quality projects.

In addition, industrial linkage is one of the critical components of cooperation between Huaihua and Hainan. With the advantages of the Yangpu Economic Development Zone in petrochemicals and port logistics, the two places have realized synergistic development in extending the industrial chain and connecting the upstream and downstream industries. With the policy advantage of a 30% value-added tariff exemption for imports in Yangpu Port, Huaihua's port-related enterprises, such as grain and oil processing enterprises, can set up sub-bases in Yangpu Port. Huaihua can also be used as a production and processing base for Yangpu Port enterprises. It reduces enterprises' tax costs and makes enterprises in Huaihua more competitive in the international market through the policy advantage of the bonded port.

Logistics cooperation is an essential part of cross-regional cooperation. Huaihua International Inland Port and Yangpu Port can cooperate intensively to build an international container hub port. They can jointly promote the coordinated development of international logistics parks along the corridor. As Hainan has deepened reform and opened up on all fronts, the two places can make significant progress in customs clearance facilitation, logistics information sharing, and business synergy. Especially in promoting the "Huaihua-Yangpu-ASEAN" two-way supply chain path, the two places can further deepen the economic and trade cooperation between the corridor and ASEAN countries through multimodal transportation and water-to-water transshipment logistics mode.

Policy synergy and linkage guarantee smooth cooperation (Li et al., 2015). Huaihua and Hainan jointly explore the feasibility of tax rebates at ports of departure at inland ports on the "Huaihua-Yangpu" route. They promote cross-border cooperation and supervision facilitation reforms in cargo transshipment and movement for foreign trade at customs offices along the "Huaihua-Qinzhou-Yangpu" route. These measures improve logistics efficiency and enhance the competitiveness of the two places in international trade.

In summary, the cross-regional strategic cooperation between Huaihua International Inland Port and Hainan Province provides new opportunities and paths for the development of Huaihua City. It also injects new impetus into constructing the Hainan Free Trade Port and developing the New International Land-Sea Trade Corridor in Western China. The cooperation realizes the synergistic development of the regional economy, mutual benefit and win-win results through information exchange, cooperation in investment promotion, industrial linkage and in-depth logistics cooperation. At the same time, it also strongly supports the economic development and internationalization of the two regions.

Promoting the New Progress of Huaihua International Inland Port by IPO

It is common for ports to conduct IPOs (Initial Public Offerings). On May 19, 2006, Tianjin Port Development Holdings Limited launched its IPO in Hong Kong and was warmly welcomed by investors. According to its sponsor, Tianjin Port's listing price was set at RMB 1.88 per share, expected to raise US$139 million (about HK$1,084 million).

After the IPO, Tianjin Port acquired substantial funds to construct port infrastructure, and it could invest billions of dollars in terminal expansion and upgrading equipment. It greatly enhanced the port's comprehensive strength and operational efficiency. Subsequently, the port attracted more attention in China and abroad, and its reputation increased dramatically, becoming a famous port brand. As a result, it has attracted many talents with rich capital market experience and professional management ability to join, like financial experts and strategic consultants. It has promoted the innovation and optimization of the port's management mode. For the region's development, it boosts a series of related industries through IPO, with Tianjin Port as the core. Logistics, shipping, trade and other industries achieve tens of billions of yuan of added value yearly, and their contribution to Tianjin's economic growth continues to rise. Expanding the port business and implementing new projects have created many jobs directly and indirectly. Every year, tens of thousands of new jobs are created for the local community, stabilizing local employment.

Following the IPO, Tianjin Port has been continuously upgraded in the national port ranking, and its competitiveness has been significantly enhanced. It has become a major shipping center and logistics hub in North China, generating a robust driving effect in neighboring regions.

There is also a precedent of IPO for international inland ports in China. Hebei Port Group Co., LTD Handan International Inland Port. Co., Ltd. was successfully listed on July 24, 2015. Handan International Inland Port. Co., Ltd. is the first modernized logistics enterprise of Hebei Port Group Co., LTD, listed in China. Jointly founded by Hebei Port Group Co., LTD and Handan Municipal People's Government, it is the "No.1 Project" of the Hebei Provincial People's Government. After Handan International Inland Port is completed, governmental bodies such as the Handan Customs and Quarantine Department will be stationed there. It can offer container dismantling and consolidation, container distribution, storage, customs clearance and other services.

Import and export declaration, customs clearance and other work in the port completed at once, without having to perform commodity inspection, animal and plant quarantine and sanitary and phytosanitary work in the coastal customs. Goods coming into the port go through customs, and goods going out of the port are cleared by customs, and the cargo transportation time to the seaports has significantly been shortened. The company's successful listing has extended the functions of coastal ports and border ports to the inland area of China. Moreover, it is strategically significant for the port and city to adjust the structure and change the mode, integrate into the opening up and development of Hebei with a new attitude, and serve the regional economic development.

The success of Hebei and Tianjin ports' IPOs proves that Huaihua International Inland Port's IPO is feasible. Following the IPO, the Huaihua government can obtain substantial capital from the capital market for infrastructure construction, business expansion, and technology upgrades at Huaihua International Inland Port. It can accelerate the development of Huaihua International Inland Port. Its debut in the capital market can increase the popularity of Huaihua International Inland Port and even Huaihua in China and the world and attract more cooperation opportunities and resources. In addition, the

IPO requests that the inland port standardize and improve its governance mechanism and enhance its operation and management standards. It has, in turn, promoted the optimization of the governance structure of Huaihua International Inland Port. The IPO is a great help in promoting the linked development of related industries in Huaihua and neighboring areas and enhancing the vitality of the regional economy. At the same time, it promotes the optimization and upgrading of Huaihua's regional trade and logistics industry. Thus, Huaihua will become a more attractive economic center and enhance its competitiveness.

Conclusion

Huaihua International Inland Port plays a crucial role in globalization and regional economic integration. This chapter analyzes its existing development strategies, reassesses its strategic positioning, and explores its new strategic directions in China and the international arena. Some constructive recommendations are made. Huaihua should be identified as an international inland port special zone. Firstly, Huaihua International Inland Port is an essential node connecting West China with the whole country and even the Southeast Asian market. Its strategic position supports the opening up and development of Hunan Province, Central and Western China. Its development has further deepened the connection between Huaihua and the international market. Especially since the Belt and Road Initiative was introduced and the RCEP came into effect, the status and role of Huaihua International Inland Port have been significantly enhanced.

Secondly, the development of Huaihua International Inland Port boosts the vitality of the local economy and promotes employment and social stability. It also significantly increases the competitiveness of enterprises within and outside the region through its efficient logistics services and optimized operational efficiency. Huaihua can attract more investment from China and abroad and accelerate the concentration of high-tech and high-value-added industries through the port's international cooperation platform. The port plays an irreplaceable role in promoting regional economic integration. It strengthens the economic ties between Hunan, Hubei, Chongqing, Guizhou and Guangxi. Besides, the port integrates regional resources, optimizes industrial structure, and enhances the region's economic efficiency and market competitiveness through its multimodal transport capability.

In addition, Huaihua International Inland Port faces many challenges and problems in its development. It must balance economic development and environmental protection, deal with uncertainties in international trade, and improve operational efficiency and service quality. These issues need to be addressed through more scientific and systematic strategic planning. Therefore, this chapter suggests that Huaihua International Inland Port should continue reinforcing its strategic position as the critical node of the New International Land-Sea Trade Corridor in Western China. It should engage in more international cooperation and technological innovation to enhance its competitiveness. At the same time, it should strengthen collaboration with high-tech and high-value-added industries in China and abroad and make good use of markets and resources in China and the international community. In this way, it can realize sustainable development and contribute to further opening up and integrating the regional economy.

Chapter 2
International Inland Ports' Competitiveness

International inland ports are a hot research topic in contemporary Chinese academia. Evaluating the competitiveness of China's international inland ports under the RCEP is crucial for understanding their position in regional economic integration, optimizing the development strategies of inland ports, and enhancing their service capacity and competitiveness. This chapter summarizes the definition, functions, research status and development of China's international inland ports. Based on the constructed system of international inland ports' competitiveness indices, subjective and objective weights are calculated using the subjective analytic hierarchy process (AHP) and objective entropy weighting method. The game theory is introduced again to compute the combined weights of each evaluation index. Grey Relational Analysis (GRA) and Technique for Order Preference by Similarity to Ideal Solution (TOPSIS) are jointly applied to evaluate the competitiveness of international inland ports. Finally, 182 international inland ports in China are empirically analyzed, and corresponding policy recommendations are proposed.

Introduction

This chapter aims to sort out and summarize the definition, functions, research status and development of China's international inland ports. Based on the established scientific evaluation system, it explores the current competitiveness status of China's international inland ports and identifies the key influencing factors. Moreover, it proposes strategies to enhance its competitiveness and contribute wisdom and strength to the economic development of the regions where China's international inland ports are located. It provides new ideas for international inland port construction planning and promotes the economic development of inland port cities in China and abroad. In October 2020, in its 14th Five-Year Plan, China proposed accelerating efforts to foster a new pattern of development focused on China's economy, which features a positive interplay between China's and international economic flows. From 2020 to 2023, China's import and export trade was restricted by the global COVID-19 pandemic. However, the construction and development of international inland ports can effectively promote trade recovery and accelerate economic development. According to the data released by China State Railway Group Co., Ltd. on July 29, 2023, the number of 10,000 trips of China-Europe freight train this year was achieved 22 days earlier than last year. At present, 86 China-Europe freight trains run at 120 kilometers per hour in China, with a total of 1,083,000 TEUs of goods delivered, a year-on-year increase of 27%. As of October 2023, China-Europe freight trains have reached 112 cities in China, more than 200 cities in 25 European countries and regions, and more than 100 cities in 11 Asian countries and regions along the route. It opens up a new channel of land transportation between Asia and Europe. The international inland ports, as transit stations, are essential transportation nodes for China-Europe freight trains. They contribute significantly to the promotion of China's economic development.

On November 2, 2021, the Regional Comprehensive Economic Partnership (RCEP) was enacted. It covers 15 member countries (10 ASEAN countries, including China, Japan, South Korea, Australia, and New Zealand). The agreement aims to reduce trade barriers among member countries, promote the free flow of goods, services and investment, strengthen economic cooperation and enhance regional economic integration. Since the RCEP came into effect, the agreement has played a significant role in stabilizing China's foreign trade and attracting foreign investment. In 2021, the total imports and exports between China and other RCEP member countries reached RMB 12.95 trillion, a year-on-year growth of 7.5%. It accounted for 30.8% of China's total imports and exports. Under this framework, China's international inland ports are vital global supply chains and trade nodes. They perform the function of cargo distribution and are the intersection centers of the flows of goods, information and capital. These inland ports are crucial in promoting the Belt and Road, the New International Land-Sea Trade Corridor and other major national strategic tasks of China.

International trade has become increasingly important to China's economic development, with imports and exports accounting for more than 30% of China's GDP (Figure 2-1). International inland ports are the extension of coastal ports in inland cities. They are the transit and distribution ports for international capital in the inland area, bearing space for transferring coastal industries to the inland areas. They are the gateway of the inland area to the international market. At the same time, they are the pioneer area and essential foundation for developing the Belt and Road. They have evolved from inland logistics hubs dependent on seaports to independent ports.

Moreover, they have become indispensable logistics hubs under the new economic development paradigm of "dual-circulation" between China's and international economies. International inland ports have become a hot topic in Chinese academic research. Therefore, assessing the competitiveness of China's international inland ports under the RCEP is strategically crucial for understanding their position in regional economic integration, optimizing the development strategy of inland ports, and enhancing their service capacity and competitiveness.

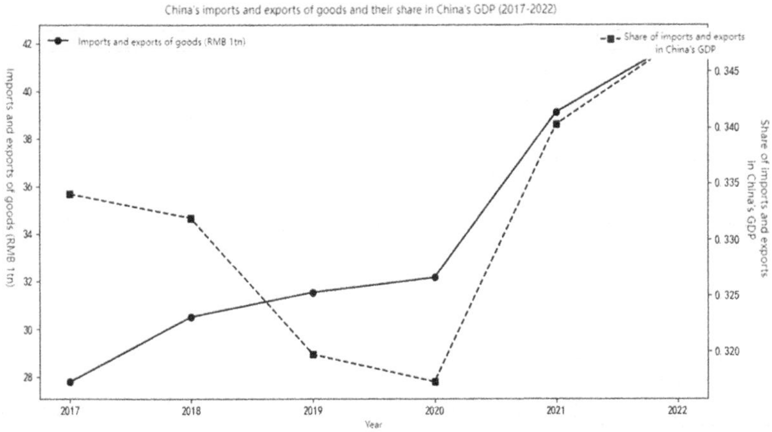

Figure 2-1 China's imports and exports of goods and their share in China's GDP (2017-2022)

Definition, Functions and History of International Inland Ports

International inland ports are ports for customs clearance of goods set up in inland central cities without water and with convenient land transportation. They have inherited the functions of coastal and border ports. They also have the functions of multimodal transportation, customs clearance, international trade, comprehensive bonded zone and value-added services, which are not available in coastal ports (Liu et al., 2020). They are the functional extension of coastal or border ports in the inland areas.

The development and functional characteristics of international inland ports have been improved continuously. According to Liu (2020), the history of China's international inland ports can be divided into the following three stages:

The first stage is the stage of economic globalization. In the 1980s, ports mainly depended on seaports, with container transportation, cargo distribution and other logistics transportation as their primary functions. The ports had a single function and business. The second stage is the stage after the Belt and Road was initiated. The concept of international inland ports was introduced by Chinese leaders in 2001, and the State Council proposed the Belt and Road Initiative in 2003. Since then, China has formally applied the new international inland port concept. At this stage, inland ports no longer depend on seaports and develop as independent inland ports. At the same time, they combine the functions of multimodal transportation, customs clearance, international trade, comprehensive bonded zone and value-added services. The third stage is when the new development pattern was proposed under the dual circulation of China's and international economies. In this stage, international inland ports link seaports and inland ports and integrate multiple business sectors. From 2020 to the end of 2023, China has been working.

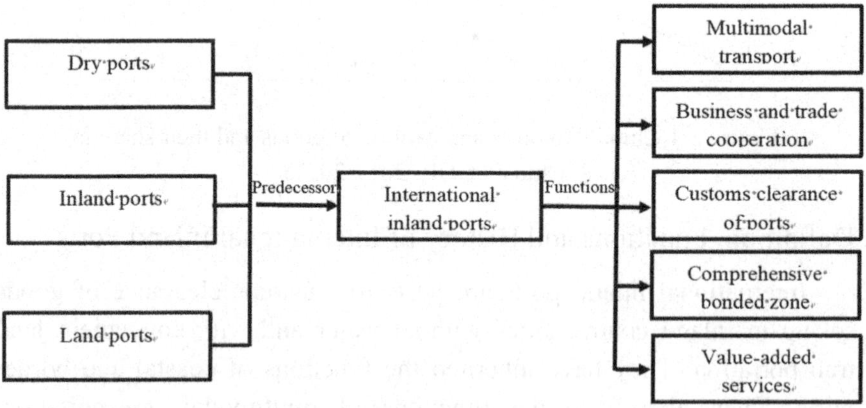

Figure 2-2 History and significant functions of international inland ports

It is a new development pattern focused on the Chinese economy, which features a positive interplay between Chinese and international economic flows. It has prompted the international inland port projects to build an integrated network platform for supply and marketing, launch China-Europe freight trains and keep them running smoothly.

Moreover, it has implemented sea-rail transportation, attracted high-value industries to cluster in the ports, improved supply chain management efficiency, and innovated supply chain financial services. Efforts have been made to develop the hub economy, platform economy and port economy of inland ports and realize multi-industry business cooperation in China and internationally. It can be modeled in Figure 2-2.

The international inland ports have evolved from inland logistics hubs dependent on seaports to independent ports. They have become indispensable logistics hubs under the new economic development paradigm of "dual-circulation" of Chinese and international economies. Also, their functions have been improved. International inland ports are constructed to facilitate loading and unloading, transporting, storing and distributing goods, and processing relevant international transport documents. They are trading ports directly open to the outside world following the relevant international transportation regulations, treaties, practices and Chinese domestic laws and regulations.

Policies for Developing China's International Inland Ports

China's international inland ports extend the coastal ports and logistics network. They are also the engines of socio-economic development or local development. 2020 is a watershed for the development of international inland ports. In the earlier period, the development of international inland ports was primarily influenced by strategic policies, such as Western Development, the Belt and Road, Free Trade Zone Development, and Port Integration. The influencing mechanisms are specified in Table 2-1 below.

Table 2-1 Policies significantly affecting the early development

Time	Policies influencing the development	Influencing mechanism
The 1990s	Western Development	The "Western Development" policy has facilitated the transfer of Chinese industries from the east to the central and western parts. Thus, it has accelerated the development of inland transportation systems in West and Central China.
After 2001	Port Integration	The "port integration" model has strengthened the market power of inland ports and provided more efficient customs clearance of goods at inland ports.
2010	Outline of the Twelfth Five-Year Plan	The concept of "coordinated land and marine development" has been proposed, emphasizing the coordinated development of the maritime economy.
2013	The Belt and Road	It promotes cooperation and investment in various industries and sectors in many countries along the Silk Road Economic Belt from historical, political and economic perspectives.
2013	Free Trade Zone	It simplifies customs clearance procedures for goods, provides "one-stop" customs clearance services, reduces the time required for customs clearance and improves the efficiency of importing and exporting goods.
2016	Three-year Action Plan for the Construction of Major National Transportation Infrastructure (2016-2018)	Vigorous construction of transportation projects in inland cities in central and western China has dramatically reduced transportation time and cost.
2019	Outline Development Plan for the Guangdong-Hong Kong-Macao Greater Bay Area	A "world-class city cluster" has been established in the Guangdong-Hong Kong-Macao Greater Bay Area to vigorously develop the marine economy, foster coordinated land and marine development, and build China into a maritime powerhouse.

In 2017, the agreement on the "Southbound Corridor," the predecessor of the "new land-sea corridor," was formally signed. In 2018, the project "Memorandum of Understanding on Cooperation on the Construction of the New International Land-Sea Trade Corridor under the China-Singapore (Chongqing) Demonstration Initiative on Strategic Connectivity" was successfully promoted. 2019 China's National Development and Reform Commission issued the New International Land-Sea Trade Corridor Master Plan. Many provinces and cities (e.g., Guangxi, Chongqing, Qinghai, Gansu, Xinjiang, Ningxia, Yunnan, and Shaanxi) have joined the "new land-sea corridor" to exchange business with foreign enterprises. It has formed a pattern of opening up to the outside world with the linkage of land and sea and the two-way mutual assistance between eastern and western China. Since 2020, the New International Land-Sea Trade Corridor has been advancing smoothly. The unimpeded operation of China-Europe freight trains promotes international inland ports to become critical transportation and logistics network nodes. It ensures seamless transportation connections between inland areas and the international community. The New International Land-Sea Trade Corridor is the most convenient and stable international logistics corridor to ASEAN in central and western China. It is an essential channel for developing the ASEAN market and overseas trade. The international inland ports are pivotal for provinces and cities to connect and integrate into the New International Land-Sea Trade Corridor. Since then, Chinese provinces and cities have actively developed international inland port projects. Capitalizing on the New International Land-Sea Trade Corridor, the international inland ports have been engaged in trade and cooperative exchanges with Southeast Asian countries such as Laos, Vietnam, Thailand, Russia, the United Kingdom, and other Nordic countries. It has contributed to the rapid development of the local economy.

Current Development of International Inland Ports

International inland ports enable inland cities to have more convenient international logistics channels, reduce the transit segments of imports and exports, and accelerate the speed of customs clearance. Moreover, it provides convenient ports and comprehensive logistics services for local international trade and improves the opening-up level of inland cities. The construction of international inland ports in various cities and the regular operation of China-Europe freight trains have driven significant changes in the trade distribution system. They have enriched the supply of global transportation services, helped form a system of land trade rules and standards and better adapted to the innovations of various trade forms.

In order to promote economic growth, China has established international inland ports in many cities since the establishment of the first inland port - Henan Highway Port, in 2006. China's representative international inland ports include Xi'an International Port Area, Zhengzhou International Inland Port, Lanzhou International Inland Port, Chengdu International Inland Port, Xinjiang International Inland Port, and Hefei International Inland Port. Over time, the functions of China's international inland ports have been expanding. Under the new economic development paradigm of "dual-circulation" of Chinese and international economies, China's international inland ports are organized to serve enterprises and consumers and link port industries in China and abroad to form an industrial chain. China-Europe freight trains are launched to reduce transportation costs. Moreover, they closely link the production and manufacturing of various industries in China and abroad, as well as inter-regional logistics, commerce, and finance, and promote the rapid development of local economies.

Research on the development of China's inland ports reveals that its development trajectory is closely related to China's participation in globalization. So far, the development of China's inland ports has gone through economic globalization, the construction of The Belt and Road, and the new economic development paradigm of "dual-circulation" of Chinese and international economies. Their development characteristics have also changed from sea-oriented thinking, initially dependent on seaports, to land-oriented thinking for independent ports. Eventually, it evolved into the two-way thinking of land-sea linkage and multi-sectoral integration. Functional characteristics have also been enriched. At present, China has built several inland port cities. The construction of international inland ports and the regular operation of China-Europe freight trains reduce the transit process of imported and exported goods and accelerate the speed of customs clearance. It provides convenient port and logistics services for local international trade. Moreover, it improves the opening-up level of inland cities and significantly promotes local economic development.

Literature Review

The research on inland ports and international inland ports started in 1986, with two research peaks. The first research peak was in 2010. After 2020, the number of research literature increased rapidly, and the number of papers in 2022 grew by 100% compared to 2021. International inland ports have become a hot research topic.

Building An Index System for Evaluating International Inland Ports' Competitiveness

Building a comprehensive index system for evaluating international inland ports' competitiveness is the key to evaluating their competitiveness. Since international inland ports have recently become new, few related studies exist. Searching for "international inland ports' competitiveness" in CNKI's general library reveals only 67 articles. The following index systems for evaluating international inland ports are derived from the relevant literature. Tang et al. (2020) constructed a competitiveness evaluation model and index system for inland ports based on infrastructure, production capacity and development environment from the literature. Chen and Huang (2011) constructed an evaluation system of international inland ports' competitiveness through literature collection and expert inquiry. It covers six aspects: infrastructure development, service provision capability, brand building level, industrial agglomeration, driving force, regional economic development and government policy.

Jiang (2023) constructed an evaluation system of international inland ports' competitiveness through a questionnaire survey. It involves infrastructure facilities, operation level, the status of leading operation platforms, economic development of the hinterland, transportation infrastructure, and the development potential of inland ports. Jiang (2022) constructed a comprehensive evaluation system for inland ports based on internal conditions, external conditions, operation level, and soft power by combining relevant data and expert ratings. Yan (2021) constructed a comprehensive competitiveness system for Xi'an International Inland

Port, ranging from basic logistics to vertical and horizontal integration through specialist inquiry. He (2018) created an index system for evaluating international inland ports' competitiveness. It involves the development of inland ports' internal infrastructure, logistics, transportation, and policy environment. Through literature, Wei (2016) constructed seven primary indexes, including conditions of equipment service of inland ports.

Moreover, he selected 17 secondary indexes to construct a comprehensive system for evaluating inland ports. From logistics business, infrastructure development, regional economy, customers and social development, Che (2015) used the balanced scorecard to establish an index system for evaluating international inland ports' logistics. The following problems exist in constructing the index system for evaluating international inland ports' competitiveness. First, the index system is complicated; in some cases, the same information is reported by more than one index. Second, according to the expert screening method, it is overly subjective as it relies solely on the meanings of the indexes and personal experience.

Selection of Evaluation Methods of International Inland Ports' Competitiveness

Various methods can evaluate international inland ports' competitiveness. Here, we mainly cover quantitative research methods. The subjective methods include AHP, G1, G2, and ANP approaches. Jiang (2023) applied the AHP method to assign weights in the index system for evaluating international inland ports' competitiveness. Sun, Wu and Ma (2022) assigned weights in national grain production using the G1 method. Zhu and Zhang (2019) detailed the application of the G2 method. Chen and Huang (2011) used ANP to empirically validate the competitiveness of Xi'an International Inland Port against the shortcomings of AHP. Objective assignment methods include entropy weighting, factor analysis, principal component analysis, grey relational degree, and cloud modeling. Yan (2021) empirically demonstrated the competitiveness of Xi'an International Inland Port by using cloud modeling. Li (2011) empirically demonstrated the competitiveness of Kunming International Inland Port by using grey relational analysis.

Cheng (2010) introduced the application of the entropy weight method in detail. Wang (2003) introduced principal component analysis and factor analysis. In selecting evaluation methods for international inland ports' competitiveness, the following problems are identified: Firstly, in the AHP method, only one expert creates a judgment matrix or uses the average value, reducing the use of decision-making by multiple groups of experts. Secondly, many articles use one method and cannot avoid the disadvantages of using only one method.

Building a System for Evaluating International Inland Ports' Competitiveness

Principles of Index Selection

An appropriate number of evaluation indexes should be selected to evaluate international inland ports' competitiveness. If too many indexes are used, excessive covariance and correlation between the indexes may cause repetition effects and interference with the results. When too few indexes are selected, the response information may not be comprehensive and cannot be evaluated. Therefore, the following principles should be followed in establishing the evaluation system of inland ports' competitiveness: (1) Applicability principle: The selected indexes should genuinely reflect the level of competitiveness of inland ports and be representative and universally applicable. (2) Principle of comparability: The selected indexes should be comparable, facilitating the comparison between different regions or types of inland ports. (3) Comprehensive principle: The selected indexes should comprehensively reflect the factors of inland ports' competitiveness, involving the economy, technology, management and other aspects. (4) Principle of operability: The selected indexes should be operable and provide guidance and decision-making support for inland ports.

Evaluation Index System of International Inland Ports' Competitiveness

According to the above principles, the index system for evaluating competitiveness is constructed by synthesizing the relevant research results of Chinese scholars, as shown in Table 2-2.

Table 2-2 Index system for evaluating international inland ports' competitiveness

Criterion layer	Index error	Unit	No.	Index direction
Internal infrastructure development of international inland ports Y1	Investment amount	RMB100mn	x1	Positive
	Number of bonded logistics centers (Type B)		x2	Positive
	Bonded logistics centers (Type B)	sq. km.	x3	Positive
	Area of special customs supervision areas	sq. Km.	x4	Positive
	Number of national logistics hubs (inland ports, airports, production, commerce)		x5	Positive
Logistics development of international inland ports Y2	Citywide postal revenue	RMB 10,000	x6	Positive
	Investment in fixed assets	RMB 10,000	x7	Positive
	Fixed Asset Investment Price Index (previous year = 100)		x8	Positive
	Total annual passenger traffic on public buses and trolleys in the city district	10,000 persons	x9	Positive
	Citywide highway passenger traffic	10,000 persons	x10	Positive
	Citywide highway freight transportation	10,000 tons	x11	Positive
	Highway mileage	km	x12	Positive

Criterion layer	**Index error**	**Unit**	**No.**	**Index direction**
Business development of international inland ports Y3	Number of wholesale and retail trade enterprises above designated size in the city_Number of legal persons		x13	Positive
	Number of enterprises invested by Hong Kong, Macao and Taiwan merchants in the city		x14	Positive
	Foreign-invested enterprises in the city		x15	Positive
	Area of free trade zones	sq. km.	x16	Positive
	Import volume of goods in the city	RMB10,000	x17	Positive
	Export volume of goods in the city	RMB10,000	x18	Positive
	Actual utilization of foreign capital	RMB100mn	x19	Positive
	Balance of RMB loans from financial institutions at the end of the year	RMB10,000	x20	Positive
Regional Economic Development Y4	Gross Domestic Product (GDP) of the city	RMB100mn	x21	Positive
	Growth rate of Gross Domestic Product (GDP) of the city	%	x22	Positive
	Share of secondary industry in the city's GDP	%	x23	Positive

Criterion layer	Index error	Unit	No.	Index direction
	Registered population of the city	10,000 persons	x24	Positive
	Total sales value of wholesale and retail trade above the designated size in the city	RMB10,000	x25	Positive
	Value added of primary industry	RMB10,000	x26	Positive
	Value added of secondary industry	RMB10,000	x27	Positive
	GDP per capita of the city	RMB10,000	x28	Positive

Notes: Index descriptions

1. Internal infrastructure development of international inland ports

Y1: This criterion layer assesses the infrastructure development of inland ports. It focuses on inland ports' physical structures and facilities, such as logistics centers and supervisory areas. These are the cornerstones that support the operation and growth of inland ports. It consists of the following index layers:

Investment amount (x1): It measures the investment size in infrastructure development within inland ports, in RMB100mn. A higher investment amount usually means better facilities and higher development potential.

Number of bonded logistics centers (Type B) (x2): It calculates the number of Type B bonded logistics centers in inland ports. These centers are essential logistics nodes in international trade, and their number reflects the logistics handling capacity of inland ports.

Area of bonded logistics centers (Type B) (x3): Type B bonded logistics centers in inland ports, in sq. km. A larger area usually represents higher logistics handling and storage capacity.

Area of particular customs supervision areas (x4): The total area of particular customs supervision areas set up in inland ports, in sq. km. The presence and size of these areas are crucial for strengthening customs supervision and improving the efficiency of customs clearance.

Number of national logistics hubs (x5): It counts the number of national logistics hubs of various types in inland ports, including inland ports, airports, production and commerce. This index reflects the importance and diversity of inland ports in the national logistics network.

2. Logistics development of international inland ports

Y2: This criterion layer emphasizes the logistical capabilities of inland ports, covering the areas of transportation, cargo handling and logistics services. A good level of logistics development can enhance the efficiency and attractiveness of inland ports. It contains the following index layers:

Citywide postal revenue (x6): It indicates the city's total postal revenue, where inland ports are located, in RMB10,000. It reflects the scale and efficiency of the postal logistics business in the region.

Investment in fixed assets (x7): the total investment in fixed assets in inland ports, in RMB10,000. This index is usually related to infrastructure construction and upgrading of logistics facilities.

Fixed Asset Investment Price Index (x8): It reflects the price change of investment in fixed assets based on the previous year (previous year = 100). It helps to understand the value and efficiency of capital investment.

Total annual passenger traffic on public buses and trolleys in the city district (x9): It records the total passenger traffic on public buses and trolleys in the city district in a year, in 10,000 persons. It indicates the level of development and use of the public transportation system.

Citywide highway passenger traffic (x10): the total amount of highway passenger traffic within the city in 10,000 persons. This index reflects the status of the highway transportation network in the city where the inland ports are located.

Citywide highway freight transportation (x11): the tons of highway freight transportation in the city where the inland ports are located, in 10,000 tons. The amount of freight transportation is directly related to the logistics capacity of the inland ports.

Highway mileage (x12): the total mileage of inland ports in km. A more extended highway network can help improve logistics efficiency and connect remote markets.

3. Business development of international inland ports

Y3: The criterion layer measures the development of inland ports in terms of business and trade. It includes the volume of trade, the diversity of business activities, and the degree of international business cooperation, and is a crucial index of the international competitiveness of inland ports. It consists of the following index layers:

Number of wholesale and retail trade enterprises above the designated size in the city (x13): It counts the number of wholesale and retail trade enterprises above the designated size. It shows the scale of trade activities and market potential of inland ports.

Number of enterprises invested by Hong Kong, Macao and Taiwan merchants in the city (x14): It counts the number of enterprises invested by Hong Kong, Macao and Taiwan merchants in the city where inland ports are located. It shows the attractiveness of inland ports to investors from these regions.

Foreign-invested enterprises in the city (x15): It records the number of foreign-invested enterprises in the city where inland ports are located. This index reflects the attractiveness and status of inland ports for international investment.

Area of free trade zones (x16): It indicates the total area of free trade zones in the region where the inland ports are located, in sq. km. Free trade zones are vital areas for promoting international trade and investment.

Import volume of goods in the city (x17) and export volume of goods in the city (x18): They record the total amount of imports and exports of goods in the city where the inland ports are located, in RMB10,000. These indices reflect the trade scale and international connectivity of inland ports.

Actual utilization of foreign capital (x19): The amount of foreign capital attracted by the city where the inland ports are located, in RMB100mn. It shows the ability of inland ports to attract foreign direct investment.

Balance of RMB loans from financial institutions at the end of the year (x20): the total amount of RMB loans from financial institutions in the city where the inland ports are located at the end of the year, in RMB 10,000. It represents the activity and development level of the financial market in the region.

4. Regional economic development

Y4: The criterion layer concerns the economic development of the region where the inland ports are located. Healthy regional economic growth is crucial to the long-term prosperity of inland ports. This index involves regional GDP, industrial value added, and population and economic status. It consists of the following index layers:

Gross Domestic Product (GDP) of the city (x21): It indicates the Gross Domestic Product (GDP) of the city district where inland ports are located, in RMB100mn. It is a crucial index to measure the size and development level of the regional economy.

Growth rate of Gross Domestic Product (GDP) of the city (x22): It reflects the annual growth rate of GDP of the area where the inland ports are located, in percent. It shows the rate of economic growth and potential of the region.

Share of secondary industry in the city's GDP (x23): It shows the share of the secondary industry (i.e., manufacturing) in the city's GDP in percent. It reflects the importance of industry and manufacturing in the regional economy.

Registered population of the city (x24): It records the total registered population of the city where the inland ports are located, which is 10,000 persons. The population size directly affects the size of the labor and consumer markets.

Total sales value of wholesale and retail trade above the designated size in the city (x25): It measures the total sales of goods in the city by wholesale and retail businesses above the designated size, in RMB10,000. It reflects the scale of business activities and market dynamics.

Value added of primary industry (x26) and value-added of secondary industry (x27): They capture the value added of the contribution of agriculture (primary industry) and industry (secondary industry) to the city's economy, in RMB10,000. These indices show the contribution of the different industries to the regional economy and the development status of these industries.

GDP per capita of the city (x28): It calculates the GDP per capita of the city where inland ports are located, in RMB10,000. It is an important index to assess the average economic well-being of the population and economic development of the region.

Research Methodology

Subjective Weighting by AHP

AHP (Feng et al., 2023) decomposes the target problem into objective, benchmark and program layers and calculates the weight of each layer or factor by comparing the relative importance of the layers and factors. The researcher can use the relevant experience or expert opinions in the field to judge and measure the importance of various factors to rank their weights. Thus, a quantitative analysis can be realized. The steps of AHP are as follows:

(1) Scoring the evaluation system according to the questionnaire for collecting experts' opinions. It concludes the judgment matrix A.

$$A = \begin{bmatrix} a_{11} & a_{12} & \cdots & \cdots & a_{1n} \\ a_{21} & a_{22} & \cdots & \cdots & a_{2n} \\ \cdots & \cdots & a_{ij} & \cdots & \cdots \\ \cdots & \cdots & \cdots & \cdots & \cdots \\ a_{n1} & a_{n2} & \cdots & \cdots & a_{nn} \end{bmatrix},$$

a_{ij} in the matrix represents the importance of A_i relative to A_j. If the former is more important, $a_{ij} > 1$. If both are equally important, $a_{ij}=1$.

The importance of the matrix elements is summarized in Table 2-3.

Table 2-3 Criteria of relative importance scale

Scale	Meaning
1	Two factors are equally important when compared
3	When comparing two factors, the former factor is slightly more important than the latter.
5	When comparing two factors, the former is significantly more critical than the latter.
7	When comparing two factors, the former is more significant than the latter.
9	When comparing two factors, the former is more important than the latter.
2、4、6、8	The median value of two neighboring factors
The reciprocal of the above figures	Two factors compared inversely are the reciprocal of the original comparison.

(2) Calculating the weight vector of the index

Step 1: normalize the matrix

The following formula is utilized:

$$\overline{a_{ij}} = a_{ij} / \sum_{i=1}^{n} a_{ij} (i, j = 1, 2, \mathrm{L}\ n) \quad \text{.......................................} (1)$$

where a_{ij} denotes the data in row i and column j of the judgment matrix A, $\overline{a_{ij}}$ denotes the data in row i and column j of the normalized matrix.

Step 2: add the elements of the matrix.

$$\overline{w_i} = \sum_{j=1}^{n} \overline{a_{ij}} (i, j = 1, 2, \mathrm{L}\ n) \quad \text{..} (2)$$

Step 3: normalize $\overline{w_i}$ in the above formula:

$$w_i = \overline{w_i} / \sum_{i=1}^{n} \overline{w_i} (i = 1, 2, \mathrm{L}\ n) \quad \text{...} (3)$$

where w_i denotes the weight of the index i

Step 4: calculate the maximum eigenvalue of the judgment matrix A

$$\lambda_{\max} = \frac{1}{n} \sum_{i=1}^{n} \frac{(Aw)_i}{w_i} \quad \text{..} (4)$$

where n denotes the order of the matrix, A denotes the judgment matrix, w_i denotes the weight of the index i. $\lambda_{\max}$ denotes the maximum eigenvalue of the judgment matrix A.

(3) Consistency test.

The vectors and eigenvalues are tested for consistency. The judgment matrix is reasonable if it can pass the test, indicating that the interpretation value exists. It is assumed that CI stands for consistency index, and the following is the operation method:

$$CI = \frac{\lambda_{\max} - n}{n - 1} \quad \text{...} (5)$$

The consistency test is summarized in Table 2-4.

Table 2-4 Random index (RI)

N	RI
1	0
2	0
3	0.52
4	0.89

N	RI
5	1.12
6	1.24
7	1.32
8	1.41
9	1.45
10	1.49
11	1.51

RI value can be derived through n to obtain the consistency ratio, i.e. $CR = CI/RI$. When CR<0.1, it passes the test.

(4) Weights of multi-expert group decision-making

With n experts ($j = 1, 2, L\ n$) scoring the index system, it can generate n judgment matrices and derive n w_{ij}. Each expert can assign different weights v_j as per their positions, and age. Based on this, the final weight of the decision of multiple experts will be derived by $w_{ij} \times v_j$. It is converted into the following formula:

$$w_{ij} = \begin{bmatrix} w_{11} & w_{12} & \Lambda & \Lambda & w_{1j} \\ w_{21} & w_{22} & \Lambda & \Lambda & w_{2j} \\ \Lambda & \Lambda & \Lambda & \Lambda & \Lambda \\ \Lambda & \Lambda & \Lambda & \Lambda & \Lambda \\ w_{n1} & w_{n2} & \Lambda & \Lambda & w_{ij} \end{bmatrix} \quad \text{......................................(6)}$$

$$v_j = [v_1, v_2, \cdots v_n]^T \quad \text{...(7)}$$

Final weight W, where $W = w_{ij} \times v_j = [W_1, W_2, \cdots W_n]$ ....(8)

Objective Weighting by Entropy Weight Method

In information theory, entropy is a tool to measure the degree of system disorder. In this study, the entropy value of each index is calculated to determine the weight of each index. The entropy value reflects the degree of difference of the index data. The more significant the difference between the index data of each evaluation object, the more information the index carries, the more critical the index is to the evaluation result, and the more weight should be given to it. The steps of the entropy weight method (Chen and Wang, 2003) are as follows:

(1) Data normalization

The data for each index are normalized to avoid the influence of the scale on the data processing.

For positive indexes:

$$u_{ij} = 0.998\frac{x_{ij} - \min\{x_{1j}, x_{2j}, ..., x_{nj}\}}{\max\{x_{1j}, x_{2j}, ..., x_{nj}\} - \min\{x_{1j}, x_{2j}, ..., x_{nj}\}} + 0.002$$

..................................(9)

For negative indexes:

$$u_{ij} = 0.998\frac{\max\{x_{1j}, x_{2j}, ..., x_{nj}\} - x_{ij}}{\max\{x_{1j}, x_{2j}, ..., x_{nj}\} - \min\{x_{1j}, x_{2j}, ..., x_{nj}\}} + 0.002$$

..............................(10)

u_{ij} denotes the value after the standardization of the index j under the evaluation object i. x_{ij} denotes the observed value of the index j under the evaluation object i. n denotes the number of evaluation objects, and m denotes the number of evaluation indexes. Coefficients 0.998 and 0.002 are designed to make the value u_{1j} greater than 0 to prevent subsequent calculations $\ln u_{1j}$. Here, 0.998 can be changed to any number closer to 1, such as 0.999 and 0.997.

(2) Calculating the index ratio

$$p_{ij} = \frac{u_{ij}}{\sum_{i=1}^{n} u_{ij}}$$

....(11)

where, P_{ij} denotes the index ratio of the program i under the index j (i=1,2, ……, n), (j=1,2, ……, m).

(3) Calculating information entropy

$$e_j = -k\sum_{i=1}^{n} p_{ij} \ln(p_{ij})$$

....(12)

where $k = \frac{1}{\ln(n)}$, satisfying $e_j > 0$; where e_j denotes the entropy value of the index j (j=1,2, ……, m).

(4) Calculating the redundancy of information entropy

$$g_j = 1 - e_j \quad \text{......(13)}$$

where g_j denotes the information entropy redundancy of the index j (j=1,2, ……, m).

(5) Calculating index weights

$$w_j = \frac{g_j}{\sum_{j=1}^{m} g_j} \quad \text{......(14)}$$

The result should meet the equation $\sum_{j=1}^{m} w_j = 1$, where w_j denotes the index's weight j (j=1,2, ……, m).

Combination Weighting Based on Game Theory

Combination weighting can reflect experts' subjective evaluation of international inland ports' competitiveness. It can also reflect the objective pattern of the survey data. The game theory (Yao, Kou and Zhang, 2023) was introduced to determine the subjective and objective weights of each index to determine the coefficients of subjective and objective weights. The basic idea is to fully consider the subjective and objective weights and look for the consistency or compromise between the two to minimize the deviation of the subjective and objective weights.

(1) Building the combined weight vector

$$w_3^T = A_1 w_1^T + A_2 w_2^T \quad \text{......(15)}$$

where w_1^T denotes the subjective weight vector, w_2^T denotes the objective weight vector, and w_3^T denotes the optimal combination weight.

(2) Introducing the idea of game theory

$$\min\left\|\sum_{v=1}^{2}A_v w_v^T - w_z^T\right\|_2 \quad (z=1,2) \tag{16}$$

The above formula is derived to yield the following formula:

$$\begin{bmatrix} w_1 \cdot w_1^T & w_1 \cdot w_2^T \\ w_2 \cdot w_1^T & w_2 \cdot w_2^T \end{bmatrix} \times \begin{bmatrix} A_1 \\ A_2 \end{bmatrix} = \begin{bmatrix} w_1 \cdot w_1^T \\ w_2 \cdot w_2^T \end{bmatrix} \tag{17}$$

The above formula is solved to get the final combination coefficient $A_h\,(h = 1,2)$.

(3) Normalizing the coefficients

$$A_h^* = \frac{|A_h|}{\sum_{h=1}^{2}|A_h|} \tag{18}$$

(4) Obtaining the optimal combination weights

$$w_3^T = A_1^* w_1^T + A_2^* w_2^T \tag{19}$$

(5) Optimizing for negative weights

When we solve for the combination weights based on game theory, we aim to find an equilibrium point where the subjective weights (w1) and objective weights (w2) are reasonably combined. Ideally, this combined weight (W) should reflect the equilibrium of the two weights, given their respective importance.

We first try to find this equilibrium by solving a linear system (A*B=C). A is a matrix consisting of weight vectors, B is a vector of coefficients we are looking for, and C is a vector associated with A. The basis of this method is least squares, which attempts to minimize the squared difference between the predicted and actual values. We find B by calculating the pseudo-inverse of A and applying it to C.

However, in some cases, this method may have negative weights, which is meaningless in many practical applications. If negative weights are assumed, the optimization method is used here to ensure that all the combination weights are non-negative. If negative weights occur, the following optimization methods are employed:

1. Defining the objective function: An objective function measures the difference between the optimized and original combined weight

vectors. The specific form of this function is the sum of differences of squares, i.e., $\sum\left(a_1 w_1 + a_2 w_2 - w_{orig}\right)^2$. a_1 and a_2 are the coefficients we are looking for, w_1 and w_2 are the original weight vectors, and w_{orig} is the original combined weight vector obtained by solving the linear system.

2. Constraints: First, it is the sum constraint $a_1 + a_2 = 1$. It guarantees that the sum of the coefficients is 1, implying that the new combined weight vector is a valid combination of w_1 and w_2. Second, there is the non-negativity constraint: $a_1 \geq 0$ and $a_2 \geq 0$. It ensures that all weights are non-negative, which makes sense in most cases.

3. The optimization method uses the 'scipy.optimize.minimize' function. It is a potent mathematical optimization tool in Python. This function finds the values of the variables that minimize the objective function while satisfying all the given constraints.

Evaluation Model of International Inland Ports' Competitiveness Based on the GRA-TOPSIS Approach

The traditional TOPSIS method (Guo, Xu and Huang, 2023) only considers the relative positions of the programs to the positive and negative ideal solutions but ignores the trends of the programs. The GRA method (Grey Relational Analysis) (Yi, 2023) mainly analyzes the similarity of the data curves and predicts the trend of changes. Therefore, this chapter combines the TOPSIS and GRA methods to validate the sample data of international inland ports empirically. The specific steps are as follows:

(1) Standardizing the original data.

The initial evaluation matrix $X = (x_{ij})_{m\times n}$ is constructed from m international inland ports and n evaluation indices. The indexes are standardized to obtain a standardized evaluation matrix. Data standardization can be performed by max-min standardization, according to e $Y = (y_{ij})_{m\times n}$ quations (9) and (10).

(2) Determining the weight of each evaluation index.

Here, the weight $w=\{w_1,w_2,K\ w_j,K\ ,w_n\}$ can be determined based on the above combination weighting approach, where $0\le w_j\le 1$ and

$$\sum_{j=1}^{n} w_j = 1$$

.

(3) Calculating the weighted evaluation matrix.

The standardized evaluation matrix $Y=(y_{ij})_{m\times n}$ is assigned to yield the weighted evaluation matrix $Z=(Z_{ij})_{m\times n}$ according to the following formula:

$$Z_{ij}=w_j\times y_{ij} \quad \text{.........(20)}$$

(4) Calculate the weighted evaluation matrix's positive and negative ideal solutions.

The positive ideal solution is the solution that maximizes the positive index and minimizes the negative index. In contrast, the negative ideal solution is the solution that minimizes the positive index and maximizes the negative index. For the weighted evaluation matrix $Z=(Z_{ij})_{m\times n}$, the positive ideal solution $Z^+=\left\{Z_1^+,Z_2^+,K\ ,Z_j^+,K\ ,Z_n^+\right\}$ is determined, and the negative ideal solution $Z^-=\left\{Z_1^-,Z_2^-,K\ ,Z_j^-,K\ ,Z_n^-\right\}$ is determined as follows:

$$Z_j^+=\left\{\max_{1\le i\le m} Z_{ij}\mid j=P,\min_{1\le i\le m} Z_{ij}\mid j=N\right\} \quad \text{.........(21)}$$

$$Z_j^-=\left\{\min_{1\le i\le m} Z_{ij}\mid j=P,\max_{1\le i\le m} Z_{ij}\mid j=N\right\} \quad \text{.........(22)}$$

In formulas (19) and (20) Z_j^+ denote the positive ideal solution of the index j, Z_j^- denotes the negative ideal solution of the index j. P is a positive index, and N is a negative index.

(5) Calculate each program's Euclidean distance to positive and negative ideal solutions.

$$d_i^+=\sqrt{\sum_{j=1}^{n}\left(Z_{ij}-Z_j^+\right)^2},i=1,2,K\ ,m \quad \text{.........(23)}$$

$$d_i^- = \sqrt{\sum_{j=1}^{n}\left(Z_{ij} - Z_j^-\right)^2}, i = 1,2,\mathrm{K}, m \quad (24)$$

(6) Calculate each program's grey relational degree to positive and negative ideal solutions. First, according to the weighted evaluation matrix, the absolute difference between the index and positive and negative ideal solutions of each program based on the following formulas:

$$\Delta_{ij}^+ = \left|y_{ij} - y_j^+\right| \quad (25)$$

$$\Delta_{ij}^- = \left|y_{ij} - y_j^-\right| \quad (26)$$

The grey relational coefficient of positive and negative ideal solutions is as follows:

$$\xi_{ij}^+ = \left(\min_i \min_j \Delta_{ij}^+ + \rho \max_i \max_j \Delta_{ij}^+\right) \Big/ \left(\Delta_{ij}^+ + \rho \max_i \max_j \Delta_{ij}^+\right) \quad (27)$$

$$\xi_{ij}^- = \left(\min_i \min_j \Delta_{ij}^- + \rho \max_i \max_j \Delta_{ij}^-\right) \Big/ \left(\Delta_{ij}^- + \rho \max_i \max_j \Delta_{ij}^-\right) \quad (28)$$

where, ρ denotes the distinguishing coefficient, $0 < \rho < 1$, generally valued as 0.5.

(7) Calculating the grey relational degree of each program and positive and negative ideal solutions:

$$r_i^+ = \frac{1}{m}\sum_{j=1}^{n}\xi_{ij}^+ \quad (29)$$

$$r_i^- = \frac{1}{m}\sum_{j=1}^{n}\xi_{ij}^- \quad (30)$$

(8) Making the Euclidean distance and the grey relational degree dimensionless.

$$D_i^+ = \frac{d_i^+}{\max\limits_{1\le i\le m} d_i^+}, \quad D_i^- = \frac{d_i^-}{\max\limits_{1\le i\le m} d_i^-} \quad (31)$$

$$R_i^+ = \frac{r_i^+}{\max\limits_{1\le i\le m} r_i^+}, \quad R_i^- = \frac{r_i^-}{\max\limits_{1\le i\le m} r_i^-} \quad (32)$$

(9) Calculate each evaluation program's comprehensive distance to the positive and negative ideal solutions. The principle of Grey

Relational Analysis and the TOPSIS method shows that the closer the evaluation object is to the positive ideal solution, the larger the Euclidean distance D_i^- and grey relational degree R_i^+ obtained by the TOPSIS method is to the positive ideal solution. The more the evaluation object deviates from the positive ideal solution, the larger the values D_i^+ and R_i^-. Then, the formula for combining the dimensionality-free Euclidean distance and grey relational degree is as follows:

$$H_i^+ = \alpha R_i^+ + \beta D_i^- \quad (33)$$

$$H_i^- = \alpha R_i^- + \beta D_i^+ \quad (34)$$

where, $0 \leq \alpha$、$\beta \leq 1$ and $\alpha + \beta = 1$, α and β represent the degree of preference for shape and distance, respectively, valued as 0.5. H_i^+ and H_i^- denote the comprehensive distance of each program to positive and negative ideal solutions

(10) Calculating the relative closeness.

$$L_i = \frac{H_i^+}{H_i^+ + H_i^-} \quad (35)$$

The integrated relative closeness reflects the similarity between each evaluation object's relative position and shape and the ideal solution. According to the ranking of integrated relative closeness, the greater the integrated relative closeness, the greater the international inland ports' competitiveness.

Overall Process

This chapter adopts the gray relational TOPSIS combination weighting method for comprehensive evaluation. The main processes include building the evaluation index system quantification of combination weighting → quantification of evaluation indices → analysis and evaluation of grey relation TOPSIS → sorting of international inland ports' competitiveness, as shown in Figure 2-3.

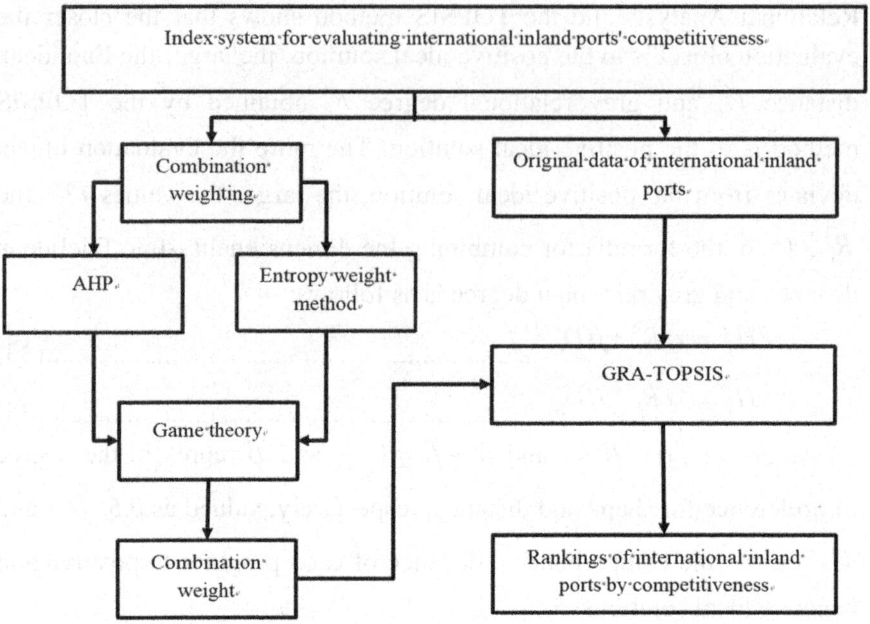

Figure 2-3 Evaluation process of international inland ports' competitiveness

Empirical Research

Data Selection

The corresponding data of 182 international inland ports in China in 2021 are selected. In 2021, there were 203 international inland ports in China. Fifteen international inland ports of local states and unions were deleted, and 189 international inland ports of prefectural cities were retained. On this basis, the six international inland ports with missing data on investment amount were further depleted. The figures for x1-x6 and x18 come from the official websites of international inland ports, international inland port associations, the White Paper on International Inland Ports 2020, and the official websites of local governments. The other data come from the statistical yearbook of each prefecture-level city government. The data are shown in Table 2-1.

Calculation of GRA-TOPSIS Evaluation Model for Combination Weighting Based on Game Theory

Weighting by AHP

In this evaluation, we invited three persons in charge of the functional departments of international inland ports, two for communicating in governmental departments, one expert advisor for international inland ports, and four college teachers studying international inland ports. They evaluated the index system of international inland ports' competitiveness. The final weights were calculated using AHP, as shown in Table 2-2.

Weighting by Entropy Weighting Method

The final weights of the indexes are calculated using the entropy weighting method in Table 2-3.

Combination Weight Calculation under Game Theory

Using formulas (15)-(19), we can derive A1=-0.656, A2=1.656. We use the scipy.optimize.minimize function in Python to optimize by adding the non-negative conditional constraints and A1+A2=1. The optimal weight distribution coefficients are A1=0.001, A2=0.999. The final combined weights are shown in Table 2-4.

Ranking and Calculation of International Inland Ports' Competitiveness by GRA-TOPSIS

The weighted evaluation matrix and the positive and negative ideal solutions are computed. The Euclidean distance between each inland port and the positive and negative ideal solutions is computed. Then, the relational degrees between the positive and negative ideal solutions are computed for each program. Finally, the score program of each international inland port under GRA-TOPSIS is calculated in Table 2-5.

Result Analysis

Cluster Analysis

According to the scores of Y1-Y4 under GRA-TOPSIS, we performed a k-means cluster analysis. The statistical information of each layer of clusters is shown in Table 2-5, and the scatter diagram of the clustering results is shown in Figure 2-4.

Table 2-5 Basic statistical analysis of the clusters

Cluster No.	count	mean	std	min	25%	50%	75%	max
1	39	0.090487	0.04207	0.035	0.056	0.094	0.111	0.188
2	7	0.136857	0.045671	0.099	0.1085	0.118	0.1605	0.203
3	8	0.112625	0.041662	0.072	0.076	0.101	0.1495	0.177
4	128	0.053984	0.2217	0.013	0.039	0.0535	0.06025	0.122

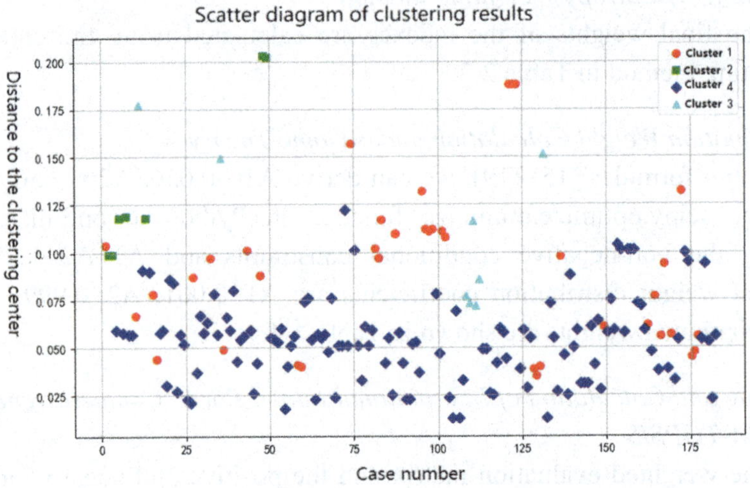

Figure 2-4 Clustering results of 182 international inland ports' competitiveness in China

According to the clustering results, the following conclusions can be drawn:

(1) The number of clusters: It can be seen that there are 128 international inland ports in Category 4, and the rest of the clusters are Category 1, Category 3, and Category 2 in descending order.

(2) Clustering mean: Since the clustering is done according to the scores of Y1-Y4 under GRA-TOPSIS (the higher the score, the better), we can compare the centroid (mean) of each cluster to determine the strength of competitiveness of each category. Among them, the mean value of Category 2 is 0.136857, which has the most robust competitiveness. The rest of the clusters are, in descending order of strength, Category 3, Category 1, and Category 4.

(3) Cluster variance (standard deviation): Since the variance (standard deviation) reflects the degree of dispersion of the clusters, the larger it is, the more dispersed the clusters are; the smaller the clusters are, the more concentrated they are, and the more similar they are. Since the standard deviation of Category 4 is 0.2217, it is the largest among the four categories. The clusters are decentralized, and the rest of the categories are not much different. In descending order of dispersion hierarchy, these clusters are Category 4, Category 2, Category 1, and Category 3.

General Analysis

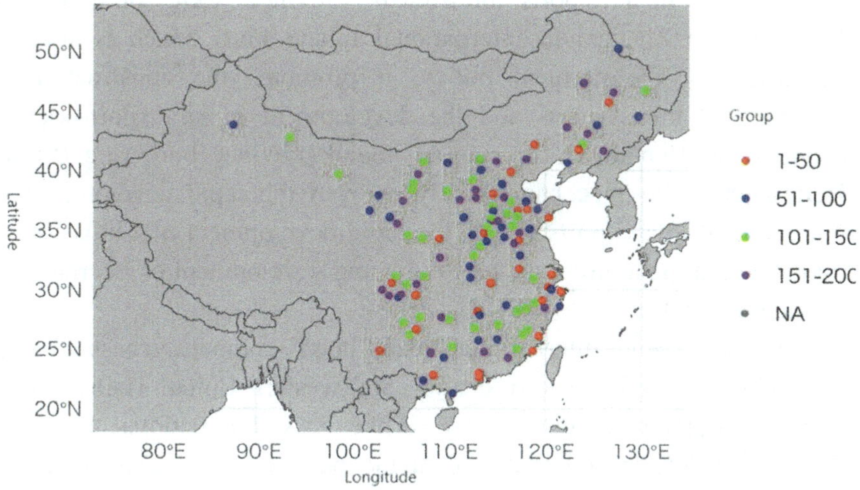

Figure 2-5 Distribution of competitiveness scores of 182 major international inland ports in China in 2021

(1) Regarding the competitiveness scores of international inland ports in various cities, the international inland ports of Beijing, Chongqing, Suzhou, Hangzhou, Chengdu, Ningbo and Xi'an are highly developed. It fits with the economic development level of the region where it is located. In Central China, the competitiveness of international inland ports in Wuhan, Changsha, and Zhengzhou is in the middle to upper levels, with similar scores. Central China has a high demand for opening up to the outside world. Cities in Central China are highly motivated to promote export-oriented economic development through

international inland ports, thus boosting regional economic development. Seventy-three international inland ports have scores lower than 0.3 but higher than 0.28. These inland ports are located in poorly developed cities that need to build international inland ports to improve their economic development.

(2) The overall competitiveness of international inland ports in provinces such as Shandong Province, Zhejiang Province, Henan Province, and Heilongjiang Province has led to the building of many international inland ports. Their overall competitiveness scores for international inland ports are high. Firstly, Eastern China has a sound economic foundation, and inland ports are mostly an extension of the seaport business, which is developing quickly. Secondly, the international inland ports in Henan Province were built earlier. According to Zhengzhou International Inland Port, which is strongly supported by the national policy, it promotes the construction of international inland ports and the development of an export-oriented economy in Henan. Thirdly, as an inland province bordering Russia, Heilongjiang Province has recently enjoyed the rapid development of international inland ports due to the rapid development of China-Russia trade. Heilongjiang presents the flourishing development of international inland ports in the whole province.

(3) Nationwide, international inland ports' competitiveness changes from high to low in eastern, central, and western China. Thanks to the national strategic policy support of the New International Land-Sea Trade Corridor, the international inland ports in Chongqing, Chengdu and Xi'an are highly competitive. They have a strong impetus to the economy of the hinterland. Moreover, they will further play an essential role in China's Belt and Road Initiative and significantly contribute to developing the export-oriented economy in western China, thus revitalizing Western China.

Recommendations

The economy of the coastal areas in southeastern China has taken off since the reform and opening up, capitalizing on the coastal economy policy. Central and western China are developing at a slow pace economically. The international inland ports have solved the bottleneck problem of creating an export-oriented economy in inland areas (Gou, 2015). Promoting the construction of international inland ports in China's inland areas can effectively promote the connection of the inland regions with the international community and accelerate the economic development of Central and Western China. In order to promote stable economic growth, Chinese leaders outlined the "new development concept" as a complete theoretical system in China's 14th Five-Year Plan.

Moreover, China should adhere to innovative, coordinated, green, open and shared development. Under the new development pattern, building international inland ports and accomplishing its construction goals is necessary. Based on the existing research results, the following suggestions are made for the bottlenecks in the development of China's international inland ports:

(1) Collaborative research on international inland ports should be conducted in multiple fields and disciplines. Most scholars focus on a single field based on the previous statistical research results. Furthermore, there is little cooperation and communication among scholars in different fields, so the research results can hardly overcome their bottlenecks to achieve a multiplying effect. Scholars should deepen cooperation and communication in future research to solve problems in their fields. Based on the existing research, they should further explore the comprehensive development of international inland ports and the social economy, regional coordination and other aspects.

(2) The development orientation of international inland ports should be clarified, and "globalized" international inland ports should be constructed by combining advanced science and information technology. Since the beginning of the 21st century, digital information technology has developed rapidly. We should use modern scientific information technology to design an intelligent network management system to accelerate the construction of China's international inland ports and facilitate the rapid development of the region's economy. In this way, it can shorten the time of cargo customs clearance, lower operating costs and improve work efficiency. Furthermore, it can drive the economic development of central and western China and the cooperative regions overseas and realize the goal of the globalization of international inland ports.

(3) The development of international inland ports should be boosted in multiple aspects and levels. China's import and export volume increased dramatically after the liberalization of the COVID-19 pandemic in 2023. While promoting economic development, we should also encourage the comprehensive capacity of international inland ports, taking into account the environment and social health.

(4) The national strategy of the New International Land-Sea Trade Corridor should be further advanced. China has about 22,000 kilometers of land borders and shares borders with 14 countries. Western China shares borders with 13 countries except North Korea, accounting for 93% of the total bordering countries. The land boundary is more than 18,000 kilometers, accounting for 91% of the total. China is separated from many Southeast Asian countries by the sea and has a continental coastline of 1,595km, accounting for about 9% of the country's coastline. The successful experience of building international inland ports in Xi'an and Chongqing indicates that the rail-sea intermodal trains of the New International Land-Sea Trade Corridor enhance the openness and development of the cities along the route and their hinterland economies. Meanwhile, the rail-sea intermodal trains have accelerated the rapid development of China's international trade with Russia, Europe, Laos and Vietnam and promoted the economic development of the regions along the route. From the empirical results, inland ports in Western China are less competitive and need national policy support.

(5) Coordination at the national level should be strengthened. At present, international inland ports are growing as a network. It will significantly enhance the resilience of the industrial and supply chains in Central and Western China. It will also solidify the support of the channels and nodes of the dual economic circulation of China and the world. At the same time, it can also be noted that most international inland ports in Western China are weakly competitive and need to be strongly supported by policies. In order to avoid excessive development and vicious competition, China's national government must coordinate and realize the digital, intelligent and balanced development of international inland ports.

Table 2-6. Distribution of 182 international inland ports in China

Province	International inland port name	No.	City	Province	International inland port name	No.	City
Jiangsu Province	Xuzhou Huaihai International Inland Port	1	Xuzhou City	Hubei Province	Hankoubei Trade and Logistics Hub	95	Wuhan City
	Jiangsu Taicang Port Suzhou High-tech Development Zone Inland Port	2	Suzhou City		Hankoubei International Multimodal Logistics Port	96	Wuhan City
	Suzhou Industrial Park Inland Port (Suzhou Comprehensive Bonded Area)	3	Suzhou City		Wuhan Asia-Europe International Comprehensive Logistics Park	97	Wuhan City
Zhejiang Province	Taizhou Smart Inland Port New Area	4	Taizhou City		Wuhan Zall Inland Port	98	Wuhan City
	Yuyao Inland Port	5	Ningbo City		Xiangyang International Inland Port	99	Xiangyang City
	Lishui Inland Port	6	Lishui City		Jingmen International Inland Port	100	Jingmen City
	West Zhejiang Railway Logistics Park	7	Ningbo City	Hunan Province	Changsha International Rail Port	101	Changsha City
	Jinhua Inland Port	8	Quzhou City		Zhongnan International Inland Port Container Consolidation Base	102	Changsha City
	Quzhou Inland Port	9	Quzhou City		Huaihua International Inland Port	103	Huaihua City
	Yiwu International Inland Port	10	Jinhua City		Hengyang Rail Port Integrated Logistics Park	104	Hengyang City
	Xiaoshan Inland Port	11	Hangzhou City		Chenzhou Xiangnan International Logistics Park (Inland Port)	105	Chenzhou City
	Shaoxing Inland Port	12	Shaoxing City		Hengyang Inland Port	106	Hengyang City
	Cixi Inland Port	13	Ningbo City		Zhuzhou CRRC Logistics Base	107	Zhuzhou City

Province	International inland port name	No.	City	Province	International inland port name	No.	City
	Keqiao Inland Port	14	Shaoxing City	Chongqing	Chongqing International Logistics Park	108	Chongqing City
	Yongkang Inland Port	15	Jinhua City		Chongqing ASEAN International Logistics Park	109	Chongqing City
Anhui Province	Hefei International Inland Port	16	Hefei City		Chongqing Lianglu Cuntan Bonded Port Area (Guoyuan Port)	110	Chongqing City
	Bengbu (Northern Anhui) Rail Inland Port	17	Bengbu City		Luzhou Port Rongchang Inland Port	111	Chongqing City
	Huaibei Qinglongshan Rail Inland Port	18	Huaibei City	Sichuan Province	Chengdu International Rail Port	112	Chengdu City
	Xuancheng Inland Port	19	Xuancheng City		Southwest (Zigong) International Inland Port	113	Zigong City
Jiangxi Province	Nanchang Xiangtang International Inland Port	20	Nanchang City		Deyang International Rail Logistics Port	114	Deyang City
	Ganzhou International Inland Port	21	Ganzhou City		Western Rail Logistics Park	115	Suining City
	Yingtan Inland Port	22	Yingtan City		Qinba (Dazhou) International Inland Port	116	Dazhou City
	Shangrao Inland Port	23	Shangrao City		Guang'an Inland Port	117	Guang'an City
	Ji'an Inland Port	24	Ji'an City		Fengming Logistics Park, Ya'an Inland Port	118	Ya'an City
	Yingtan Modern Logistics Park	25	Yingtan City		Emei Inland Port	119	Leshan City
	Jiangxi Yingtan International Comprehensive Port Economic Zone	26	Yingtan City		Neijiang International Logistics Port	120	Neijiang City

Huaihua International Inland Port

Province	International inland port name	No.	City	Province	International inland port name	No.	City
Shandong Province	Linyi International Inland Port	27	Linyi City	Guizhou Province	Guiyang Gaimao Rail Port	121	Guiyang City
	Liaocheng Guanxian Inland Port	28	Liaocheng City		Qingzhen Land-Sea International Logistics Port	122	Guiyang City
	Yangxin Inland Port Logistics Park	29	Binzhou City		Guizhou Tietou Doulaying International Land-Sea Logistics Port	123	Guiyang City
	Zaozhuang Inland Port	30	Zaozhuang City		Guizhou Bijie International Inland Port	124	Bijie City
	Jining Inland Port	31	Jining City		Guizhou East Inland Port	125	Tongren City
	Zibo Inland Port	32	Zibo City		Guizhou Qianbei New Modern Logistics City	126	Zunyi City
	Ganghui International Logistics Park	33	Linyi City		Guizhou (Anshun) International Inland Port	127	Anshun City
	Dezhou Inland Port	34	Dezhou City	Yunnan Province	Kunming South Asia International Inland Port Logistics Park	128	Kunming City
	Qingdao International Inland Port	35	Qingdao City		Kunming Baoxiang 10,000-ton Cold Chain Port	129	Kunming City
	Jinan International Inland Port	36	Jinan City		Tengjun International Inland Port	130	Kunming City
	Binzhou (Boxing) Inland Port	37	Binzhou City	Shaanxi Province	Xi'an International Port Area	131	Xi'an City
	Yanzhou International Inland Port	38	Jining City		Baoji Port Area	132	Baoji City
	Weifang International Inland Port	39	Weifang City		Yulin Inland Port Hairong Logistics Park	133	Yulin City
	Heze Inland Port New Industrial Town	40	Heze City		Ankang Shanggang Inland Port	134	Ankang City

Province	International inland port name	No.	City	Province	International inland port name	No.	City
	Tai'an Inland Port	41	Tai'an City	Gansu Province	Julong Agricultural Logistics Port	135	Jiuquan City
	Taishan Inland Port	42	Tai'an City		Gansu (Lanzhou) International Inland Port	136	Lanzhou City
Fujian Province	Fujian Quanzhou Jinjiang Inland Port	43	Quanzhou City		Lanzhou New Area Zhongchuanbei Station Logistics Park	137	Lanzhou City
	Longyan Inland Port	44	Longyan City		Gansu (Tianshui) International Inland Port	138	Tianshui City
	Sanming Inland Port	45	Sanming City		Gansu (Wuwei) International Inland Port	139	Wuwei City
	Fujian Wuyishan Inland Port	46	Nanping City		Gansu (Minzhou) International Inland Port	140	Dingxi City
	Fujian Xiangfu International Logistics Park	47	Fuzhou City	Qinghai Province	Qinghai Shuangzhai Silk Road (International) Logistics City	141	Xining City
Beijing City	Pinggu International Inland Port	48	Beijing City	Ningxia Hui Autonomous Region	Yinchuan International Highway & Railway Logistics Port	142	Yinchuan City
	Beijing Tongzhou Logistics Industrial Park	49	Beijing City		Lingwu Inland Port Logistics Park	143	Yinchuan City
Shanxi Province	Datong International Inland Port	50	Datong City		Yinchuan Inland Port Logistics Center Jinqiao Logistics Park	144	Yinchuan City
	Houma Baote Inland Port	51	Linfen City		Zhongwei International Inland Port	145	Zhongwei City
	Wutai Inland Port	52	Xinzhou City		Huinong Inland Port	146	Shizuishan City

Province	International inland port name	No.	City	Province	International inland port name	No.	City
	Fanglvc Bonded International Inland Port	53	Linfen City	Xinjiang Uygur Autonomous Region	Urumqi International Inland Port	147	Urumqi City
	Pinglu Inland Port	54	Shuozhou City		Hami North Highway-Railway Intermodal Logistics Park	148	Hami City
	Zhongding Logistics Park	55	Jinzhong City	Heilongjiang Province	Harbin International Inland Port	149	Harbin City
	Jinbei Rail Logistics Park	56	Datong City		Qiqihar International Inland Port	150	Qiqihar City
	Xiaoyi Modern Logistics Park Inland Port	57	Lvliang City		Heihe Yuexing China-Russia Cross-border Logistics Hub	151	Heihe City
Hebei Province	Shijiazhuang Inland Port	58	Shijiazhuang City		Yingkou Port Suihua Inland Port (Beilin Logistics Inland Port)	152	Suihua City
	Shijiazhuang International Inland Port	59	Shijiazhuang City		Mudanjiang Inland Port Logistics Park	153	Mudanjiang City
	Handan International Inland Port	60	Handan City		Suifenhe International Comprehensive Logistics Park	154	Mudanjiang City
	Wuan Bonded Logistics Center	61	Handan City		Qiqihar International Logistics Park	155	Qiqihar City
	Xingtai Inland Port	62	Xingtai City		Suifenhe Fumin Railway Trading and Logistics Park	156	Mudanjiang City
	Baoding Inland Port Logistics Park	63	Baoding City		Dongning Trading and Logistics Park	157	Mudanjiang City
	Zhangjiakou Inland Port	64	Zhangjiakou City		Suifenhe Trading and Processing Logistics Park	158	Mudanjiang City
	Chengde Inland-Sea Logistics Industry Cluster	65	Chengde City		Heihe International Comprehensive Logistics Park	159	Heihe City

Province	International inland port name	No.	City	Province	International inland port name	No.	City
	Hengshui Inland Port	66	Hengshui City		Heihe Highway-Railway-Waterway Intermodal Transportation Logistics Park	160	Heihe City
	Hengshui International Inland Port	67	Hengshui City		Tongjiang Highway-Railway Transshipment and Transportation Logistics Park	161	Jiamusi City
	Qingdao Bonded Port Area Handan (Jize) Functional Zone	68	Handan City		Harbin International Airport Logistics Park	162	Harbin City
	Dingzhou Inland Port	69	Baoding City	Jilin Province	Tonghua International Inland Port Area	163	Tonghua City
Inner Mongolia Autonomous Region	Inner Mongolia North Inland Port International Logistics Center	70	Ulanqab City		Changchun International Inland Port	164	Changchun City
	Ulanqab Wanyi Integrated Logistics Park	71	Ulanqab City		Siping Inland Port	165	Siping City
	Ulanqab Integrated Logistics Industrial Park	72	Ulanqab City	Liaoning Province	Shenyang Comprehensive Free Trade Zone (Offshore Zone)	166	Shenyang City
	Qisumu China-Europe Railway Express Logistics Hub Base	73	Ulanqab City		Yingkou Port Faku Inland Port	167	Yingkou City
	Chifeng International Inland Port (Hongshan Logistics Park)	74	Chifeng City		Tieling International Inland Port	168	Tieling City
	Baotou International Inland Port Logistics Park	75	Baotou City		Shenyangdong Station Inland Port	169	Shenyang City

Province	International inland port name	No.	City	Province	International inland port name	No.	City
	Jiuyuan (International) Logistics Park Multimodal Transportation Center	76	Baotou City	Guangdong Province	Meizhou International Inland Port	170	Meizhou City
	Bayannur Inland Port (Modern Agricultural and Livestock Products Logistics Park)	77	Bayannur City		Shaoguan Inland Port	171	Shaoguan City
	Wuhai International Inland Port Public Bonded Warehouse	78	Wuhai City		Foshan International Inland Port	172	Foshan City
	Horqin Industrial Park Inland Port Bonded Logistics Park	79	Tongliao City		Heshan International Inland Port	173	Jiangmen City
	Tongliao Inland Port, Panjin Port	80	Tongliao City		Lianjiang Inland Port New Logistics Town	174	Zhanjiang City
Henan Province	Zhengzhou International Inland Port	81	Zhengzhou City	Guangxi Zhuang Autonomous Region	Nanning International Rail Port	175	Nanning City
	Zhengzhou "Inland Port" (Henan Bonded Logistics Center)	82	Zhengzhou City		China-Singapore Nanning International Logistics Park	176	Nanning City
	Zhengzhou Shangjie Central Inland Port	83	Zhengzhou City		Nanning International Comprehensive Logistics Park	177	Nanning City
	Kaifeng International Inland Port	84	Kaifeng City		Nandan Inland Port Bonded Logistics Park	178	Hechi City
	Dongfanghong (Luoyang) International Inland Port Center	85	Luoyang City		Liuzhou Rail Port	179	Liuzhou City
	Nanyang International Inland Port	86	Nanyang City		Hechi Inland Port	180	Hechi City
	Shangqiu International Inland Port	87	Shangqiu City		Guilin Suqiao Inland Port	181	Guilin City

Province	International inland port name	No.	City	Province	International inland port name	No.	City
	Hebi International Inland Port	88	Hebi City		Guangxi Chongzuo (ASEAN) International Logistics Park	182	Chongzuo City
	Pingdingshan International Inland Port	89	Pingdingshan City				
	National (Anyang) Inland Port Logistics Hub New Area	90	Anyang City				
	Anyang Xiangdao Inland Port	91	Anyang City				
	Xinxiang International Inland Port	92	Xinxiang City				
	Puyang Inland Port	93	Puyang City				
	Yuzhong Inland Port Integrated Logistics Port	94	Xuchang City				

Table 2-7. Weights of evaluation indexes

Criterion layer	Weight	Index layer	Weight	Combined weight
Y1	0.4956	x1	0.4910	0.2433
		x2	0.0411	0.0204
		x3	0.1040	0.0515
		x4	0.0629	0.0312
		x5	0.3010	0.1492
Y2	0.3462	x6	0.2317	0.0802
		x7	0.0388	0.0134
		x8	0.0388	0.0134
		x9	0.0835	0.0289
		x10	0.0237	0.0082
		x11	0.2929	0.1014
		x12	0.2908	0.1007

Criterion layer	Weight	Index layer	Weight	Combined weight
Y3	0.1067	x13	0.1234	0.0132
		x14	0.0577	0.0062
		x15	0.0613	0.0065
		x16	0.3510	0.0375
		x17	0.1990	0.0212
		x18	0.1443	0.0154
		x19	0.0483	0.0052
		x20	0.0149	0.0016
Y4	0.0516	x21	0.3189	0.0165
		x22	0.1289	0.0067
		x23	0.0258	0.0013
		x24	0.0475	0.0025
		x25	0.1443	0.0074
		x26	0.0187	0.0010
		x27	0.0458	0.0024
		x28	0.2702	0.0139

Table 2-8. Index weights

Criterion layer	Weight	Index layer	Weight	Ranking
Internal infrastructure development of international inland ports Y1	0.213215	x1	0.047122	12
		x2	0.041252	13
		x3	0.048971	9
		x4	0.048031	11
		x5	0.027839	18
Logistics development of international inland ports Y2	0.220809	x6	0.075022	1
		x7	0.018	20
		x8	0.001038	28
		x9	0.037617	14
		x10	0.056911	4
		x11	0.017002	21

Criterion layer	Weight	Index layer	Weight	Ranking
		x12	0.015219	22
Business development of international inland ports Y3	0.417527	x13	0.030452	17
		x14	0.056556	5
		x15	0.063788	3
		x16	0.055688	6
		x17	0.072073	2
		x18	0.05091	8
		x19	0.053693	7
		x20	0.034367	16
Regional Economic Development Y4	0.148447	x21	0.037481	15
		x22	0.002528	27
		x23	0.003632	26
		x24	0.012622	23
		x25	0.048323	10
		x26	0.011669	24
		x27	0.024025	19
		x28	0.008167	25

Table 2-9. Weight matrix

No.	Subjective weight	Objective weight	Combined weight	Ranking
x1	0.491	0.047122	0.047122	12
x2	0.0411	0.041252	0.041252	13
x3	0.104	0.048971	0.048971	9
x4	0.0629	0.048031	0.048031	11
x5	0.301	0.027839	0.027839	18
x6	0.2317	0.075022	0.075022	1
x7	0.0388	0.018	0.018	20
x8	0.0388	0.001038	0.001038	28
x9	0.0835	0.037617	0.037617	14

No.	Subjective weight	Objective weight	Combined weight	Ranking
x10	0.0237	0.056911	0.056911	4
x11	0.2929	0.017002	0.017002	21
x12	0.2908	0.015219	0.015219	22
x13	0.1234	0.030452	0.030452	17
x14	0.0577	0.056556	0.056556	5
x15	0.0613	0.063788	0.063788	3
x16	0.351	0.055688	0.055688	6
x17	0.199	0.072073	0.072073	2
x18	0.1443	0.05091	0.05091	8
x19	0.0483	0.053693	0.053693	7
x20	0.0149	0.034367	0.034367	16
x21	0.3189	0.037481	0.037481	15
x22	0.1289	0.002528	0.002528	27
x23	0.0258	0.003632	0.003632	26
x24	0.0475	0.012622	0.012622	23
x25	0.1443	0.048323	0.048323	10
x26	0.0187	0.011669	0.011669	24
x27	0.0458	0.024025	0.024025	19
x28	0.2702	0.008167	0.008167	25

Table 2-10. Scores of 182 international inland ports and rankings by province

Province	International inland port name	City	Score	Province-level score	Ranking
Jiangsu Province	Xuzhou Huaihai International Inland Port	Xuzhou City	0.3827	1.5011	19
	Jiangsu Taicang Port Suzhou High-tech Zone Inland Port	Suzhou City	0.5592		

Province	International inland port name	City	Score	Province-level score	Ranking
	Suzhou Industrial Park Inland Port (Suzhou Comprehensive Bonded Area)	Suzhou City	0.5592		
Zhejiang Province	Taizhou Smart Inland Port New Area	Taizhou City	0.3136	4.5831	3
	Yuyao Inland Port	Ningbo City	0.4866		
	Lishui Inland Port	Lishui City	0.2850		
	West Zhejiang Railway Logistics Park	Ningbo City	0.4869		
	Jinhua Inland Port	Quzhou City	0.2906		
	Quzhou Inland Port	Quzhou City	0.2906		
	Yiwu International Inland Port	Jinhua City	0.3653		
	Xiaoshan Inland Port	Hangzhou City	0.5463		
	Shaoxing Inland Port	Shaoxing City	0.3347		
	Cixi Inland Port	Ningbo City	0.4867		
	Keqiao Inland Port	Shaoxing City	0.3347		
	Yongkang Inland Port	Jinhua City	0.3621		
Anhui Province	Hefei International Inland Port	Hefei City	0.3922	1.3081	22
	Bengbu (Northern Anhui) Rail Inland Port	Bengbu City	0.3229		
	Huaibei Qinglongshan Rail Inland Port	Huaibei City	0.2826		
	Xuancheng Inland Port	Xuancheng City	0.3104		
Jiangxi Province	Nanchang Xiangtang International Inland Port	Nanchang City	0.3397	2.1388	14
	Ganzhou International Inland Port	Ganzhou City	0.3335		
	Yingtan Inland Port	Yingtan City	0.2922		
	Shangrao Inland Port	Shangrao City	0.2933		

Province	International inland port name	City	Score	Province-level score	Ranking
	Ji'an Inland Port	Ji'an City	0.2930		
	Yingtan Modern Logistics Park	Yingtan City	0.2932		
	Jiangxi Yingtan International Comprehensive Port Economic Zone	Yingtan City	0.2939		
Shandong Province	Linyi International Inland Port	Linyi City	0.3422	5.2582	1
	Liaocheng Guanxian Inland Port	Liaocheng City	0.2936		
	Yangxin Inland Port Logistics Park	Binzhou City	0.3237		
	Zaozhuang Inland Port	Zaozhuang City	0.2857		
	Jining Inland Port	Jining City	0.3056		
	Zibo Inland Port	Zibo City	0.3676		
	Ganghui International Logistics Park	Linyi City	0.3365		
	Dezhou Inland Port	Dezhou City	0.2918		
	Qingdao International Inland Port	Qingdao City	0.4606		
	Jinan International Inland Port	Jinan City	0.3819		
	Binzhou (Boxing) Inland Port	Binzhou City	0.3235		
	Yanzhou International Inland Port	Jining City	0.3059		
	Weifang International Inland Port	Weifang City	0.3400		
	Heze Inland Port New Industrial Town	Heze City	0.3164		
	Tai'an Inland Port	Tai'an City	0.2916		
	Taishan Inland Port	Tai'an City	0.2915		
Fujian Province	Fujian Quanzhou Jinjiang Inland Port	Quanzhou City	0.3982	1.6986	16
	Longyan Inland Port	Longyan City	0.2974		
	Sanming Inland Port	Sanming City	0.3005		

Province	International inland port name	City	Score	Province-level score	Ranking
	Fujian Wuyishan Inland Port	Nanping City	0.2890		
	Fujian Xiangfu International Logistics Park	Fuzhou City	0.4136		
Beijing City	Pinggu International Inland Port	Beijing City	0.5923	1.1847	24
	Beijing Tongzhou Logistics Industrial Park	Beijing City	0.5925		
Shanxi Province	Datong International Inland Port	Datong City	0.3157	2.4228	9
	Houma Baote Inland Port	Linfen City	0.3148		
	Wutai Inland Port	Xinzhou City	0.2850		
	Fanglve Bonded International Inland Port	Linfen City	0.3160		
	Pinglu Inland Port	Shuozhou City	0.3005		
	Zhongding Logistics Park	Jinzhong City	0.2888		
	Jinbei Rail Logistics Park	Datong City	0.3149		
	Xiaoyi Modern Logistics Park Inland Port	Lvliang City	0.2871		
Hebei Province	Shijiazhuang Inland Port	Shijiazhuang City	0.3622	3.7614	5
	Shijiazhuang International Inland Port	Shijiazhuang City	0.3632		
	Handan International Inland Port	Handan City	0.3273		
	Wuan Bonded Logistics Center	Handan City	0.3276		
	Xingtai Inland Port	Xingtai City	0.2902		
	Baoding Inland Port Logistics Park	Baoding City	0.3121		
	Zhangjiakou Inland Port	Zhangjiakou City	0.2866		
	Chengde Inland-Sea Logistics Industry Cluster	Chengde City	0.2845		

Province	**International inland port name**	**City**	**Score**	**Province-level score**	**Ranking**
	Hengshui Inland Port	Hengshui City	0.2833		
	Hengshui International Inland Port	Hengshui City	0.2845		
	Qingdao Bonded Port Area Handan (Jize) Functional Zone	Handan City	0.3275		
	Dingzhou Inland Port	Baoding City	0.3124		
Inner Mongolia Autonomous Region	Inner Mongolia North Inland Port International Logistics Center	Ulanqab City	0.3101	3.4525	6
	Ulanqab Wanyi Integrated Logistics Park	Ulanqab City	0.3100		
	Ulanqab Integrated Logistics Industrial Park	Ulanqab City	0.3331		
	Qisumu China-Europe Railway Express Logistics Hub Base	Ulanqab City	0.3100		
	Chifeng International Inland Port (Hongshan Logistics Park)	Chifeng City	0.3803		
	Baotou International Inland Port Logistics Park	Baotou City	0.3321		
	Jiuyuan (International) Logistics Park Multimodal Transportation Center	Baotou City	0.3178		
	Bayannur Inland Port (Modern Agricultural and Livestock Products Logistics Park)	Bayannur City	0.3057		
	Wuhai International Inland Port Public Bonded Warehouse	Wuhai City	0.2886		
	Horqin Industrial Park Inland Port Bonded Logistics Park	Tongliao City	0.2829		
	Tongliao Inland Port, Panjin Port	Tongliao City	0.2819		
Henan Province	Zhengzhou International Inland Port	Zhengzhou City	0.4249	4.6186	2
	Zhengzhou "Inland Port" (Henan Bonded Logistics Center)	Zhengzhou City	0.4241		
	Zhengzhou Shangjie Central Inland Port	Zhengzhou City	0.4278		

Province	International inland port name	City	Score	Province-level score	Ranking
	Kaifeng International Inland Port	Kaifeng City	0.3017		
	Dongfanghong (Luoyang) International Inland Port Center	Luoyang City	0.3299		
	Nanyang International Inland Port	Nanyang City	0.3093		
	Shangqiu International Inland Port	Shangqiu City	0.3483		
	Hebi International Inland Port	Hebi City	0.2838		
	Pingdingshan International Inland Port	Pingdingshan City	0.2903		
	National (Anyang) Inland Port Logistics Hub New Area	Anyang City	0.2942		
	Anyang Xiangdao Inland Port	Anyang City	0.2942		
	Xinxiang International Inland Port	Xinxiang City	0.2924		
	Puyang Inland Port	Puyang City	0.2841		
	Yuzhong Inland Port Integrated Logistics Port	Xuchang City	0.3135		
Hubei Province	Hankoubei Trade and Logistics Hub	Wuhan City	0.4414	2.3856	12
	Hankoubei International Multimodal Logistics Port	Wuhan City	0.4311		
	Wuhan Asia-Europe International Comprehensive Logistics Park	Wuhan City	0.4310		
	Wuhan Zall Inland Port	Wuhan City	0.4313		
	Xiangyang International Inland Port	Xiangyang City	0.3364		
	Jingmen International Inland Port	Jingmen City	0.3144		
Hunan Province	Changsha International Rail Port	Changsha City	0.4309	2.4037	11
	Zhongnan International Inland Port Container Consolidation Base	Changsha City	0.4305		

Province	International inland port name	City	Score	Province-level score	Ranking
	Huaihua International Inland Port	Huaihua City	0.2931		
	Hengyang Rail Port Integrated Logistics Park	Hengyang City	0.3033		
	Chenzhou Xiangnan International Logistics Park (Inland Port)	Chenzhou City	0.3278		
	Hengyang Inland Port	Hengyang City	0.3032		
	Zhuzhou CRRC Logistics Base	Zhuzhou City	0.3149		
Chongqing	Chongqing International Logistics Park	Chongqing City	0.5527	2.2156	13
	Chongqing ASEAN International Logistics Park	Chongqing City	0.5510		
	Chongqing Lianglu Cuntan Bonded Port Area (Guoyuan Port)	Chongqing City	0.5614		
	Luzhou Port Rongchang Inland Port	Chongqing City	0.5505		
Sichuan Province	Chengdu International Rail Port	Chengdu City	0.5055	2.8366	7
	Southwest (Zigong) International Inland Port	Zigong City	0.3173		
	Deyang International Rail Logistics Port	Deyang City	0.2897		
	Western Rail Logistics Park	Suining City	0.2912		
	Qinba (Dazhou) International Inland Port	Dazhou City	0.2926		
	Guang'an Inland Port	Guang'an City	0.2855		
	Fengming Logistics Park, Ya'an Inland Port	Ya'an City	0.2802		
	Emei Inland Port	Leshan City	0.2878		
	Neijiang International Logistics Port	Neijiang City	0.2868		
Guizhou Province	Guiyang Gaimao Rail Port	Guiyang City	0.4132	2.4199	10

Province	International inland port name	City	Score	Province-level score	Ranking
	Qingzhen Land-Sea International Logistics Port	Guiyang City	0.4134		
	Guizhou Tietou Doulaying International Land-Sea Logistics Port	Guiyang City	0.4136		
	Guizhou Bijie International Inland Port	Bijie City	0.2905		
	Guizhou East Inland Port	Tongren City	0.2883		
	Guizhou Qianbei New Modern Logistics City	Zunyi City	0.3118		
	Guizhou (Anshun) International Inland Port	Anshun City	0.2891		
Yunnan Province	Kunming South Asia International Inland Port Logistics Park	Kunming City	0.3987	1.1955	23
	Kunming Baoxiang 10,000-ton Cold Chain Port	Kunming City	0.3978		
	Tengjun International Inland Port	Kunming City	0.3991		
Shaanxi Province	Xi'an International Port Area	Xi'an City	0.4846	1.3793	20
	Baoji Port Area	Baoji City	0.3047		
	Yulin Inland Port Hairong Logistics Park	Yulin City	0.3059		
	Ankang Shanggang Inland Port	Ankang City	0.2840		
Gansu Province	Julong Agricultural Logistics Port	Jiuquan City	0.2907	1.8488	15
	Gansu (Lanzhou) International Inland Port	Lanzhou City	0.3396		
	Lanzhou New Area Zhongchuanbei Station Logistics Park	Lanzhou City	0.3214		
	Gansu (Tianshui) International Inland Port	Tianshui City	0.2942		
	Gansu (Wuwei) International Inland Port	Wuwei City	0.3222		
	Gansu (Minzhou) International Inland Port	Dingxi City	0.2807		

Province	International inland port name	City	Score	Province-level score	Ranking
Qinghai Province	Qinghai Shuangzhai Silk Road (International) Logistics City	Xining City	0.3166	0.3166	27
Ningxia Hui Autonomous Region	Yinchuan International Highway & Railway Logistics Port	Yinchuan City	0.3101	1.5182	18
	Lingwu Inland Port Logistics Park	Yinchuan City	0.3101		
	Yinchuan Inland Port Logistics Center Jinqiao Logistics Park	Yinchuan City	0.3101		
	Zhongwei International Inland Port	Zhongwei City	0.2800		
	Huinong Inland Port	Shizuishan City	0.3079		
Xinjiang Uygur Autonomous Region	Urumqi International Inland Port	Urumqi City	0.3284	0.6211	26
	Hami North Highway-Railway Intermodal Logistics Park	Hami City	0.2927		
Heilongjiang Province	Harbin International Inland Port	Harbin City	0.3805	4.5307	4
	Qiqihar International Inland Port	Qiqihar City	0.2827		
	Heihe Yuexing China-Russia Cross-border Logistics Hub	Heihe City	0.3212		
	Yingkou Port Suihua Inland Port (Beilin Logistics Inland Port)	Suihua City	0.2826		
	Mudanjiang Inland Port Logistics Park	Mudanjiang City	0.3299		
	Suifenhe International Comprehensive Logistics Park	Mudanjiang City	0.3296		
	Qiqihar International Logistics Park	Qiqihar City	0.2827		
	Suifenhe Fumin Railway Trading and Logistics Park	Mudanjiang City	0.3295		
	Dongning Trading and Logistics Park	Mudanjiang City	0.3296		
	Suifenhe Trading and Processing Logistics Park	Mudanjiang City	0.3296		
	Heihe International Comprehensive Logistics Park	Heihe City	0.3207		

Province	International inland port name	City	Score	Province-level score	Ranking
	Heihe Highway-Railway-Waterway Intermodal Transportation Logistics Park	Heihe City	0.3207		
	Tongjiang Highway-Railway Transshipment and Transportation Logistics Park	Jiamusi City	0.3109		
	Harbin International Airport Logistics Park	Harbin City	0.3805		
Jilin Province	Tonghua International Inland Port Area	Tonghua City	0.2818	0.9162	25
	Changchun International Inland Port	Changchun City	0.3484		
	Siping Inland Port	Siping City	0.2860		
Liaoning Province	Shenyang Comprehensive Free Trade Zone (Offshore Zone)	Shenyang City	0.3632	1.3784	21
	Yingkou Port Faku Inland Port	Yingkou City	0.3471		
	Tieling International Inland Port	Tieling City	0.3051		
	Shenyangdong Station Inland Port	Shenyang City	0.3630		
Guangdong Province	Meizhou International Inland Port	Meizhou City	0.2886	1.6642	17
	Shaoguan Inland Port	Shaoguan City	0.2869		
	Foshan International Inland Port	Foshan City	0.4033		
	Heshan International Inland Port	Jiangmen City	0.3535		
	Lianjiang Inland Port New Logistics Town	Zhanjiang City	0.3320		
Guangxi Zhuang Autonomous Region	Nanning International Rail Port	Nanning City	0.3654	2.6000	8
	China-Singapore Nanning International Logistics Park	Nanning City	0.3645		
	Nanning International Comprehensive Logistics Park	Nanning City	0.3628		
	Nandan Inland Port Bonded Logistics Park	Hechi City	0.2820		

Huaihua International Inland Port

Province	**International inland port name**	**City**	**Score**	**Province-level score**	**Ranking**
	Liuzhou Rail Port	Liuzhou City	0.3291		
	Hechi Inland Port	Hechi City	0.2822		
	Guilin Suqiao Inland Port	Guilin City	0.2945		
	Guangxi Chongzuo (ASEAN) International Logistics Park	Chongzuo City	0.3197		

Chapter 3
Spillover Effects of the International Inland Port

Previous studies have shown that the construction and development of international inland ports have a significant economic spillover effect on the neighboring regions. The construction and development of Huaihua International Inland Port inevitably exerts economic spillover effects on the adjacent regions. It is necessary to analyze and predict the trend of economic data before and after the construction of the inland port in the study area to evaluate accurately the role and effect of the inland port in driving the economic development of the local and neighboring regions. Then, the impact of inland ports as a variable is quantified by analyzing the difference between the predicted and actual results, thus providing a basis for formulating scientific policies. Local governments' general public budget revenue (GPBR) is an important indicator for measuring the economic development of a region. The paper uses the local governments' GPBR of Huaihua International Inland Port Economic Development Zone, Hecheng District, and Zhijiang Dong Autonomous County from January 2019 to June 2023. Based on this, time series decomposition and SARIMA modeling are carried out. It analyzes the impact of Huaihua International Inland Port on the region and its economic spillover effect on the surrounding regions. The results found that the impact presented by the model is consistent with the actual situation. Therefore, the evaluation results are highly accurate and reliable.

Introduction

In the economic development of non-coastal regions worldwide, much attention has been paid to the construction and development of inland ports, especially international inland ports. They contribute more positively to the development of the regional economy (Pablo, Ivan, and Violeta et al., 2023). China's vast central and western regions are far from the coastline. Therefore, building and developing international inland ports has become essential for regional economic development. International and domestic practice shows that building international inland ports facilitates the development of the regional export-oriented economy.

Furthermore, they can promote industrial accumulation and transfer and advance the high-quality development of logistics. They can also accelerate the integration of industry and urban development and stabilize society. In particular, they exert an economic spillover effect on the neighboring regions. Therefore, international inland ports should be highly emphasized and researched. The construction and development of Huaihua International Inland Port in Hunan Province of China is taken as an example. It applies the SARIMA time series analysis model to analyze the local governments' GPBR. Thus, it can quantitatively evaluate the economic benefits of the construction of the Huaihua International Inland Port and then investigate the spillover effect of such benefits on the economic development of the surrounding regions.

The history of economic development of countries has proved that the export-oriented economy must be developed vigorously for long-term and stable economic development. Under the premise of promoting regional economic development and growth, the export-oriented economy must fully consider international market demand and expand exports. While effectively utilizing the resource advantages in China, it should make full use of foreign resources and factors of production and adopt an export-oriented development path. Moreover, it should actively participate in the economic structure, economic operation mechanisms, and systems based on the international division of labor and international competition (Per, Lokesh, and Violeta, 2023). The construction and development of international inland ports can more effectively promote the local communities to fully play their location advantages and the strengths of transportation and logistics platforms.

Further, it can drive the concentration of advantageous industries and resource elements and bring into play the effects of the scale of enterprises, population, and inland. Moreover, it can actively develop export-oriented, chained, high-performance industrial clusters, constantly enhancing the overall industrial competitiveness of international inland ports and ultimately boosting regional economic development. The achievements of countries worldwide have shown that international inland ports can help optimize the urban layout and build high-class port towns and cities. Moreover, they can promote the integrated development of urban and rural areas and new urbanization, thus increasing employment opportunities, raising incomes, and stabilizing society (Sinan, 2023). In short, international inland ports can fully use international and Chinese resources and markets. It can further open Western China to the outside world and engage it deeply in the global economic division of labor and economic cycle.

In recent years, Chinese government leaders have put forward significant propositions. China should build a new development pattern, create a center of inland reform, and open up from the perspective of a national development strategy. They have called for earnest efforts in the central and western inland regions. Since the beginning of the 21st century, several international inland ports have been built and operated in Western China. They have contributed significantly to Western China's economic and social development (Liu, 2023). After repeated research and demonstration, the Hunan Provincial People's Government has decided to develop Huaihua International Inland Port in Huaihua City, a city in Western Hunan Province. It aims to promote the economic development of the Huaihua area and take a new path for the economic development of Hunan Province and even the Greater South China region (Zhang, 2023). Huaihua International Inland Port Project is a node project for building the New International Inland-Sea Trade Corridor and connecting the "Belt and Road." It will become an important engine to drive the coordinated development of the western Hunan region and a critical window for shaping a new pattern of opening up the Hunan Province to the outside world in all aspects. At the same time, it will vigorously promote the regional development of South China.

Since the early establishment of the international inland port, local officials in Huaihua City have regarded it as a significant strategic measure for the city's economic and social development. All social sectors in Huaihua recognize that the construction and development of the international inland port is a significant historic opportunity to promote the city's high-level opening and high-quality development

(Yang et al., 2023). However, since the commencement of the project in September 2021, no method has been developed to fully quantify the impact of the construction of the port on the local economy. It hinders the validity testing of the government's decision-making and significantly affects its and enterprises' future investment plans. The Huaihua International Inland Port must be quantitatively analyzed to overcome this dilemma. This can provide a basis for further decision-making for the smooth progress of the project.

This chapter uses the time series analysis model, SARIMA model, as the research method and tool. The financial indicator of local governments' GPBR is modeled and analyzed. Then, it quantitatively evaluates the impact of the construction of Huaihua International Inland Port on the economy of the Economic Development Zone and the surrounding areas. Regarding the theoretical significance and contribution of this study, it empirically tests the validity of the SARIMA model. Furthermore, the analysis is extended to the judgment of large-scale economic projects and their spillover effects. It is expected to give theoretical guidance to China and other countries for analyzing international inland ports' results and spillover effects.

Literature Review

Internationally, there is still a significant gap in the research on inland ports. On the contrary, China has a considerable advantage in this field. The concept of inland ports was also coined by Ping Xi (2001), the father of inland ports in China. The SARMA model is a commonly used method for modeling stationary time series. At present, many scholars have adopted the SARIMA model, a time series model, to forecast the results of economic development. Many favorable forecasting results have been produced.

Inland Ports

To promote the development of a local export-oriented economy in recent years, the inland areas of China have seen a boom in constructing international inland ports. Building international inland ports, especially those in line with the current national strategy and local policy supports, will highly facilitate the financing of local state-owned enterprises.

With the implementation of the Belt and Road Initiative in the last decade, numerous studies have been conducted on the export-oriented economy, especially the inland port economy, in China. Chinese scholars have investigated the utility of the export-oriented economy to countries, regions, enterprises, and individuals through case studies, indicator development, and modeling. Li (1985), Liang (1985), Wang (1985), and Zhang (1985) intensively researched the establishment of special economic zones to boost the development of local export-oriented economy. Their studies focus on the reforms of economic institutions and mechanisms, economic development models, and factors of production. Since then, the theories on developing a local export-oriented economy have expanded. Fu, Liao (2013), Wu (2021), Lu (2022), Zhao (2022), and Shu (2022) examined the export-oriented economy in Hainan, Shanghai, Shenzhen, Alashankou, Xiangyang, Shandong, and Hubei. Then, they put forward appropriate recommendations for the development of these areas.

Regarding the study of the inland port economy, Xi et al. (2001) presented the idea of establishing an international inland port in Western China, i.e., Xi'an Inland Port. In addition, the central and local governments have emphasized inland port development since around 2010. A boom in the development of inland ports has also been observed in various inland areas far from the coastline. Related studies have also been launched continuously. Based on Xi's research, Zhu and Dong (2009) made a new expression of the essence and connotation of international inland ports. They indicated that international inland ports are established in inland areas, relying on information technology and convenient transportation corridors. These ports are logistics nodes with integrated functions such as container distribution, freight forwarding, third-party logistics, and port supervision.

Furthermore, they are inland hubs with perfect coastal port functions and convenient outbound transportation operation systems. Chen and Huang (2011) constructed an evaluation index system to assess the competitiveness of international inland ports regarding internal and external development circumstances. They also conducted an empirical study using the Fuzzy-ANP evaluation approach. While elaborating on the functional positioning of Xi'an Inland Port, Zhang et al. (2015) further analyzed the necessity and feasibility of enhancing the function of

Xi'an Inland Port as an international transit hub. They presented path analysis and countermeasure suggestions that may serve as a reference for inland areas. Specifically, it can gather more inland hub ports and expand cargo sources. Adopting the data envelopment analysis approach, Yang and Li (2019) constructed an evaluation system for the coordinated development of logistics capacity and socio-economic development in cities of international inland ports.

Moreover, they conducted an empirical study on representative cities with international inland ports in China. With the construction of Huaihai International Inland Port, He and He (2023) examined the planning and layout of the port, its functional position, project progress, institutions, and mechanisms. Based on this, they considered that the three systems of inland port construction (industrial system, open system, logistics system) help to support and guarantee the management service mechanism.

Economic Indicators Based on the SARIMA Model

In the research on time series on the GDP (Gross Domestic Product) and Consumer Price Index (CPI), Sun (2018) et al. modeled China's quarterly GDP data from 2000 to 2016 by using a seasonal time series model. They forecast the quarterly data for 2017. The fitting and forecasting results of the GDP forecasting model based on SARIMA are highly reliable and accurate. Chen (2021) sampled 66 quarters of GDP data from Q1 2003 to Q2 2019 in Guizhou Province. He modeled this time series by the SARIMA model. Furthermore, he forecast the GDP from Q3 2019 to Q3 2020. The results show a high fitting accuracy, and the forecasting results of the GDP forecasting model based on SARIMA provide a practical reference for setting economic development targets in Guizhou Province.

Geng and Ye (2018) constructed a CPI model of SARIMA with the sample data of Sichuan's CPI from 2009 to 2016. They made a short-term forecast of the CPI from January to July 2017 in Sichuan Province. The analysis indicated that the model has a high forecasting accuracy. Li (2020) modeled and forecasted the monthly CPI of Henan Province using SARIMA, SARIMA-LSTM, and LSTM models. It was found that the SARIMA-LSTM model was the most effective and could truly reflect Henan Province's CPI. Besides, the model is highly effective in forecasting the actual CPI.

Research on Industry Trends Based on the SARIMA Model

In this regard, extensive scholarly attention has been drawn regarding the simulation of SBP tariff forecasts utilizing a SARIMA model. It derives the aging status for specific operational strategies and features of incremental cost segments (Olk et al., 2019). Chen et al. (2019) developed a statistical model to predict international undergraduate enrollment in the central and western regions. During the COVID-19 pandemic, Wickramasinghe et al. (2020) forecast the economic losses caused by the pandemic. Andreana et al. (2021) estimated the disruptive impact of the COVID-19 outbreak on macro-regional air transportation. Turkish agricultural economists Çevrimli et al. (2023) used Box-Jenkins and Winter's exponential smoothing approach to develop models for time series data on Turkey's honey prices between 1998 and 2018.

Moreover, they assessed the application of such models to forecast the changes in the exchange rate of the Turkish lira to the US dollar in 2019-2020. Polish researchers Sitkiewicz et al. (2021) applied predictive models and neural networks to analyze electricity consumption in Poland. Indonesian researchers Fajari et al. (2021) used the SARIMA approach to identify the best model for forecasting the average rice price of wholesales or retail trade from July 2020 to June 2021 in Indonesia. Furthermore, the data used in this model are average figures.

Chinese researchers forecast vegetable prices in Shanghai from January to June 2020 using the SARIMA model, comparing and analyzing the forecast data (adjusted for the Chinese New Year) with the actual wholesale vegetable prices in Shanghai. The average error rate of static forecast for this model was 7.3%, and that for dynamic estimates was 4.6%. It shows that the SARIMA(3, 1, 3)×(2, 1, 0)12 model can well represent the volatility characteristics of vegetable prices in Shanghai. That is, vegetable prices in Shanghai are closely correlated with those in the previous three months and the same period in the last two years. Hence, the SARIMA model can help analyze and predict the future trend of Shanghai vegetable prices and guide the development of the vegetable industry (Zheng, 2020). At the same time, the researchers also selected the consumer vouchers issued in Hangzhou and Ningbo, Zhejiang Province. Using the SARIMA model, they analyzed the economic stimulating effects of the general-purpose consumer vouchers (Hangzhou) and industry-specific consumer vouchers (Ningbo), respectively. They identified significant differences in the outcomes across models. The overall effect of general-purpose vouchers is weaker than that of industry-specific vouchers. The results of the two types of vouchers differ significantly in the catering, tourism, retail, and accommodation sectors. It is then suggested that consumer vouchers should be designed with strong connections with specific industries based on the characteristics of the regional economy and regional consumer groups. It is further recommended that consumer vouchers have a significant time decay effect, and local governments should not issue them repeatedly over the long term (Wu and Wu, 2021).

Zhou et al. (2020) investigated time series trends in other industries in China using the SARIMA model. They selected the daily business volume data of a branch office of a courier company. They built a SARIMA model based on time series analysis using R language and optimized the linear fitting of the model residuals. Given that the time series model only applies to short-term forecasting, they built a sliding window model with a forecasting period of three days. Then, they forecast a courier company's daily express delivery business volume, with an average error of the forecast results of 7.0%. According to An and Ho (2022), the data from the forecasting model can better assist the express delivery industry in addressing possible risks and uncertainties. It provides an essential reference for the future development of the regional economy and express business.

Song (2022) applied two forecasting methods, SARIMA and ANFIS, to forecast the demand for electricity materials. Then, he used the BP neural network to integrate the results of these two forecasting methods to derive the final results. At the same time, he verified the reliability and accuracy of the method by applying it to Shenzhen Power Supply Co., Ltd. In recent years, bicycle-sharing programs have been introduced in many cities in China. Using the monthly active users (MAU) of Hellobike, Dong, and Lou (2023) built SARIMA and ARIMA-GARCH models to predict its user size. They found that the MAPE values of both models were less than 5%, with a slight forecasting deviation and a satisfactory forecasting effect. The ARIMA-GARCH model can better capture the fluctuating aggregation characteristics of MAU data and achieve higher prediction accuracy. Also, it can better reflect the short-term changes in the size of bike-sharing users.

For meteorological monitoring and forecasting, Zhang et al. (2021) applied the CAR (Continuous Time Autoregressive) model based on the O-U mean-reversion process, the SARIMA (Seasonal Autoregressive Integrated Moving Average) model, and the wavelet neural network algorithm. They fitted the model by selecting the temperature of representative cities with geographical characteristics, such as Mohe, Beijing, Urumqi, Wuhu, Kunming, and Haikou. Moreover, they tested the model's prediction accuracy using the indicators of unbiased absolute percentage error, absolute percentage error, and average absolute proportion error.

Research on Import and Export Trade Based on SARIMA model

Wang and Guan investigated the import and export trade using the SARIMA model. Using the time-series test method, they analyzed the correlation between China's monthly historical data of total import and export trade from 1994 to 2016. Then, they established the corresponding SARIMA model. The time-series forecast model of China's monthly total import and export trade showed prominent U-shaped trends and quarterly variations. Based on the monthly data of trade in Chinese herbal medicines of five Central Asian countries from January 2010 to November 2021, Wang and Zhu (2022) established a forecasting method with the SARIMA model. They discovered a seasonal pattern in the demand for Chinese herbal medicines in Central Asia. The need for Chinese herbal medicines in Central Asia peaks in the fall (July and September) and will see sustained growth. The forecast will provide a reference for the future action strategies of the government, enterprises, and medicinal herb growers in the trade of Chinese herbal medicines.

Research on Regional Growth Based on the SARIMA Model

In recent years, Chinese scholars have paid much attention to how infrastructure development contributes to regional economic growth. Based on a comprehensive consideration of the synergistic effects of multidimensional factors on regional economic growth in China, Zhang (2012) built a model of spatial spillovers of transportation infrastructure on regional economic development. Based on spatial econometrics, he empirically analyzed China's provincial panel data from 1993 to 2009. It was concluded that the output elasticity of China's transportation infrastructure to regional economic growth was about 0.05-0.07. He affirmed the critical effect of transportation infrastructure on regional economic growth in China. Pan (2012) investigated the spatial distribution pattern and characteristics of per capita GDP in Chinese provinces and regions from 1988 to 2009 by applying exploratory spatial data analysis tools.

On the one hand, there is a positive spatial autocorrelation in the whole area, which increases with time. On the other hand, the local correlation analysis also shows that China's localized spatial agglomeration becomes increasingly visible. The empirical analysis also revealed that the spatial spillover effect decreases with the increased distance between regions.

In summary, many Chinese and foreign scholars have applied time series modeling to forecast various economic phenomena. However, there are very few studies on local international inland ports. Very few studies have been conducted on the economic spillover effects of the Huaihua International Inland Port on the neighboring regions. This study can compensate for the absence of research and pioneer such research. Specifically, three representative districts and counties in Huaihua City (Huaihua International Inland Port Economic Development Zone, Hecheng District, and Zhijiang Dong Autonomous County) were selected. Using the SARIMA model and the GPBR statistics of the three regions, a short-term prediction and analysis of the economic spillover effect of Huaihua International Inland Port are made. It is intended to provide a reference for the smooth progress of the project.

Modeling and Data Analysis

In this chapter, the SARIMA model was built for forecasting and analysis. Seasonal data are analyzed because the statistical analysis of economic indicators across China is conducted on a seasonal basis. The data for each month is recurrent and repetitive, with a cycle of one year. Such data are consistent with the characteristics of seasonal data.

Introduction to the SARIMA Model

First of all, we introduce the SARIMA model, which is expressed as follows:

$$\Theta_P(B^S)\theta_p(B)(1-B^S)^D(1-B)^d y_t = \Phi_Q(B^S)\phi_q(B)\varepsilon_t \text{ .... (1)}$$

It is usually abbreviated as $\mathrm{SARIMA}(p,d,q)(P,D,Q)_s$ model. The parameters can be roughly categorized into two types. One is seasonal parameters, including seasonal autoregressive order *P*, the number of seasonal differences *D*, the order of seasonal moving average *Q*, and the length of the seasonal cycle *s*. The other is non-seasonal parameters, including non-seasonal autoregressive order *p*, the number of one-step differences *d*, and the order of non-seasonal moving average *q*. The indicator analyzed in this chapter is local governments' general public budget revenue (GPBR), which is ten thousand yuan. The data were obtained from the monthly economic statistics report published on the local government's website. Moreover, the data were briefly cleansed. The raw data were the cumulative GPBR as of the end of the current month. It was subtracted from the previous month's data to get the GPBR of the current month. Missing values were complemented with the average of the figures of the previous and next periods.

The statistical criteria of GPBR is fiscal revenue, which is mainly based on local tax revenue. It comprises the revenue of the local government, the tax rebates and transfer payments from the superior government to the local government, and the revenue turned over by the subordinate government. It can represent the development of the local economy well. Therefore, this indicator is chosen to analyze the impact of the construction of Huaihua International Inland Port on the economy of the region, as well as the spillover effect on the surrounding areas.

The data analyzed in this study were selected from Huaihua International Inland Port Economic Development Zone data. In addition, only the data of the nearby Hecheng District (excluding the data of the Economic Development Zone) and Zhijiang Dong Autonomous County were selected. The impacts of the Huaihua International Inland Port on other regions will be analyzed and introduced in the subsequent research results. The time frame of this study is from January 2019 to June 2023, as shown in Fig. 1.

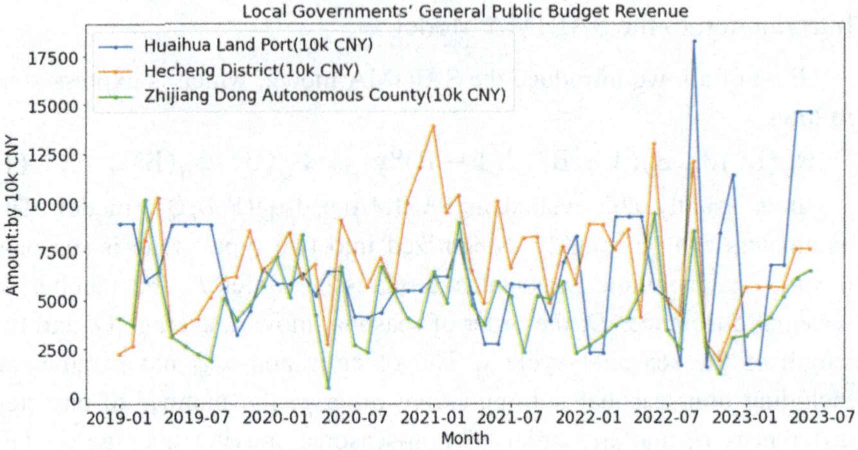

Figure 3-1. Local governments' general public budget revenue.

Time Series Decomposition

There are many models to decompose time series, such as additive model, multiplicative model, hybrid model, X11 decomposition, SEATS decomposition, STL decomposition, and fbprophet decomposition. The multiplicative model is one of the most used decomposition models in the economic field and is expressed as follows:

$$X_t = T_t + S_t + R_t, t = 1,2,... \quad .... (2)$$

Where, X_t is the time series value, T_t is the trend term, S_t is the seasonal term, and R_t is the random variable.

The multiplicative model applies to analyzing data where the effects of the various factors on the time series are not independent. In addition, the seasonal fluctuations and trends in the data may change over time. Most economic indicators are consistent with this assumption, and the local governments' GPBR analyzed in this chapter is no exception. Thus, this model is used to decompose the time series of the GPBR of Huaihua International Inland Port Economic Development Zone (the Economic Development Zone), Hecheng District, and Zhijiang Dong Autonomous County, respectively. The decomposition results are shown in Fig.2, 3, and 4.

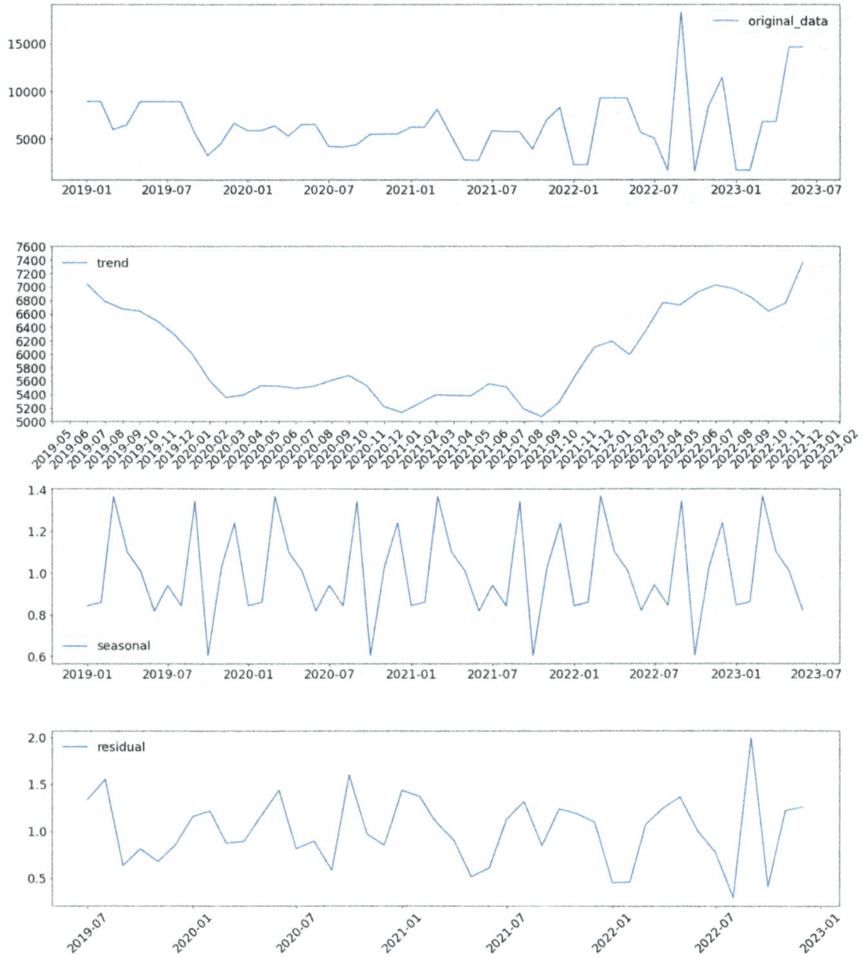

Figure 3-2. The raw data, trend, seasonal and random terms of the Economic Development Zone's GPBR

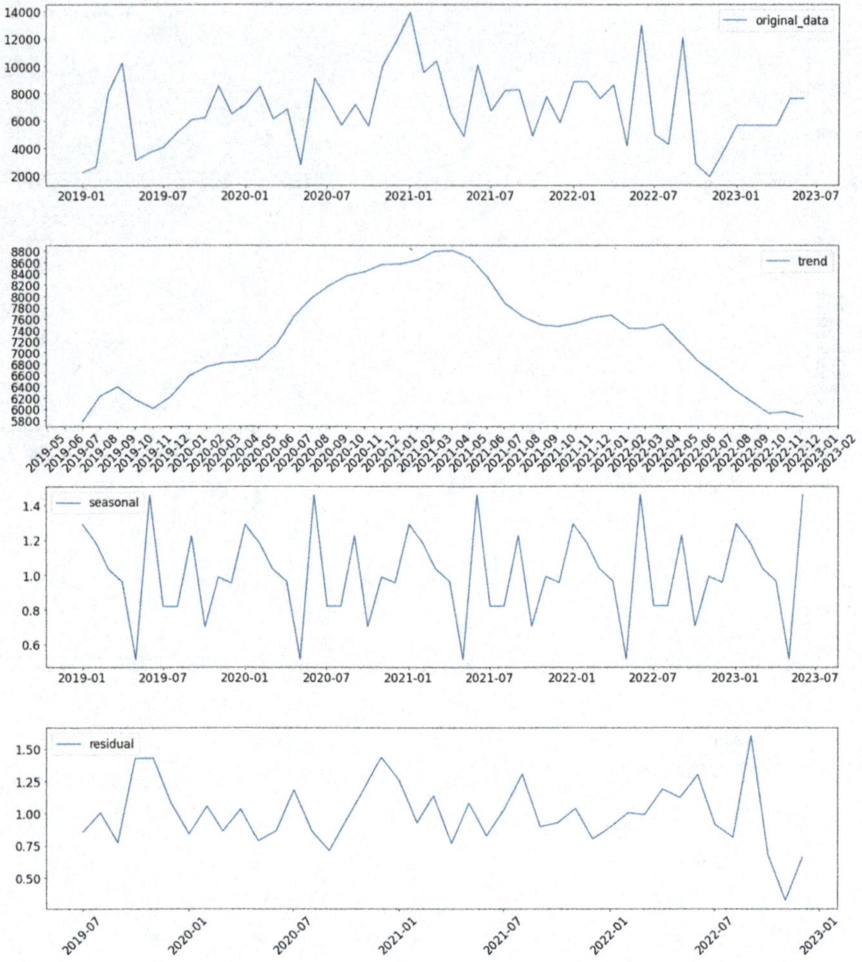

Figure 3-3. The raw data, trend, seasonal and random terms of Hecheng District's GPBR

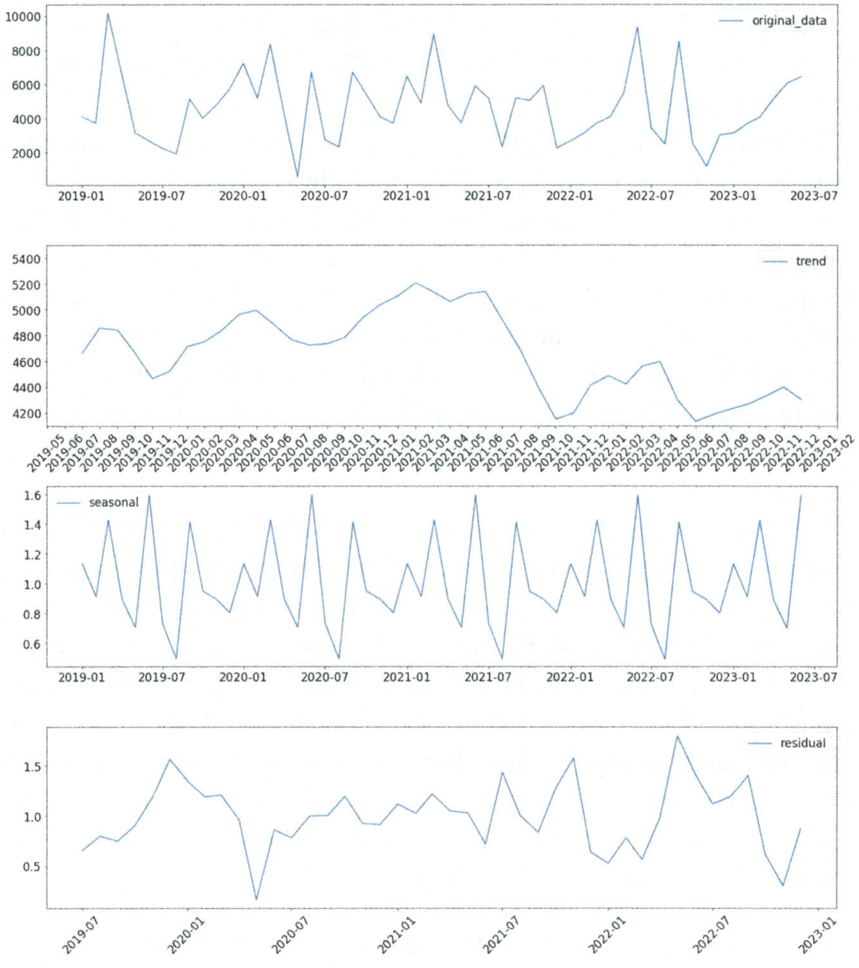

Figure 3-4. The raw data, trend, seasonal and random terms of Zhijiang County's GPBR

The Economic Development Zone's GPBR declined from 2019, stabilized by 2020, and remained low. The trend changes from September 2021, when the curve rises rapidly. The trend agrees with the reality. From January 2020 to September 2021, the COVID-19 pandemic had a strong negative impact on the local economy. The Port commenced construction in September 2021, bringing great opportunities to all aspects of the Economic Development Zone. In particular, there has been rapid progress in its economic development. Local governments' GPBR faithfully captures these messages and indirectly verifies the credibility of its proxy for economic growth. The decomposed series of seasonal factors reveals that local governments' GPBR is characterized by marked seasonal fluctuations (Fig. 2).

Hecheng District's GPBR consistently rose from 2019 to early 2021, remained stable from 2021 to 2022, and always significantly declined from early 2022. The reason may be that the construction of Huaihua International Inland Port has created many policy dividends for the Economic Development Zone, such as tax incentives, financial subsidies, and financial support. It attracted many businesses and enterprises in the Hecheng District in the short term, resulting in a significant decline in tax revenues. The decomposed series of seasonal factors shows that Hecheng District's GPBR is also characterized by marked seasonal fluctuations (Fig. 3).

Zhijiang Dong Autonomous County's GPBR rose from late 2019, peaking in 2021 and declining in the first half 2021 until October 2021. Since then, the data has remained essentially flat, stopping the decline. In 2021, the development of the Huaihua International Inland Port boosted Zhijiang's economy. Analyzing Zhijiang Dong Autonomous County as a typical case demonstrates the positive economic spillover effect of the Huaihua International Inland Port on the surrounding areas. The decomposed series of seasonal factors still shows that significant seasonal fluctuations characterize Zhijiang's GPBR. The second quarter is the peak of the annual wave (Fig. 4).

Stationarity Test on the Data before the Inland Port

September 2021, the commencement date of the Huaihua International Inland Port, is used as the dividing node to analyze the economic impacts of the port better. The local governments' GPBR data were divided into pre- and post-construction. The pre-construction data were modeled statistically.

From Fig. 1, we cannot directly observe the stationarity of local governments' GPBR in the Economic Development Zone, Hecheng District, and Zhijiang Dong Autonomous County before constructing the international inland port. Therefore, the Autocorrelation Function (ACF), Partial Autocorrelation Function (PACF), and Unit Root Test were needed. ADF test, which is the most commonly used unit root test, is used in this chapter. The original hypothesis of the test is that the time series is non-stationary.

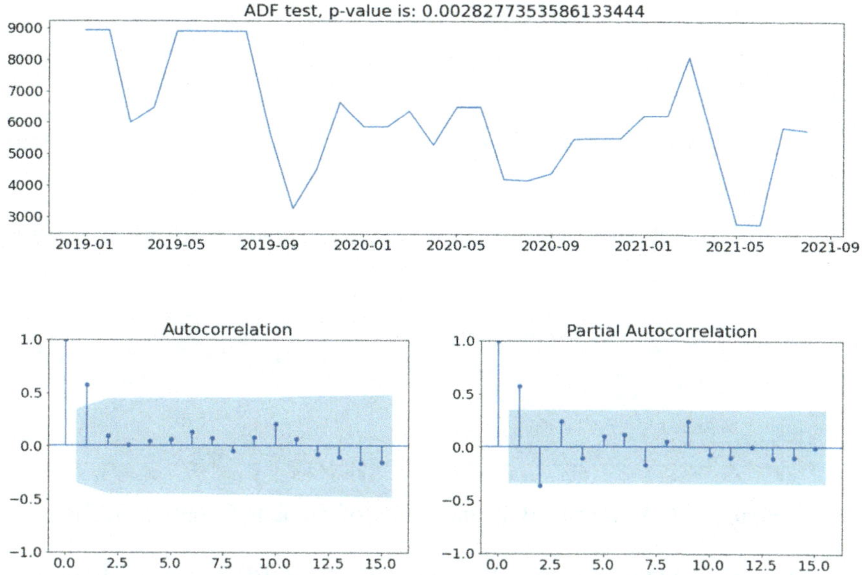

Figure 3-5. ADF test, ACF, and PACF of the Economic Development Zone's GPBR

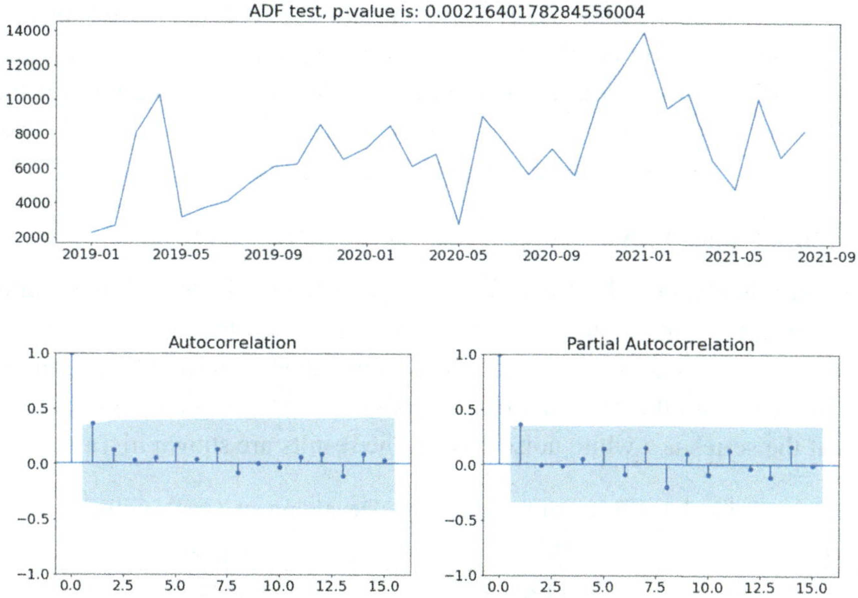

Figure 3-6. ADF test, ACF, and PACF of Hecheng District's GPBR

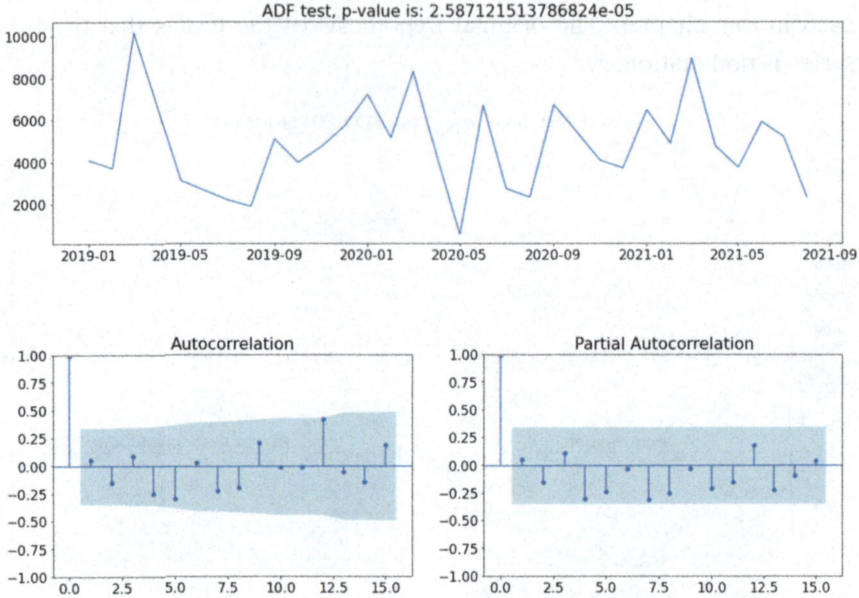

Figure 3-7. ADF test, ACF, and PACF of Zhijiang County's GPBR

After the ADF test, the P-values of the GPBR of the Economic Development Zone, Hecheng District, and Zhijiang County were approximately 0.0028, 0.0022, 2.5871×10^{-5}, approaching 0. The observation of the three ACF charts and three PACF charts reveals that the autocorrelation coefficients of the three-time series rapidly decrease and converge to zero in the range of small lag order. To summarize the above results, we can reject the original hypothesis and conclude that the time series data of the three regions' GPBR are stationary.

White Noise Test

In this chapter, the Ljung-Box test, or LB test, is used to determine whether the time series of local governments' GPBR is a white noise series. If it is a white noise series, no valuable information can be extracted from the data, and the analysis ends. The original hypothesis is that the series is a white noise series. The results are shown in Tables 1-3.

Table 3-1. LB test of the Economic Development Zone's GPBR

lags	lb_stat	lb_pvalue
1	11.661932	0.000638

Table 3-2. LB test of Hecheng District's GPBR

lags	lb_stat	lb_pvalue
1	4.649948	0.031054

Table 3-3. LB test of Zhijiang County's GPBR

lags	lb_stat	lb_pvalue
1	0.116588	0.732765
2	0.847313	0.654649
3	1.178102	0.758261
4	3.510623	0.476265
5	6.884644	0.229362
6	6.942189	0.326227
7	8.941521	0.256882
8	10.530701	0.229733
9	12.687700	0.177254
10	12.687710	0.241660
11	12.689614	0.314095
12	22.656133	0.030791

The P-values of the LB test for the GPBR of the Economic Development Zone and Hecheng District were 0.000638 and 0.031054, respectively, less than 0.05. Hence, the original hypothesis can be rejected. The p-value of the LB test of Zhijiang County's GPBR in period 12 was 0.030791, less than 0.05. Therefore, the original hypothesis can be rejected, and the time series can be considered to have long-run autocorrelation. It can be concluded that the analyzed time series of GPBR of the Economic Development Zone, Hecheng District, and Zhijiang Dong Autonomous County were not white noise. Therefore, the data is of value for modeling and analysis.

Building SARIMA Model

The time series data of local governments' GPBR are characterized by pronounced seasonality and non-stationarity. Thus, we choose to build a SARIMA model to predict and analyze the GPBR of the three regions. The results show a good fit of the model. The fitted value (fitted), the actual value (GPBR), and the forecast value (forecast) and actual value were in good agreement (Fig. 8, Fig. 9, and Fig. 10).

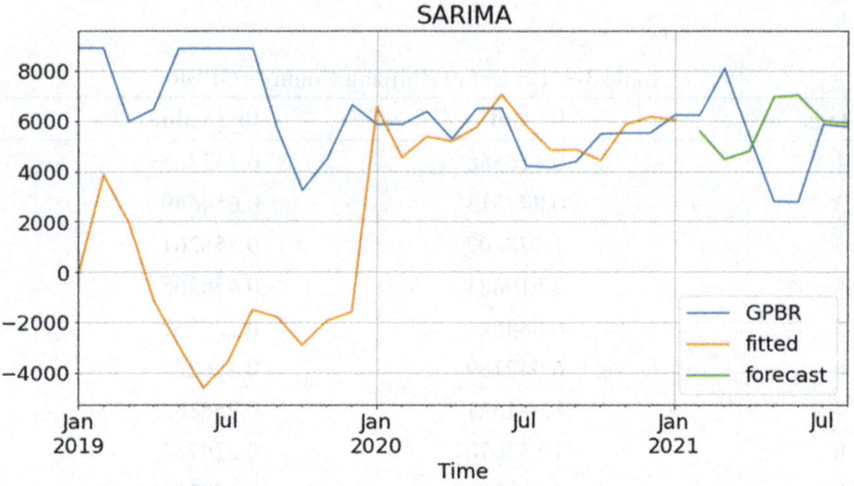

Figure 3-8. SARIMA model of the Economic Development Zone's GPBR

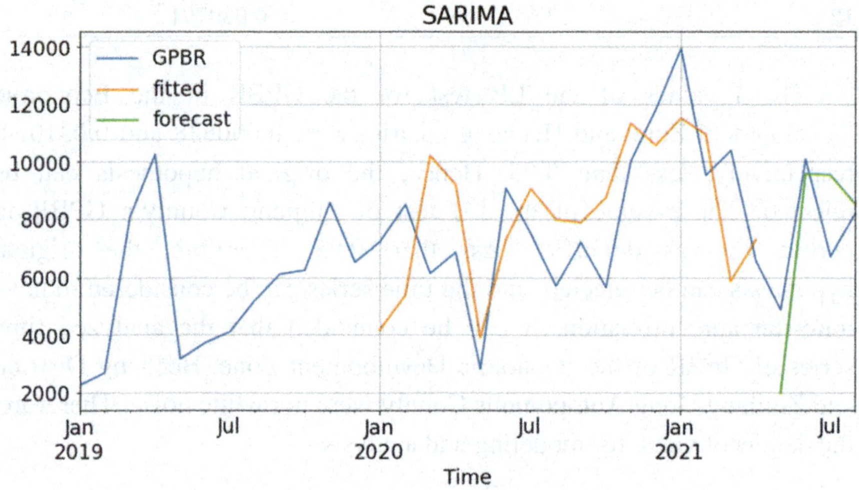

Figure 3-9. SARIMA model of Hecheng District's GPBR

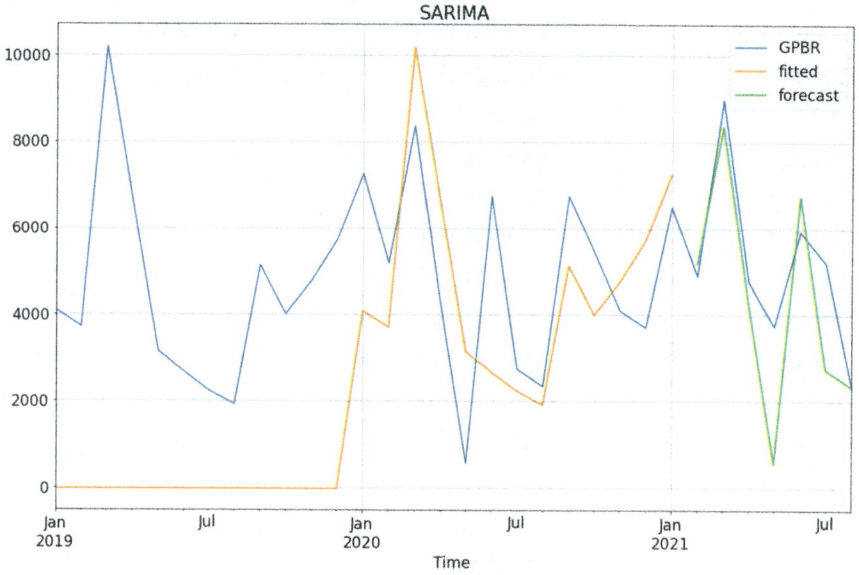

Figure 3-10. SARIMA model of Zhijiang County's GPBR

Model Forecast

The above-trained model forecasts the GPBR of Huaihua International Inland Port Economic Development Zone, Hecheng District, and Zhijiang Dong Autonomous County. The forecast period is from September 2021 to June 2023 after the construction of Huaihua International Inland Port. The forecast results of the three regions are shown in Tables 3-4-3-6.

Table 3-4. GPBR Forecast of the Economic Development Zone

Date	**Forecast value**	**Actual value**
2021-09	4372.286019	5768
2021-10	3804.994219	3955
2021-11	4181.109671	6963
2021-12	5338.063379	8310
2022-01	6451.228931	2328
2022-02	6344.324401	2328
2022-03	5531.949036	9256
2022-04	5139.610420	9256
2022-05	6519.891363	9256

Date	Forccast value	Actual value
2022-06	6409.827838	5629
2022-07	5467.245126	5088
2022-08	5680.340777	1684
2022-09	4662.738444	18288
2022-10	4360.330180	1604
2022-11	4557.871645	8427
2022-12	5398.716455	11429
2023-01	6233.516347	1707
2023-02	5967.171490	1707
2023-03	5247.894585	6790
2023-04	5126.618528	6790
2023-05	6723.224401	14635
2023-06	6672.271168	14635

Table 3-5. GPBR forecast of Hecheng District

Date	Forecast value	Actual value
2021-09	7897.886948	8272
2021-10	6795.275292	4898
2021-11	8099.734177	7765
2021-12	9044.130686	5861
2022-01	9650.609281	8862
2022-02	7578.969744	8862
2022-03	8700.973634	7627
2022-04	7081.150918	8618
2022-05	6629.962392	4168
2022-06	7773.204408	13002
2022-07	6649.191339	4990
2022-08	7669.305370	4267
2022-09	7332.401239	12079
2022-10	7149.726570	2855
2022-11	7089.414733	1914
2022-12	7069.502188	3716
2023-01	7062.927866	5664

Date	Forecast value	Actual value
2023-02	7060.757289	5664
2023-03	7060.040651	5664
2023-04	7059.804046	5664
2023-05	7059.725929	7614
2023-06	7059.700138	7614

Table 3-6. GPBR forecast of Zhijiang County

Date	Forecast value	Actual value
2021-09	4922.648847	5228
2021-10	4121.446660	5064
2021-11	3427.543075	5968
2021-12	2822.501259	2293
2022-01	4353.652109	2698
2022-02	4016.050298	3175
2022-03	6142.551173	3736
2022-04	4570.450715	4114
2022-05	4647.986247	5228
2022-06	4009.081328	5064
2022-07	4709.247999	5968
2022-08	3202.561646	2293
2022-09	3747.378393	2698
2022-10	3550.373032	3175
2022-11	3621.610035	3736
2022-12	3595.850784	4114
2023-01	3605.165312	5519
2023-02	3601.797185	9396
2023-03	3603.015097	3481
2023-04	3602.574701	2528
2023-05	3602.733948	8549
2023-06	3602.676364	2581

It is necessary to define the influence ratio first. It can help to estimate more intuitively and accurately the impact of the construction of

Huaihua International Inland Port on the Economic Development Zone, Hecheng District, and Zhijiang Dong Autonomous County. The specific formula is as follows:

$$\text{Influence ratio} = \frac{\sum \text{Actual value} - \sum \text{Forecast value}}{\sum \text{Forecast value}} * 100\% \quad ....(3)$$

The actual cumulative GPBR of the Economic Development Zone was RMB 1,558,330,000, and the cumulative forecast value was about RMB 1,201,910,000. Therefore, the influence ratio was about 29.65%. The actual cumulative GPBR of Hecheng District was RMB 1,456,400,000, and the cumulative forecast value was about RMB 1,645,740,000, so the influence ratio is about −11.51%. The actual cumulative GPBR of Zhijiang County was RMB 966,060,000, and the forecast cumulative value was about RMB 870,790,000. Therefore, the influence ratio was about 10.94%.

Conclusion

The construction of Huaihua International Inland Port contributes significantly to the economic growth of the Economic Development Zone. In the 22 months after the construction of the inland port, the GPBR of the Economic Development Zone increased by RMB 356,400,000 than expected, with a positive influence ratio of more than 29.65%. It reflects the vital role of the inland port as an economic booster. In contrast, the GPBR of Hecheng District decreased by RMB 189,340,000 than expected in the 22 months, with an influence ratio of about −11.51%. It shows a significant negative economic spillover effect. Due to the construction of Huaihua International Inland Port, enormous resources and policies have been favorably deployed, attracting many enterprises registered or planning to be recorded in the Hecheng District. Therefore, it affects the local tax revenue in the short term. With the gradual maturity of Huaihua International Inland Port, we expect that the total economic size of Huaihua City will grow bigger and bigger. The short-term negative impact on Hecheng District will be diminished, and the positive economic spillover effect will become apparent.

Zhijiang Dong Autonomous County is geographically close to the Economic Development Zone, but their economic endowments differ. Zhijiang showed completely different changes from Hecheng District. Its

GPBR increased by RMB 95,270,000 more than expected in 22 months, with an influence ratio of 10.94%. The construction of Huaihua International Inland Port has significant positive spillover effects on Zhijiang's economy. First, Zhijiang County has the only civil aviation airport in Huaihua City. Huaihua International Inland Port has seen the development of air-rail and air-rail-road multimodal transportation. It increases the passenger and freight transportation capacity of Huaihua Zhijiang Airport and drives the development of Zhijiang's logistics and transportation industries. Secondly, the agricultural products of Zhijiang County can be exported through Huaihua International Inland Port, boosting the growth of agricultural output value. Thirdly, the construction of Huaihua International Inland Port enhances the national and international visibility of Huaihua City. It also positively affects Zhijiang's tourism and service industries.

Due to the problems of too many missing data, outliers in the raw data, and small data volume, the model error in this study is not accurate enough. As Huaihua International Inland Port's construction is prolonged, the data will increase, and the model can be corrected accordingly. This analysis is only based on local governments' GPBR, and some representative economic indicators should be analyzed in the future. Regarding research objects, only the Economic Development Zone, Hecheng District, and Zhijiang Dong Autonomous County were selected. This study was initially planned to include Zhongfang County in Huaihua City. However, the data for this county is not yet complete, so it is not included in this study. The follow-up study is intended to explore further the economic spillover effects of the international inland port on the 13 cities and counties of Huaihua and the greater western Hunan region. In this way, we can understand the construction of Huaihua International Inland Port more comprehensively and in detail. Thus, it can help the government make policies and enterprises make decisions.

Chapter 4
Huaihua International Inland Port and China-Laos Trade

This chapter investigates the construction status of the Huaihua International Inland Port in Hunan Province, China, its development potential and its position in China's macroeconomic development strategy. It then examines the importance of the port to the bilateral economic and trade development between China and Laos. It comprehensively analyzes the infrastructure, supporting services, legal protection and enterprise financing of Huaihua International Inland Port. Moreover, it reveals the current challenges and dilemmas the port is facing. It also provides a forward-looking perspective on the potential and prospects of Huaihua International Inland Port. In addition, it demonstrates how to accelerate the construction of the international inland port by strengthening infrastructure construction, improving policies and regulations, and providing financial financing to support the revitalization and upgrading of the industries in Huaihua. Combined with the new development stage of China-Laos trade and the requirement of high-quality development, it is concluded that Huaihua International Inland Port will open up a new way for China-Laos bilateral economic and trade exchanges, thus adding a new impetus to the economic development of the region centered on Huaihua.

Introduction

This study examines the construction and development of Huaihua International Inland Port and its impact on bilateral trade between China and Laos. It will promote the development of the economic model of inland ports in China and the bilateral economic and trade exchanges between China and Laos. The accelerated economic globalization and the logistics network era have made inland ports an integral part of the international trade logistics system. In recent years, an inland port construction boom has appeared in China in response to the economic globalization trends. Especially after The Belt and Road Initiative was introduced, the development of international inland ports has attracted even more attention. Some international inland ports in China have achieved remarkable results, such as Xi'an, Chongqing, Urumqi, and Huaihua. Nowadays, these international inland ports have formed the strategic layout of the New International Land-Sea Trade Corridor in Western China. Based on the international inland ports, they have operated China-Europe, China-Thailand, and China-Vietnam freight trains. The construction of the inland ports expands the scope of imports and exports of neighboring regions and stimulates the rapid economic development of these regions.

In the western part of China's Hunan Province, Huaihua is in the center of Hunan, Hubei, Chongqing, Guizhou, and Guangxi border regions. This unique geographic location makes Huaihua a bridgehead from Central China to Southwest China. At the same time, it is also an important node city in China's "The Belt and Road" strategy, connecting Europe and other Asian regions to the north and ASEAN to the south. Due to its transportation advantages, coupled with the construction and development of the international inland port, Huaihua has seen rapid socio-economic development. Its spillover effect has substantially driven the rapid growth of the regional economy of neighboring cities (Hou et al., 2023). In addition, Huaihua is the node city for China-Europe freight trains, China-ASEAN freight trains, and China-Central Asia freight trains. It is also the starting point in China for China-Thailand freight trains and the first city in central China to launch two-way China-Laos and China-Vietnam international trains. Given this, developing an inland port economy could make Huaihua a national transportation hub for China to Europe and ASEAN.

Laos has great potential for trade with China along the route of China's Belt and Road Initiative. Firstly, Laos has a favorable geographical location, bordering China in the north, Vietnam in the east, Cambodia in the south, and Thailand and Myanmar in the west. It is a crucial transportation hub connecting the China-ASEAN Free Trade Area (CAFTA) by waterway, railroad and land. Secondly, Laos and China have many economic and trade cooperation projects. Depending on the economic volume they cover, they are mainly organized in the following four dimensions: cooperation under The Belt and Road, the China-ASEAN Free Trade Area (CAFTA), the Lancang-Mekong Cooperation, the China-Laos Economic Corridor (Zhang, 2021). Thirdly, Laos and its five neighboring countries are engaged in the Great Mekong Subregion (GMS) Cooperation to develop the economy and society of the basin jointly. Thus, they will head towards the broader goal of developing the East-West Economic Corridor (EWEC). This corridor runs westward from Da Nang, a deep-water port in central Vietnam, to Laos, Thailand, and Myanmar (Sounvilevth, 2010). It is necessary to strengthen the economic and trade cooperation projects with Laos through international logistics transportation based on the Huaihua International Inland Port. It will help promote the economic and social development of Central China. Besides, it can accelerate the construction of China-ASEAN Free Trade Area and regional integration, boost the trade market in Southeast Asia and enhance the economic and trade exchanges between China and Southeast Asia.

Based on the above knowledge, this chapter analyzes the existing literature and theories on the trade potential between China and Laos. Accordingly, it explores the trend of bilateral trade between China and Laos from the perspective of the construction and development of international inland ports. According to the experience and model of other international inland ports, it also puts forward appropriate suggestions for developing Huaihua International Inland Port. It aims to facilitate the construction of Huaihua International Inland Port, promote bilateral trade between China and Laos, and offer solutions to other cities worldwide that are building international inland ports.

Regarding China's macroeconomic development strategies, the international inland ports built and built are essential nodes for implementing "The Belt and Road" strategy. Inland ports are interconnected with the ports so that the platform information can be linked and shared in a mutually trusting way. It is a crucial link in building and developing the inland port, which requires further communication, consultation, improvement, and sharing. Relevant departments should seriously discuss and put it into practice and work together to build a modernized platform for inland ports and contribute to the high-quality development of the hub economy. In this way, they can enhance the quality of national logistics hubs and promote connectivity between inland port cities in China and abroad.

Moreover, they can drive the construction of international logistics channels, enhance the synergy among inland ports, hubs and enterprises, and realize the sustainable development of the inland port industry and hub economy. There are few research results on the bilateral trade between China and Laos from the perspective of inland port construction. Few scholars have analyzed the impact of the China-Laos Railway on China-Laos trade. This chapter explores the construction and development of the Huaihua International Inland Port to capture the factors affecting the potential of bilateral trade between China and Laos. It provides useful theoretical references for promoting bilateral trade between China and Laos.

Existing studies have shown that the further development of China's inland port economic model is conducive to domestic economic growth. Moreover, it contributes to The Belt and Road Initiative, boosting world economic growth (Wu, 2020). Promoting Laos' foreign trade by engaging in close economic and trade exchanges with China is strategically significant. Laos faces the realistic problems of a relatively backward domestic economy and the urgent need to open up to the outside world further. Facilitating foreign trade and opening up to the outside world is a national strategic plan made by the Lao PDR after learning from the experience of China's reform and opening up. China is the largest trading partner of Laos, in addition to ASEAN. Closer economic and trade exchanges with China can further promote the opening up of Laos to the outside world and enhance its international competitiveness. In addition, it will improve the livelihood of the Lao people and enable them to lead a happier life.

Literature Review

The research on international inland ports is well-documented in international academic journals and has various perspectives. Over the past three decades, the global academic community has extensively studied the development of inland ports based on different geographical and institutional contexts (Witte, Wiegmans & Ng, 2019). Roso et al. (2010) defined "international dry port" at the beginning of the 21st century. Roso (2008) investigated the factors affecting the implementation of inland ports by surveying and defining the barriers to establishing inland ports as closed intermodal terminals. Ng et al. (2014) consider the development of inland port facilities as a distinct aspect of port geography, mainly viewed as an extension of port studies. In a study of inland ports in North America and Europe, Wiegmans et al. (2015) found that the perceptions of inland ports vary significantly across countries and regions. Witte et al. (2017) explored the multilevel nature of inland ports. They proposed that inland ports should be analyzed comprehensively and systematically from the perspectives of infrastructure, spatial, governance and economic structures.

For a long time, Monios and Wilmsmeier (2012) studied inland ports mainly from the perspective of operation and planning. However, in recent years, scholars have focused on the spatial and economic impacts of inland ports on their neighboring areas. In addition, inland facilities with or without intermodal terminals and logistics companies can connect directly to inland ports with high-capacity transportation by rail, road, or inland waterways. Thus, customers can conveniently store, load, and transport their containers or standardized freight units. The inland port should have harbor-like functions and characteristics (Roso et al., 2009; Wiegmans et al., 2015). In addition, a Dutch scholar, Fazi (2016), researched the container routing of inland ports by building a mathematical model. Indonesian scholars Syahchari et al. (2021) found through a questionnaire survey that cooperation in the supply chain and stakeholder commitment to services positively affect the performance of port companies. By analyzing its national political and economic status, Indonesian scholars Niemann et al. (2016) developed targeted B2B marketing strategies for Indonesia's Cikarang Dry Port (CDP).

Four distinct research topics and orientations exist on the Huaihua International Inland Port. First, based on the New International Land-Sea Trade Corridor in Western China, it analyzes Huaihua's location advantages and proposes strategies for building and developing the international inland port (Li, 2021). Second, from the logistics orientation and management perspective, suggestions are made to build a logistics platform for Huaihua International Inland Port (Shu et al., 2021). Third, scholars adopt different research methods and paradigms to study the industrial opportunities and challenges facing the Huaihua

International Inland Port (Yang et al., 2023). Fourth, the driving effect of the inland port economy on the financing of local state-owned enterprises in Huaihua is studied (Liu, 2023). Xiao et al. (2023) studied the construction of Huaihua International Inland Port and its impact on residents' housing demand. They found that the Huaihua International Inland Port will accelerate the population agglomeration and urbanization in southwest Hunan, leading to phased changes in residents' housing demand. Hou et al. (2023) conducted an empirical study on the economic spillover effect of Huaihua International Inland Port. Their results showed that the construction and development of Huaihua International Inland Port will inevitably have specific economic spillover effects on the neighboring areas.

China and Laos have achieved fruitful results in communication and cultural exchanges in recent years. Regarding communication cooperation, the first high-tech project between China and Laos, the LaoSat 1 spacecraft, was successfully launched in November 2015 in China. Laos has made a breakthrough in autonomous satellite communications and cross-border services. Laotians can watch satellite TV programs, enriching their lives. In addition to cooperation in traditional areas such as infrastructure, production capacity, commerce, and culture, China and Laos have strengthened their collaboration in the digital economy, ecology and environment, and clean building. Both countries strive to transform the China-Laos Economic Corridor into a digital, green, and clean corridor (Ahmad & Gul, 2018).

There is little research in the international academic community on the bilateral economic and trade exchanges between China and Laos. The research literature on China-Laos railroad cargo transportation is even scarcer, and the only research papers are mainly conducted from the perspectives of logistics management and rail route planning. There is also a fatal flaw in these papers, as the latest data after the opening of the China-Laos Railway has not yet been analyzed. A review of the existing academic research found that international academic research on the China-Laos Railway mainly focuses on geopolitical security (Wrobel, 2019). Many scholars have analyzed and discussed it as a typical project of China's Belt and Road Initiative (Pratiwi, 2020). Chinese scholars' research on China-Laos trade and the international inland port has three main perspectives. First, from a macro standpoint, it mainly deals with the impact of the international inland port on China's trade with Laos or other related countries. Zhang (2023) studied the China-Laos Railway from the perspective of multiple community building. Lu and Lan from The Research Group of The People's Bank of China Honghe Central Sub-branch (2023) examined the impact of the opening of the China-Laos Railway on China's economic development. Second, there are two views from the meso perspective.

On the one hand, it analyzes China's development of international inland ports (Yang & Deng, 2023). He et al. (2024) utilized the cite-space method to summarize Chinese scholars' research and analysis on international inland ports. On the other hand, there is an analysis of trade potential between China and Laos (Chansana, 2022). Third, at the micro level, specific studies are conducted on constructing China's major international inland ports. The volume of literature at this level is impressive. Dong and Gao (2016) examined the railroad routes and location economics of the Shangjie Inland Port in Zhengzhou under The Belt and Road. Zhang (2024) studied the development of the Maohan-Boten Economic Cooperation Zone in Yunnan with the China-Laos Railway as the core. Cui (2023) provides suggestions for the Manzhouli International Inland Port from the logistics orientation and management perspective.

While combing and analyzing the existing research stock, this chapter takes the construction and development of Huaihua International Inland Port as the starting point. It focuses on China-Laos railroad transportation and bilateral trade. Combined with research results in China and abroad and relevant new data, it will analyze the economic impact of the port on China-Laos trade. Furthermore, it will explore whether it can provide construction experience and methods for other inland port cities to provide a new perspective for the empirical research of the current inland port economy.

Huaihua International Inland Port's Strategic Position and Current Status

In August 2019, China's National Development and Reform Commission developed a national strategic plan for developing the Huaihua International Inland Port. Thus, the construction and development of Huaihua International Inland Port is supported by Huaihua City and Hunan Province. After several years of construction and initial operation, the port increasingly demonstrates its strategic importance. The port has attracted many investment enterprises and introduced many cooperative projects. It has also achieved such successes as being the only ASEAN hub in Hunan Province. However, in the construction and development process, the port still has problems with its imperfect infrastructure and inadequate legal protection. It also faces the challenges of insufficient enterprise financing ability, shortage of professionals and insufficient core competitiveness. It is urgent for the authorities concerned to think about how to grasp the strategic positioning of the Huaihua International Inland Port, seize the opportunity to develop the inland port economy, meet the challenges and solve the current problems.

Strategic Significance and Positioning

In August 2019, China's National Development and Reform Commission issued the Master Plan of the New International Land-Sea Trade Corridor in Western China ("The Plan"). It indicates that Western China's New International Land-Sea Trade Corridor has been elevated to China's national strategy. The Plan positioned Huaihua as a critical node city on the eastern route of the main corridor. Since then, the Hunan Provincial People's Government has taken the Huaihua International Inland Port as a strategic project for the province's economic development. Moreover, it fully supports its development into a strategic platform for interfacing deeply with the Regional Comprehensive Economic Partnership Agreement (RCEP) and ASEAN countries, an ASEAN cargo consolidation center, and a landmark project for reforming and opening up the inland region. Huaihua International Inland Port is explicitly designated as the only international inland port in Hunan Province.

In recent years, the Hunan Provincial People's Government has attached great importance to and strongly supported the construction of Huaihua International Inland Port. It is regarded as a significant project to fully implement the strategy of "Three Highlands and Four New Missions." Moreover, a new pattern of opening up to the outside world should be accelerated, focusing on The Belt and Road Initiative for

Hunan Province. Furthermore, the Huaihua International Inland Port should contribute to the new positioning and mission of Huaihua's development. The Three Highlands refer to shaping a national advanced manufacturing industry, nurturing innovative technology with a competitive edge, and expanding opening-up and reform. The Four Missions mean realizing integrated development, assuming new responsibilities in promoting the development of China's central region and Yangzi River Economic Belt, striving to write a new chapter for Hunan to adhere to, and developing socialism with Chinese characteristics in the new era. At present, Huaihua is highly united in thought and action in implementing the major decisions and deployments of the provincial government. The city's leaders and people work together to advance the Huaihua International Inland Port.

In conclusion, Huaihua International Inland Port has been strategically positioned very high. From China's macroeconomic development perspective, Huaihua International Inland Port is a vivid practice that implements Chinese leaders' proposal of building a new development pattern and creating a high ground for reforming and opening up the inland area. It is a node project for building the New International Land-Sea Trade Corridor in Western China and connecting with The Belt and Road. For Hunan Province, Huaihua International Inland Port is an essential window for building a new pattern of opening up the province to the outside world in an all-round way. It is a vital bridge between Changsha, the provincial capital, and the New International Land-Sea Trade Corridor in Western China and ASEAN. It is also an important engine to promote the coordinated development of the western Hunan region. For Huaihua City, the port is related to its economic and social development. Promoting the city's high-standard opening and high-quality development is a significant historical opportunity. It is the first project that must be undertaken and must be accomplished.

Origin and Achievements

As mentioned above, in August 2019, China's National Development and Reform Commission issued the Master Plan for the New International Land-Sea Trade Corridor in Western China. Huaihua is an essential node city on the "Chongqing-Huaihua-Liuzhou-Beibu

Gulf" main channel. Huaihua Municipal People's Government fully implements the strategic positioning and mission of Three Highlands and Four New Missions. In response to the model of developing city clusters and metropolitan areas, it has seized the opportunity and determined to push forward the construction of Huaihua International Inland Port as a strategic project. "City clusters and metropolitan areas" are strategic plans for the development of small and medium-sized cities introduced by the State Council of China in the "Outline of the Strategic Plan for Expanding Domestic Demand (2022-2035)" on December 14, 2022. It refers to fostering and developing some modern metropolitan areas, where central cities have a strong capacity for driving the development of their surrounding areas and are highly integrated with surrounding cities. Also, it will improve the coordinated development of the commuting circles. It should make medium- and large-sized cities more suitable for living and working and support the cultivation of new small- and medium-sized cities.

Moreover, it should improve the urban system, strengthen the ecological restoration and functional improvement of cities under laws and regulations, and rationalize cities' scale, population density and spatial structure. Currently, Huaihua, as a small and medium-sized city in central and western China, is speeding up the construction of Huaihua International Inland Port, accelerating its integration into the New International Land-Sea Trade Corridor in Western China. It has initially constructed an open pattern of "serving the whole country, interfacing with ASEAN, and trading with the world."

In July 2021, Hunan positioned Huaihua as the only ASEAN cargo consolidation center among the five international cargo consolidation centers. Since the end of June 2023, Huaihua International Inland Port Economic Development Zone has received more than 180 luggage enterprises from Shanghai, Hebei, Jiangxi, Guangdong and other places for investigation and negotiation in Huaihua. Twenty-three enterprises have been signed and settled, with a total investment of more than 3 billion yuan. Tapioca starch from Laos is an "old friend" of Hunan Province and has been imported into Hunan Province through the Hunan-Guangdong-Africa Rail-Sea Intermodal Freight Train. It is made into "pearls" in bubble tea, medical capsules, and alcohol. On February 2, 2024, the Huaihua Hezhong Integrated Human Resource Market was opened, and the Spring Breeze Campaign of 2024 was launched. More than 40 enterprises from Huaihua International Inland Port Economic Development Zone, Huaihua International Hi-Tech Zone, Hecheng District, and Zhongfang County offered more than 1,800 jobs to job seekers. Thus, Huaihua International Inland Port has attracted many enterprises to invest in Huaihua and create many jobs. The port serves as a logistics hub in the hinterland, facilitating the importation of goods by other industries. Because of this, the China-Laos Railway effectively radiates to China's inland hinterland and the market of the Indo-China Peninsula countries. The regions along the railway can enjoy mutual complementarity of resources.

According to Huaihua Bureau of Commerce statistics, from January to September 2023, Huaihua International Inland Port introduced 30 new projects, with a total investment of 7.737 billion yuan. Among them were three industrial projects with output values of over 1 billion yuan and five projects involved in "three types of top 500 enterprises" (Fortune Global 500 enterprises, top 500 Chinese enterprises, and top 500 Chinese private enterprises). As of October 26, 2023, the import and export throughput of Huaihua International Inland Port reached 474,000 tons, with a value of 1.6 billion yuan. During the Chinese New Year 2024, Huaihua held 221 matchmaking sessions for various Hunan businesses to return to invest in Huaihua. 1,426 Hunan merchants were interviewed, and 160 projects were under negotiation. A total of 95 projects were signed, with an investment amount of 24.819 billion yuan. It has built a "1+N" industrial system led by bags and leather goods and supported by business services, modern logistics, precooked dishes and electronic components. Huaihua has taken a new development path by integrating ports, industries, and cities. Driven by the Huaihua International Inland Port, Huaihua's foreign trade and economy have accelerated. According to statistics, in 2023, 479 projects with a total investment of 146.8 billion yuan were introduced into Huaihua. Among them were 45 industrial projects with over 1 billion yuan output and 28 projects involving "three types of top 500 enterprises." The amount of foreign capital used was 61.18 million U.S. dollars, an increase of 422.5 percent. Huaihua ranked 4th in Hunan Province in terms of total amount and 2nd in terms of growth rate. Huaihua was the first to break the barrier of zero foreign capital in actual use within all counties and municipalities (parks) under the jurisdiction of Huaihua City. The constructive breakthrough of these international projects has provided a strong impetus for the high-quality economic and social development of Huaihua City.

Problems and Challenges

Need for Improvement of Infrastructure and Supporting Services

Huaihua International Inland Port, a logistics hub of China-Europe freight trains and The Belt and Road has limited cargo transportation and port throughput capacity. On the one hand, in the era of high electronic informationization, Huaihua International Inland Port has not created an online program suitable for logistics chain storage and management. No international distribution center has been established to integrate and coordinate logistics and industries. On the other hand, if the port is to be developed into an international inland port for free trade, there is still a gap in infrastructure and service functions with the requirements of a free trade port. The port's supporting services are insufficient, and no integrated logistics center has been formed yet. The logistics industry has not matured; it remains in the traditional transportation, storage, and transfer mode. In addition, Huaihua has no platforms such as a Pilot Free Trade Zone, Comprehensive Bonded Zone, Cross-border E-commerce Comprehensive Pilot Zone or Market Purchasing Platform. The port cannot benefit fully from some of the bonded and tax rebate policies, rendering it impossible to operate the relevant business normally.

Inadequate Legal Protection

Currently, the free trade zone mainly conducts business activities under the guidance of national policy documents, which are of low legal effect. It is not a long-term solution to depend on administrative regulations for guidance. If a free trade inland port is to be built, it concerns China's national interests and relations with other countries, and various legal disputes are related to China. It should have a complete legal system, unlike the free trade zone. Therefore, there must be a high-ranking law as the legal support to ensure the smooth implementation of various matters in the free trade port and the prompt resolution of multiple conflicts.

Inadequate Corporate Financing Capacity

The financing of Huaihua International Inland Port is weak in two aspects. On the one hand, Huaihua International Inland Port is a new project, and its future development is still uncertain. Some of its projects and industrial programs are still undefined. For lending institutions, the first choice of loan recipients must be promising projects. Therefore, the port will encounter difficulties applying for construction and liquidity loans for industrial projects. Lenders could not secure the release of large loans. On the other hand, the main financing body of the port, Huaihua International Inland Port Co., Ltd., is newly incorporated, with a severe deficiency of assets and low capital flow. It is not conducive to the advancement of financing (Liu, 2023).

Shortage of Professionals and Leading Enterprises

On the one hand, Huaihua currently has a short supply of high-quality talents in customs and logistics, especially interdisciplinary professionals in foreign trade who systematically master international logistics, international trade, and related information system technologies. Enterprises generally report a lack of qualified personnel for international trade, making it difficult to develop international markets and handle related international business. On the other hand, there are no leading foreign trade enterprises in Huaihua, including leading production enterprises. Many advantageous and unique products can only be exported through the purchase by enterprises inside and outside the province. For example, Huaihua's fruits rank first in production and quality in Hunan Province, but their export value falls at the bottom of the province.

Low Core Competitiveness

While the construction of inland ports in China was booming earlier, Huaihua International Inland Port was a late starter. The first batch of international inland ports, represented by Xi'an International Inland Port, was already under construction as early as 2003. However, Huaihua International Inland Port was proposed to be constructed in 2019. With its long history and high reputation, Xi'an boasts a reasonable industrial structure and solid industrial cluster. As the capital city of Shaanxi

Province, Xi'an has a solid capital base for construction. In addition, many cities in China are currently constructing international inland ports, like Shangjie District in Zhengzhou, Urumqi in Xinjiang, and Mohan in Yunnan Province. Mohan in Yunnan is geographically close to Laos. The "Boten-Manhan" line has been opened along the China-Laos Railway, and the "Yunnan-Manhan-Boten" economic cooperation zone has been established. Huaihua, situated in western Hunan Province, should consider raising the necessary funds to construct the inland port and stand out in the boom of inland ports. It should create its city card and enhance the core competitiveness of Huaihua International Inland Port.

The Strategic Significance of Huaihua International Inland Port for China-Laos Trade

Huaihua International Inland Port is progressing rapidly, and its achievements are as fruitful as the fall harvest. The Chinese and Lao governments have widely recognized the strategic significance of the port for China-Laos trade. On the one hand, the construction and development of the seaport catalyze the industrial revitalization of Huaihua and bring new opportunities for China-Laos trade. On the other hand, the port links Hunan, Hubei and Jiangxi provinces and promotes China-Laos trade to enter a new stage of high-quality development. In addition, Huaihua International Inland Port is a crucial component connecting China and Laos on the China-Laos Railway. It facilitates the expansion of cargo flow from China's southeastern provinces and accelerates the flow of goods in international trade. At the same time, it also provides Laos, which used to be a landlocked country, with a new path of multimodal transportation for trade.

New Opportunities for China-Laos Trade from Huaihua's Industrial Revitalization

Hunan Provincial People's Government has issued Opinions on Promoting the Development of the Western Hunan Region to Form a New Pattern in the New Era. It explicitly supports Huaihua in building a national logistics hub and backbone base for cold chain logistics and Huaihua International Inland Port. It will highlight Huaihua's role as a gateway city in Western China's New International Land-Sea Trade

Corridor, connecting Southwest China and the Silk Road Economic Belt. Since then, Huaihua has ushered in an opportunity to open its markets, connect the logistics network, and activate commerce; in December 2022, Hunan, Hubei, and Jiangxi provinces signed the Agreement on Capitalizing on the New International Land-Sea Trade Corridor in Western China and the China-Laos Railway and Integrating into the New Pattern of The Belt and Road Initiative. They will promote the seamless integration, cooperation and sharing of various modes of transportation, such as highway, railway, water and air transport. It will further solidify the foundation of Huaihua International Inland Port's multimodal transportation and stimulate a logistics clustering effect. Thus, Huaihua becomes Hunan and central China's ASEAN freight distribution center. 70% of goods shipped along the New International Land-Sea Trade Corridor departed from Huaihua to ASEAN, with one international freight train operating daily.

In recent years, China has been paying equal attention to "bringing in" and "going global" and has listed railroad projects as a long-term strategy for Chinese enterprises to invest in overseas infrastructure projects. Laos is the first stop on China's southwest land route to Southeast Asia, and it is one of the first countries to support China's Belt and Road Initiative. Laos has a crucial position in China's comprehensive cooperation with Southeast Asia. The China-Laos Railway has deepened the investment and cooperation between China and the countries along the route. It has become an "artery" connecting Laos to China in the north and Thailand, Malaysia, and other ASEAN countries in the south. The operation of the China-Laos Railway has accelerated the level of connectivity between China and countries along the Belt and Road. At the same time, it comprehensively promotes the regional economic integration of the GMS countries and provides a strong impetus for the economic and social development of the region (Guo, 2023).

The China-Laos Railway is an indispensable link to maintain the economic and trade cooperation between China and Laos. Promoting economic and trade cooperation between the two countries is strategically essential. Geographically, China and Laos are friendly neighbors and partners connected by mountains and rivers. History has proven that the friendly relations between the two countries are longstanding and constantly revitalized. China and Laos share the same revolutionary experience and struggle. They are both socialist countries with similar development concepts and goals, making them a solid community with a shared future. In particular, the completion and opening of the China-Laos Railway has brought significant spillover effects, promoting the connectivity of the Mekong River region and boosting regional economic development. China and Laos have consistently demonstrated mutual understanding and support in multilateral cooperation mechanisms and have worked together to safeguard regional and international peace and development. With a shared future, China-Laos relations have promising prospects for growth.

A New Stage of High-Quality Development for China-Laos Trade

In February 2018, the first China-Laos Cooperation Forum of The Belt and Road Initiative was held in Vientiane, Laos. In April 2019, China and Laos signed a document on transport facilitation at the second Belt and Road Forum for International Cooperation. The top leaders of both countries also witnessed the signing of 10 bilateral agreements on economic, trade, investment and agricultural cooperation. Laos is the only landlocked country in Southeast Asia with no direct access to the sea. For this reason, Laos is very eager to break through the "blockade" and strengthen its ties with other countries, including China. The construction of the 414-kilometer-long China-Laos Railway began in December 2016 and was completed in 2021. The completed Vientiane-Vangvieng section of the China-Laos expressway gives Laos its first expressway, significantly improving the transportation situation in Laos. Upon the completion of the Vientiane-Pakse Expressway, it will open up the north-south expressway of Laos and shorten the time from Vientiane to Pakse from 10 hours to less than 7 hours. It will significantly improve Laos' transportation facilities and investment environment and give a solid impetus to accelerated socio-economic development.

China is Laos's most significant source of foreign investment, largest exporter, largest donor, and second largest trading partner. Laos is China's third largest investment destination among ASEAN countries. In 2018, total bilateral trade expenditures (22.9 billion yuan) increased by 12.2%. China's exports to Laos amounted to 9.6 billion yuan, an increase of 0.3%. China's imports from Laos amounted to 13.3 billion yuan, an increase of 22.7%. From January to August 2018, China's non-financial direct investment in Laos amounted to 990 million U.S. dollars, a year-on-year increase of 30.3%, with the total investment ranking second in Asia (Ahmad & Gul, 2018). In recent years, China has stepped up its economic and trade cooperation programs with Laos through international logistics transportation based on Huaihua International Inland Port. So far, the Huaihua International Land Port has launched regular freight train services along the China-Laos Railway and the China-Vietnam Railway. It has also launched regular sea-rail intermodal services to Beibu Gulf and the ports of Zhanjiang and Nansha. In 2023, the Huaihua International Land Port handled 455 trains, surpassing the provincial annual target. The port ranked first in central China and was at the forefront nationwide in the number of China-Laos freight trains.

In addition to the Huaihua International Inland Port, the Zhongnan International Inland Port and the Nanchang Xiangtang International Inland Port are also being actively finalized. The construction of these inland ports has opened up new paths in promoting China-Laos trade. Because of this, the international freight train service from Huaihua to Vientiane on the China-Laos Railway has been expanding and extending to Central China. Hence, goods can be exported from Central and Western China to Laos faster and more efficiently. It can also greatly facilitate the import and export trade relations between China and Southeast Asian countries and provide more options for imports from Southeast Asian countries. At the same time, the cooperative transportation mode of international trains linking Hunan, Hubei, and Jiangxi will also provide a model and reference. It will help build a new development pattern for the export-oriented economy of China's provinces and regions and strengthen the horizontal alliance and cooperation among ASEAN countries. It can also promote trade exchanges and economic development between China and Southeast Asia.

On December 12, 2023, the first freight train of the Hunan-Yunnan Lancang-Mekong Express, from Huaihua to Kunming and finally to Vientiane, departed from Huaihua International Inland Port. The train was loaded with 50 equivalent units (TEUs) of cargo, including mini-buses, plastic particles, and ammonium sulfate, with a total weight of 466 tons valued at 5.7 million yuan. The train was expected to reach Vientiane in four days.

It is a significant achievement of the inter-provincial strategic cooperation between Hunan and Yunnan in China to integrate the joint construction of the Indian Ocean International Logistics Corridor deeply. The two provinces have given full play to their regional advantages in jointly tapping into the ASEAN market. Therefore, the China-Laos Railway can effectively benefit the inland regions of China and the Indochina Peninsula countries, and regions along the railway can enjoy mutual complementarity of resources. The "Lancang-Mekong Express" provides regular freight services between Kunming and Vientiane, offering more predictable arrival times and faster customs clearance and speed than other international freight trains running along the China-Laos Railway.

New Path for China-Laos Trade

China and Laos are highly complementary regarding natural resources and industrial structure and have close bilateral trade exchanges (Sitthikone, 2023). On the one hand, China's industrial structure has almost completed its transformation into a technology-oriented industrial structure, while Laos is still a labor-intensive agricultural country. Due to China's large population base and quantity, China has a high demand for importing agricultural products from Laos. At the same time, Laos abounds in mineral resources, making up for the gap in China's imports of mineral resources. On the other hand, traditional Chinese enterprises relocate their labor-intensive industries to Laos during their transformation and upgrading process. It increases investment in Laos and introduces rich experience in industry management to Laos. In addition, China has offered international trade aid to Laos, and Laos has maintained a considerable surplus in bilateral trade with China (Table 4-1).

Table 4-1 China-Laos bilateral trade statistics (in 100 million yuan)

Year	2016	2017	2018	2019	2020	2021	2022	2023
Total volume	154.54	204.30	229.79	270.36	246.02	280.88	380.44	500.65
China's exports	65.13	96.56	96.40	121.58	103.58	107.86	156.86	236.66
Lao exports	89.41	107.74	133.39	148.77	142.43	173.02	223.58	263.99
China's deficit	24.28	11.18	36.99	27.19	38.85	65.16	66.72	27.33

With the sustained economic growth of the two countries and the continuous improvement of Laos' domestic infrastructure, the scale of bilateral trade between China and Laos has gradually expanded, and the dependence on bilateral trade has increased. Resource products like tapioca starch dominate the commodities exported from Laos to China. China's exports to Laos are dominated by industrial articles, such as audio-visual equipment (Table 4-2). Cargo transportation is integral to bilateral trade in goods (Zhang, Ding, & Zhu, 2021).

Table 4-2 Main products exported from China to Laos (2023)

Main products	**Imports (100 million yuan)**	**Percentage**
Machinery and mechanical appliances; electrical equipment; parts thereof; sound recorders and reproducers, television image and sound recorders and reproducers, and parts and accessories of such articles	80.38	33.96%
Metals and articles of metals (mainly articles of iron and steel)	34.07	14.40%
Articles of low value in simplified customs procedures	31.82	13.45%
Products of the chemical and allied industries; plastics and articles thereof; rubber and articles thereof (mainly fertilizers, articles of plastics and rubber))	30.00	12.68%
Vehicles, aircraft, vessels and associated transport equip ment (mainly locomotives, coaches, and vans)	28.68	12.12%

Main products	Imports (100 million yuan)	Percentage
Textiles and textile articles; footwear, headgear, umbrellas, sun umbrellas, walking sticks, seat-sticks, whips, riding crops and parts thereof; prepared feathers and articles made in addition to that; artificial flowers; articles of human hair (mainly chemical fibers, clothing, footwear, gaiters)	10.22	4.32%
Articles of stone, plaster, cement, asbestos, mica or similar materials; ceramic products; glass and glassware	4.93	2.08%
Other	16.55	6.99%
Total	236.66	100%

The Sino-Lao Railway combines the transport advantages of road, river and air transport (Table 4-3). To some extent, it can neutralize the disadvantages of these three modes of transport, as it has a larger capacity, is second only to air transport in terms of speed, and has greater cargo flexibility. Huaihua International Inland Port, a node city in the New International Land-Sea Trade Corridor in Western China, is an important logistics hub for land transportation between China and Laos. The opening of the railroad in 2021 has significantly increased the flow of goods between the two countries. On the other hand, Huaihua International Inland Port's industrial development and favorable policies facilitate the mutual flow of goods in international trade.

Table 4-3 Comparison of traditional modes of transportation for China-Laos trade

	Road transport	Inland water transport	Air transport
Advantages	High capacity and flexibility of cargo types	High capacity and flexibility of cargo types	High transportation rates
Disadvantages	Relatively low transportation rates	Low transportation rates	Small capacity, limited types of cargo, limited destinations

Strengthening the Development of Huaihua International Inland Port for Bilateral Economic and Trade Development between China and Laos

Under "The Belt and Road" strategy, the interconnected international trade pattern has become the dominant trend in future economic and trade cooperation. More efforts should be made to improve the Huaihua International Inland Port and build a functional and complex logistics platform. In this way, it can create a city name card for Huaihua with characteristics of the inland port and make it a lubricant for the China-Laos Railway, promoting China-Laos bilateral trade and inspiring unlimited vitality of China-Laos trade. The following are some suggestions for the problems and challenges mentioned above.

Enhancing Infrastructure Development

Huaihua should increase the investment in infrastructure development on the main channel of China-Laos Railway to promote its operation and development. As more provinces have access to the China-Laos Railway, it is necessary to speed up the construction of Huaihua International Inland Port and develop the transportation advantage into a city card of Huaihua, making it a key node city along the China-Laos Railway. At the same time, the construction of logistics hubs, freight yards and special lines should be accelerated to facilitate logistics chain management and enhance the carrying capacity of freight transportation, logistics and warehousing in areas along the railway. It can substantially increase the transportation rates of goods in the China-Laos trade and reduce the loss of time cost during transportation. It can also further advance the construction of corridor capacity enhancement projects.

Improving the Institutional Guarantee

Constructing a free trade inland port also requires fully protecting the "soft environment." The effective operation of the port business can only be ensured by managing the port under the law (Jiang & Guo, 2019). As China-Laos trade is characterized by cross-border trade, it involves the trade interests of the two countries and their relations, and there are possible differences in the laws and regulations of the two countries. Therefore, a complete legal system of inland port trade must be established to protect China's reasonable and legitimate rights and interests. It guarantees the application of the legal system in China-Laos trade and resolves the problems that may arise in the legal interface between the two countries.

On November 30, 2023, the Sixth Meeting of the Standing Committee of the 14th National People's Congress of Hunan Province voted to approve the Regulations on Promoting the Huaihua International Inland Port (the Regulations). The Regulations provide a robust legal guarantee for building an international inland port in Huaihua. The Standing Committee of Huaihua Municipal People's Congress adheres to the linkage between legislative decisions and significant decisions of the CPC Municipal Committee. It incorporates the Regulations into the legislative planning. The Regulations support the declaration and construction of comprehensive bonded zones to improve the port functions and the green and intelligent information construction to enhance the operational efficiency of the platform. Moreover, it specifies the acceleration of constructing specialized logistics parks and local railroad lines to develop modern logistics. It reflects Huaihua City's efforts to build Huaihua International Inland Port and the attention paid to its construction by the CPC Hunan Provincial Committee and the Provincial People's Government.

Providing Various Financing Channels for Industrial Revitalization

Policies for structural refinancing should be introduced to support the transfer of industries from the east to the west. It should alleviate the problems faced by China's industrial transformation and development, such as the slowdown in growth caused by the transition with traditional growth drivers being replaced by new ones. It should stimulate the development potential of western provinces and regions and integrate them into the neighboring regional markets such as ASEAN and Central Asia. Moreover, financial conditions should be created to transfer industries to East and Central China (Lu, Lan, The Research Group of The People's Bank of China Honghe Central Sub-branch, 2023). In addition, emerging enterprises can raise funds through initial public offering (IPO) to accelerate their listing progress and contribute to their development. In using IPO to raise funds, enterprises should pay attention to the compliance, feasibility, and reasonableness of the investment project in terms of overall planning. It is recommended that the overall planning of the listing of Huaihua International Inland Port be accelerated. A few cases of inland ports are currently listed, so we can refer to the IPO of seaports. In the case of Tangshan Port, for example, since 2010, Tangshan Port Industrial Group Co., Ltd. has raised 1.64 billion yuan through IPO to construct three berths (No. 20-22) in Jingtang Port. It has significantly improved the development speed and quality of Jingtang Port and strengthened the momentum of enterprise development. Tangshan Port is a model of successful IPO application, which is worthy of reference for Huaihua International Inland Port's overall listing plan.

Huaihua has set up a workshop on "Advanced Manufacturing and Innovative Development of Traditional Chinese Medicine" with some advantages. Wu Feichi, a member of the Hunan Provincial Committee of the Chinese People's Political Consultative Conference (CPPCC), serves as the Secretary General of the Hunan-Jiangxi-Guangdong-Hong Kong-Macao TCM Industrial Chain Collaborative Development Alliance. A Chinese Academy of Engineering member, Academician Liu Liang, set up the Academician Workstation in Huaihua. On February 28, 2023, the TCM enterprises were organized to participate in the China (Huaihua)-RCEP Traditional Medicine Industry Matchmaking Conference, and 12 projects were signed on the spot, with a total investment of 4 billion yuan. In the future, more and more port-related industrial enterprises will definitely "settle" in Huaihua International Inland Port.

At the same time, it is suggested that Huaihua International Inland Port should more actively attract investments through the platform. In May 2023, at the first Hunan (Huaihua) RCEP Economic and Trade Expo, 113 projects were signed, with a total investment of 75 billion yuan. During the 2023 Hunan-Guangdong-Hong Kong-Macao Greater Bay Area (GBA) Investment and Trade Conference Week, 31 Huaihua-related projects were signed, with a total investment of 22.49 billion yuan. As it strives to build a new high ground for reforming and opening up the inland area, the Huaihua Bureau of Commerce must continuously optimize the investment structure and objectives from a new historical starting point and boost new vitality for developing the international inland port.

Intensifying China-Laos Bilateral Economic and Trade Cooperation

First, it should rely on the opportunity to construct a national logistics hub and multimodal transportation demonstration base in the inland port. The synergy between inland ports, airports and seaports should be reinforced to build an all-round logistics service system. With the construction of the distribution center in Huaihua for China-Europe freight trains, leading enterprises should promote the linkage of different types of logistics enterprises and enhance the overall logistics service level of the cluster. Advanced logistics technologies, such as big data, artificial intelligence and the Internet of Things, should be adopted to improve the efficiency of logistics operations.

Second, the Huaihua Free Trade Zone should be established, with preferential tax and industrial policies. Preferential benefits in free trade port zones are crucial to attracting investment and expanding trade. They are also one of the competitive edges of the major ports. After completing Huaihua Free Trade Inland Port, it will promote the combination of The Belt and Road, the Pilot Free Trade Zone and the Western Development Strategy. It should prioritize the development of international trade, modern logistics, financial industry, and e-commerce. In the meantime, an industrial system dominated by port-related industries and modern service industries should be built to create a new high ground for reform and opening up of the inland and exert its leading and exemplary role. It should be supported by industrial policies to encourage enterprises to settle and operate in the port area, jointly supporting and driving the development of potential new industries in the port area.

Third, China's logistics and distribution center should be built and developed in the ports of Laos. It should enable the management and labor force movement from China's Huaihua International Inland Port to Laos' ports in China-Laos trade. Specifically, China should provide scientific and efficient management training for the inland port and the logistics and distribution center. Laos should provide an abundant labor force to directly coordinate with China's product management and manage the logistics and warehousing of the distribution center in Laos. By connecting the logistics and distribution centers to the local enterprises in Laos, the flow of Chinese products in Laos can be accelerated, and the market share of Chinese products in Laos can be increased.

Conclusion

This chapter analyzes the current situation of Huaihua International Inland Port, its potential, and its importance to China-Laos trade. From a new perspective, it examines the strategic position and role of the international inland port economy in China-Laos trade and the development and current situation of Huaihua International Inland Port. It also proposes solutions to the problems and challenges faced. It draws on the successful experience of the first international inland ports (e.g., Xi'an International Inland Port) and optimizes the development plan tailored to the actual situation in Huaihua. It can provide a reference for building and developing other international inland ports in China. The plan is highly realistic and feasible for practical operation.

The previous development achievements show that Huaihua International Inland Port opens up a new way for China-Laos trade and injects a new impetus for regional economic development. The China-Laos Railroad will make Laos a "land-linked country" in East Asia, facilitating the transportation of goods between the two countries and third countries. It will also benefit the two countries' cultural exchanges and business cooperation. Huaihua, as a critical node city on the main corridor of the China-Laos Railway, should seize the opportunity to develop its transportation advantage into its business card and drive the development of related industries along the route. Huaihua will become the bridgehead and the forefront of China's economic and trade relations with Laos, with great potential. However, there is no denying that Huaihua International Inland Port still faces challenges in infrastructure development, legal guarantee and enterprise financing.

As the Huaihua International Inland Port is in its infancy, many limitations exist in the bilateral economic and trade exchanges between China and Laos. The academic literature on the theoretical exploration of the subject of this chapter is insufficient. In particular, there are very few studies on constructing international inland ports in leading countries and Laos's economic and social development. Hence, the theoretical discussion in this chapter is shallow, the data collection is insufficient, and the data analysis is imperfect. It fails to explore the essence and problems behind the data. We fully realize that Huaihua International Inland Port is still in its initial stage, a complete system of relevant information and data has not yet been formed, and a limited amount of data is available for research and analysis. It is suggested that in future similar research, we should deepen the research on related theories, keep abreast of the real-time development of Huaihua International Inland Port, and dig into various data in depth. We should further understand the theoretical significance and practical value of the topic of Huaihua International Inland Port and China-Laos trade and make new contributions in this field.

Chapter 5
The Impact on Local Residents' Housing Demand

Abstract: Studies have shown that constructing international inland ports can create an impetus for the local community's comprehensive economic and social development. It can also promote population concentration and accelerate urbanization in inland areas. Population inflow affects residents' housing demand. An in-depth study should be conducted on the impact of the construction of Huaihua International Inland Port on the housing demand of the residents in the southwestern Hunan area. From the perspective of the development trajectory of Huaihua International Inland Port, it analyzes how the port affects the local economy, employment, government revenue, and urbanization progress. Combined with analyzing residents' housing status in Huaihua City of Hunan Province, China, it predicts their future housing demand in Huaihua City. The results show that residents' housing demand will change in stages.

Keywords: International inland port; Housing demand; Urbanization; Southwestern Hunan area

Introduction

In today's society, the demand for housing is a hot topic of great concern. With the rapid development of the economy and urbanization, housing has become a significant factor affecting people's quality of life and economic and social stability. The southwestern Hunan area, covering Huaihua City and the neighboring Shaoyang City and Yongzhou City, is located in the southwestern part of Hunan Province. It boasts a vital location advantage in southwest China's economic and social development. The region has been a significant transportation artery in Hunan Province since ancient times, with abundant natural resources and unique minority cultures. With the construction of the Huaihua

International Inland Port in recent years, the region has seen favorable economic and social development opportunities. Besides, the region has gradually become an essential bridge for the trade interconnection between the inland of southwest Hunan and the coastal areas. With the gradual improvement and development of Huaihua International Inland Port, the economic and social development of the southwestern Hunan area will undergo profound changes, with the effect of population inflow. The continuous influx of population significantly affects residents' housing demand.

This chapter examines the housing situation in Huaihua City and the new trend of residents' demand through a literature review, questionnaire survey and statistical analysis. It also predicts and analyzes residents' future housing demand trends and characteristics. The housing market in Huaihua City is developing healthily, and housing prices are low and stabilizing. Residents have strong affordability and high accessibility to housing. With the continuous progress of the international inland port project, the incoming population will increase significantly and gradually cover the outgoing population. Residents' housing demand also changes in phases. Shortly, there will be fewer inflows to cover the outflows. The incoming people mainly rent apartments to fulfill their demands. A large population inflow will cover its outflow in the medium to long term. The local housing stock can hardly satisfy the growing market driven by the population increase, and affordable and commercial housing will dominate the residential mode in this phase. In the long run, the population inflow will continue and stabilize, and the influx of high-quality talent will overwhelm the population. It will shift from the primary housing demand to the demand for improved, high-quality and characteristic housing properties.

This chapter analyzes the impact of the Huaihua International Inland Port on residents' housing demand in the southwestern Hunan area. It investigates the trends of residents' housing demand in the area. Moreover, it explores the new trends of residents' housing demand in the southwestern Hunan area and provides suggestions for relevant government departments and enterprises to formulate reasonable decisions and plans. Thus, it can promote the balance of local housing supply and demand, improve the residents' living conditions and quality of life, and provide a forward-looking planning layout for addressing residents' housing demand. At the same time, it also provides a valuable reference for other similar regions in the planning and designing future residential housing. Firstly, it analyzes and reviews the existing literature on international inland ports. It sorts out the different effects of international inland port projects on local economic and social development. It learns about the current situation of international inland port research, captures the significance of relevant theories on urbanization and population agglomeration, and constructs relevant theoretical frameworks. Secondly, it examines the spillover effect of the development of Huaihua International Inland Port on the urbanization of Southwest Hunan. Analyzing the history of Huaihua International Inland Port predicts the city's urbanization trend. Thirdly, it indicates how residents' housing demand will change in southwestern Hunan cities and summarizes the current housing market status and residents' affordability for housing consumption in Huaihua City. As the international inland port develops, it analyzes residents' housing demand and offers policy suggestions in stages. Finally, it summarizes the study and identifies the deficiencies and the areas for future research.

Literature Review

Accelerating the development of international inland ports is integral to China's "Belt and Road" strategy to accelerate trade facilitation. In recent years, China has made specific achievements in constructing and developing inland international ports. International inland ports have played a significant role in facilitating international trade and transportation and further promoting the inland economic development of central and western China. They bring great impetus to local economic and social development, drive the spatial aggregation of population, and contribute to inland urbanization. The massive population inflow will affect residents' demand for housing. However, due to the low urbanization and high property stock in the inland areas, the increased housing demand from population inflow cannot exceed the supply in the short term (Liang, 2023; Liu et al., 2023). No systematic analysis and research has been conducted on the phased impact of the construction of Huaihua International Inland Port on residents' housing demand in the southwestern Hunan area. Thus, it is a theoretical and practical issue for in-depth investigation.

The international inland port, also known as a dry port, was interpreted by the United Nations in 1982 as an inland transportation hub that issues bills of lading for imported and exported goods. In 1991, international inland ports provided customs services as inland customs clearance stations. In 2014, the China Ports & Harbors Association defined an inland port as an international commercial port with customs clearance, logistics, container dispatching, warehousing and other functions established in an inland city under international transportation laws and practices. International inland ports are logistics operation platforms built in inland hubs. They are also cargo distribution centers with complete functions of freight forwarding, container distribution and coastal ports, broadening the hinter inland of deep-sea ports. At the same time, they represent the extension of inland functions to boost the export-oriented economy in the inland areas, making them a necessary path for developing the port industry (Wang, 2009; Witte et al., 2016; Rodriguez, 2010).

The Belt and Road Initiative is essential for China to integrate the international and regional economies. In promoting the Belt and Road Initiative, international inland ports have become increasingly prominent in the global economy, and trade has become a pivotal node to enable countries' connectivity (Lv, 2020). At present, to accelerate the smooth implementation of the Belt and Road Initiative, China has ushered in a favorable strategic opportunity for developing international inland ports. More than 70 international inland port projects have been constructed and are pending to be built. They grew rapidly and gradually shaped the economic circle of inland ports.

Moreover, it is highly valued in China and abroad (Li, 2020). Inland port construction is a complex and dynamic systematic project. A perfect inland port system has a far-reaching impact on local economic and social development. On the one hand, inland ports rely on the Internet of Things, big data platforms, and other high-tech technologies for the real-time transmission of logistics information. Through multimodal transportation, the effectiveness of the supply chain is enhanced in many ways. The trade volume of cities will significantly increase, and the regional advantages of inland port cities will manifest.

On the other hand, inland port projects will stimulate the rapid development of the city's economy. The logistics and service industries will empower the city's economy, generating direct income and boosting employment and consumer demand (Zhong, 2021). Establishing international inland ports has provided a broader platform for developing an open economy. Inland port cities will give full play to their regional and functional advantages, accelerate the progress of urbanization, and gain more dividends in the wave of population mobility.

Population mobility has historically been closely related to the level of urbanization. Generally speaking, areas with higher population mobility are more urbanized. The progress of urbanization drives the spatial aggregation of the population (Henderson, 2009; Liu et al., 2022; Liu et al., 2021). In places where the population leaves, some of the labor force cannot find suitable jobs in the local job market, so they must move to the big cities. The outflow of these people vacates jobs for other local working populations and contributes to the saving of social resources.

Also, it advances the rational and effective allocation of social resources and ultimately maximizes the economic efficiency of the region. The proportion of floating population is significantly related to the total factor productivity of the areas with population inflow. Studies have shown that population mobility can effectively enhance regional economic efficiency and promote the transformation and upgrading of the economic growth model (Feng et al., 2023; Chen et al., 2015). At the same time, related studies also show that the floating population has positive and lagging effects on industrial structure (Uilbert,1982; Moomaw,1996). When the floating population transfers to the secondary and tertiary industries, the proportion of the local output value of the secondary and tertiary industries will increase (Mou, 2016; Chen, 2016). The increase in the labor force population also drives the consumption in the housing market. The inflow of high-level talents improves local employment and human capital structures and optimizes and upgrades the industrial system (Udall, 1980). The optimization and upgrading of industrial systems can affect the housing market in two ways. On the one hand, the optimized and upgraded industrial structure generates more jobs and more lucrative returns, further attracting the inflow of high-quality talents from the surrounding areas. On the other hand, from the perspective of long-term development, these high-quality talents are more willing to stay in big cities, thereby affecting the housing prices in areas with net population inflows (Tian et al., 2021; Wu et al., 2023).

It was found that industries in the region of net population inflow usually experience structural optimization and upgrading due to the mechanical growth of the population. This means that areas of net population inflow have shifted from low-end to medium- and high-end industries. In this process, incoming individuals are less uncertain about their future income, and their expected income and consumption ability are primarily guaranteed. It thus facilitates residents' housing demand to be released efficiently (Lang et al., 2022). The housing market factors are analyzed from perspectives on population structure and size. It can be easily observed that population mobility increases the number of people in the areas of population inflows, and the enlarged population base directly leads to higher demand for housing (Teng, 2021; Gong et al., 2021; Garriga, 2023). At the same time, population mobility also changes the age structure, employment structure, and education structure of the population in the areas of inflow. Changes in population structure inevitably lead to changes in housing demand. First, population immigration optimizes the age structure of the places with the influx, reduces the old-age dependency ratio, and increases the local housing demand. Thus, it drives up the housing prices (Jager et al., 2017; Thenuwara W, 2019; Wang et al., 2022). Second, population immigration improves the industrial structure of workers in the areas with inflows. That is, the proportion of the employed population in the secondary and tertiary industries to the total employed population grows, and population immigration also raises the per capita education level in the areas of inflows. These two factors contribute to higher per capita income levels. Ultimately, population mobility contributes to higher housing consumption and prices by affecting employment and education structures (Zhou et al., 2020).

Chinese scholars generally believe that elevated levels of urbanization boost housing demand (Li et al., 2021; Liu et al., 2021). The impact of urbanization on housing demand is mainly reflected in three aspects. First, along with the expansion of the city scale, it is necessary to accelerate the city's construction and various types of infrastructure. Therefore, it places greater demand on all types of properties. Second, many rural people have moved into the cities for work and life, with a strong potential market for housing, which becomes a demand for rented accommodation in the short term. However, with the rising wage levels and increased savings, the demand for rented housing will gradually be transformed into a request for purchased accommodation. Third, the old urban areas need renovation and significant projects due to the advancement of urban construction. Hence, the expropriation, demolition and compensation of old urban areas may lead to considerable housing demand among the original inhabitants (Ma, 2019; Yao, 2021).

However, some Chinese scholars argue that the influx of rural residents to cities due to urbanization does not significantly increase housing demand and is subject to regional differences. The main reason is that high housing prices in urban areas discourage incoming residents from settling in the cities. Furthermore, rural residents have not become the primary source of housing demand (Liu et al., 2022; Hong et al., 2021). Currently, the inelastic demand dominates, supplemented by the need for upgraded housing. In addition, the demand for upgraded housing is gradually increasing. With the increasing scale of urban population and inland use, expanding the spatial boundaries of cities at all levels and in all categories is restricted. The space available for development and utilization in cities is reduced, and urbanization will contribute less to housing demand. People's housing needs and solutions are becoming more and more diversified and differentiated. Residential product supply types, modes and quality will be transformed and upgraded (Chen, 2011; Ran, 2022).

Huaihua International Inland Port is located in Huaihua City, an ethnic area in the southwestern part of Hunan Province, China. It is often known as the southwestern Hunan area, at the intersection of China's strategies for Western development and the rise of Central China. Huaihua City is a crucial area in the national poverty alleviation strategy, with insufficient urban agglomeration capacity and a narrow radius. Without industries that are a solid driving force, it is economically backward, with poor urbanization and low housing demand. Huaihua was once a representative city of population outflow (Zhang, 2021). However, in recent years, Huaihua City has been developing, relying on the strategy of "Three High inlands and Four New Missions[1]" for the province. Establishing a new international inland port is attractive to the floating population in central and western China. The threshold of urban household registration is low, and the housing units are highly available. The population inflow from urbanization significantly affects housing demand in cities. This chapter investigates the impact of the introduction of international inland port projects on local urbanization in a fourth-tier city in southern Hunan (Sidi, X, & Guang, T., 2023) and the changes in housing demand from population mobility. It is undoubtedly significant to the local economy and people's livelihood. The construction and development of Huaihua International Inland Port is expected to serve as a model for building international inland port projects in inland areas. It is also helpful in developing the real estate industry in the urbanization of small and medium-sized cities in China.

The Spillover Effect on the Urbanization of Southwest Hunan

The international inland port enables a convenient international logistics corridor for inland areas and is vital to implementing China's Western development strategies and Central China's rise. Given its unique location, transportation, foreign trade and economic advantages, Huaihua has developed an international inland port project. It has greatly benefited the areas radiated by the project, boosting their economic growth, urbanization, and population inflow. However, the project is still in its initial stage, and its effect is not evident. It is reasonable to believe that with the continuous progress of the project, its impact will be more and more noticeable.

[1] The Three Highlands refer to shaping a national advanced manufacturing industry, nurturing innovative technology with a competitive edge, and expanding opening-up and reform; four missions include realizing integrated development, assuming new responsibilities in promoting the development of China's central region and Yangtze River Economic Belt, striving to write a new chapter for Hunan to adhere to, and developing socialism with Chinese characteristics in the new era.

Construction and Development Status of Huaihua International Inland Port

An international inland port is a logistics node with the same convenient transportation channels as coastal ports, border ports or airports. It has all the functions of ports and harbors, such as logistics, customs clearance, inspection, and value-added services. It is an inland extension of coastal or border ports' functions. In August 2019, China's National Development and Reform Commission unveiled a Master Plan for the New Western Inland-Sea Corridor. Huaihua is an essential node city on the main corridor extending from Chongqing, Huaihua, Liuzhou to Beibu Gulf. Huaihua International Inland Port is a node project for building a new western inland-sea corridor that connects with the Belt and Road. It is an essential window for Hunan to construct a unique pattern of opening up to the outside world in all aspects. Also, it serves as a bridge to facilitate the flow of goods and people between Changsha, the new western inland-sea corridor, and the ASEAN region. It is a crucial engine to promote the coordinated development of the west of Hunan region. It creates a great historical opportunity for high-level opening up and high-quality growth of the local area. The construction of Huaihua International Inland Port relies on the government's significant concerns and support. It is also closely related to Huaihua's advantages in location, transportation, economy and trade, and foreign cooperation (Lian, 2023).

As the border city of Hunan, Hubei, Chongqing, Guizhou and Guangxi, Huaihua City has distinct advantages in location. The Chinese government defines Huaihua as a node city linking the Silk Road Economic Belt and the Maritime Silk Road under the Belt and Road Initiative. The core area connects the Guangdong-Hong Kong-Macao Bay Area, Hanzhong City Cluster, Qianzhong City Cluster, Chengdu-Chongqing Twin City Circle, Yangtze River Delta Economic Zone and Beibu Gulf Economic Zone. Huaihua is also an important node on the eastern route of China's "New Western Inland-Sea Corridor" and is the only city in central China incorporated into the Corridor. It is also a node city of the transportation channel of the "South Wing" of the Yangtze River Economic Belt and a city of ecological innovation.

Huaihua boasts a modern three-dimensional transportation system. Huaihua is China's only high-speed railway hub, not a provincial capital city. It is an essential node of the main framework in the National Comprehensive Three-dimensional Transportation Network Planning Outline. Huaihua Municipal People's Government and Guangxi Beibu Bay International Port Group Co, Ltd. signed a cooperation agreement on "Building a New Western Inland-Sea Corridor." The corridor connects Hunan and central China inland, Southeast Asia, and South Asia by sea. They work together to build the sea-rail intermodal logistics corridor linking Huaihua, Beibu Gulf and the ASEAN countries. Currently, Huaihua is located on the eastern route of the new western inland-sea corridor, undertaking 70% of the rail-sea intermodal transportation logistics shipments. The import and export volume of Huaihua International Inland Port reached 8 billion, and the throughput will be 10 million tons in the future. In H1 of 2023, Huaihua launched 163 trains with 8,142 TEUs to and from the ASEAN countries, with about 250,000 tons of cargo, up 842% YoY. It ran 13 inbound freight trains loaded with cassava starch with a cargo weight of 5,337 tons, exceeding the annual import volume in 2022. Huaihua has become the only international freight assembly center among the five major global cargo centers in Hunan Province.

Huaihua has mature platforms for foreign cooperation. During China-ASEAN cooperation, Hunan Chambers of Commerce in seven ASEAN countries (including Thailand, Laos and the Philippines) have set up offices and trading companies in Huaihua. New industrial cooperation platforms have been established. They include the ASEAN-Hunan Industry Alliance, China (Huaihua)-ASEAN Green Agricultural Products Matchmaking Conference, China (Huaihua)-RCEP Traditional Medicine Industry Matchmaking Conference, Hunan (Huaihua) RCEP Economic and Trade Expo, and Huaihua Business Conference. These new modes of foreign cooperation can provide relevant mechanisms and experiences for regional cooperation under the Belt and Road Initiative.

Huaihua has sustained the integration of its economic and trade interests and has established partnerships with ASEAN countries in Chinese medicine, manufacturing, processing, and agriculture. Over the past decade, Huaihua's import and export volume has risen 7.9 times from RMB 556 million in 2013 to RMB 4.4 billion in 2022. The number of enterprises performing foreign trade has increased by 2.5 times from below 40 in 2013 to 100 in 2022. From January to September 2023, Huaihua's imports and exports to RCEP countries amounted to RMB 1.4 billion, up 170.8%. Exports were RMB 1.13 billion, up 299.4%, and imports were RMB 270 million, up 15.1%. Imports and exports to ASEAN countries amounted to RMB 860 million, up 443.4%. Exports were RMB 840 million, up 484.8%, and imports were RMB 20.605 million, up 39.5%.

In short, Huaihua International Inland Port serves China's neighborhood diplomacy policy on the one hand. It builds a center for humanistic exchanges with ASEAN countries, the Silk Road Economic Belt, and a modern integrated service center. Also, it helps to develop Hunan as a link and bridge for mutual promotion and organic connection between China and other countries along the Belt and Road. On the other hand, Huaihua has become an international corridor and three-dimensional transportation hub connecting ASEAN countries and Southwest China. It builds a more advanced economic and industrial cooperation platform and creates a distribution center for technology, capital, talents and other resources. Thus, it will contribute significantly to the economic and social development of the southwestern Hunan area (Hunan Provincial People's Government, 2022).

Expected Facilitating Effect of Huaihua International Inland Port on Southwest Hunan's Urbanization

In 2022, the Hunan Provincial People's Government released the "Implementation Plan on Deeply Integrating into the Belt and Road and Supporting the Development of Huaihua International Inland Port" on its portal. It aims to build Huaihua into an essential base for opening up inland areas, a first-class international inland port in Central and Western China, and a first-ranking station in China for trains to and from ASEAN countries. Thus, the port industry of Huaihua International Inland Port can be propelled to achieve an output value of RMB 100 billion. Huaihua International Inland Port naturally gathers the flow of cargo, capital, information, and passengers as the gateway for cargo transportation. It boosts industries and trade and promotes the rapid economic development of Huaihua city, kicking off the era of inland ports.

In 2022, Huaihua City realized an annual GDP of RMB 187.764 billion, up 3.8% from the previous year. The added value was RMB 28.230 billion or up 3.6% in the primary industry, RMB 56.687 billion or up 5.2% in the secondary industry, and RMB 102.848 billion or up 3.1% in the tertiary industry. It demonstrates a sustained improvement in the economy. Regarding foreign trade, the international inland port realized total imports and exports of RMB 1.44 billion in 2022, with a year-on-year growth of 312.6%. It drives Huaihua's total imports and exports to grow by 135.6%, as shown in Figure 5-1. Backed by the open platform of Huaihua International Inland Port, Huaihua has been selected as one of China's national logistics hubs for trade and commerce services. It enabled Huaihua to realize a total social logistics volume of RMB 530 billion, a year-on-year growth of 5.5%.

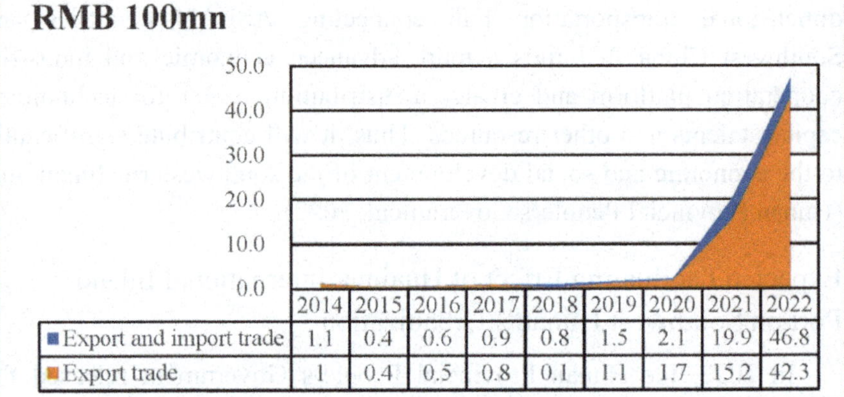

	2014	2015	2016	2017	2018	2019	2020	2021	2022
Export and import trade	1.1	0.4	0.6	0.9	0.8	1.5	2.1	19.9	46.8
Export trade	1	0.4	0.5	0.8	0.1	1.1	1.7	15.2	42.3

Figure 5-1 Huaihua's imports and exports, 2014 - 2022

In terms of employment, since the construction of the international inland port, the employed population has risen continuously in Huaihua City. However, due to the impact of the COVID-19 pandemic in 2020, it fell sharply, but it has been growing in the past two years, as shown in Figure 5-2.

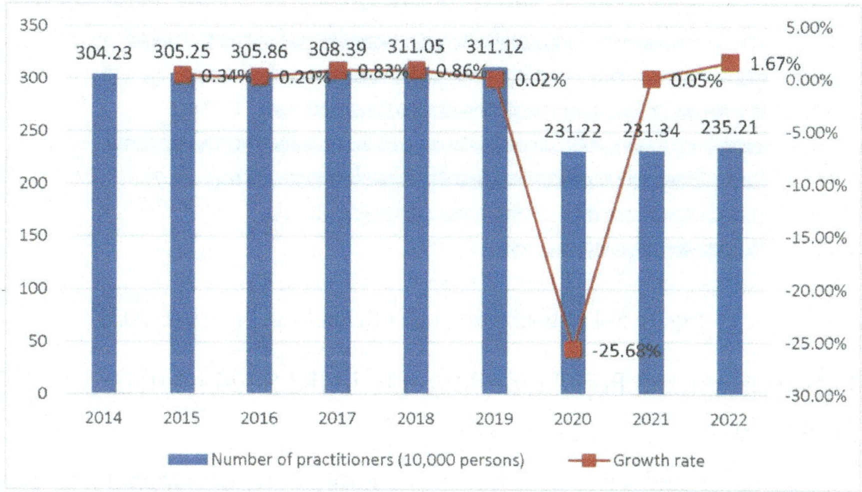

Figure 5-2 Employed population in Huaihua City, 2014 - 2022

In terms of government revenue, the government public budget revenue went up from RMB 7.891 billion in 2016 to RMB 11.956 billion in 2022, showing a steady upward trend. The revenue growth rate from 2020 onwards increased significantly, as shown in Figure 5-3.

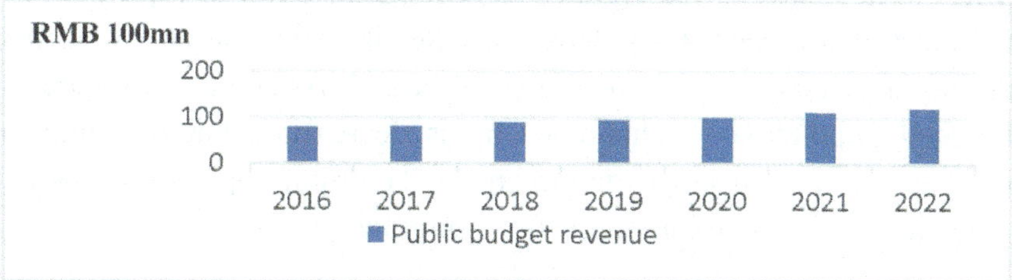

Figure 2-3 Government public budget revenue in Huaihua City, 2016-2022

Regarding urbanization progress, the western Hunan region is economically underdeveloped in Central and Western China, with a low level of urbanization. Affected by the pandemic, the urbanization rate fell in 2020, as shown in Figure 5-4. However, the recovery from the pandemic and the construction of the international inland port project created positive policy signals and economic confidence in the southwestern Hunan area. In 2022, the urbanization rate of Huaihua City was 48.77%, significantly higher than other areas in southwestern Hunan.

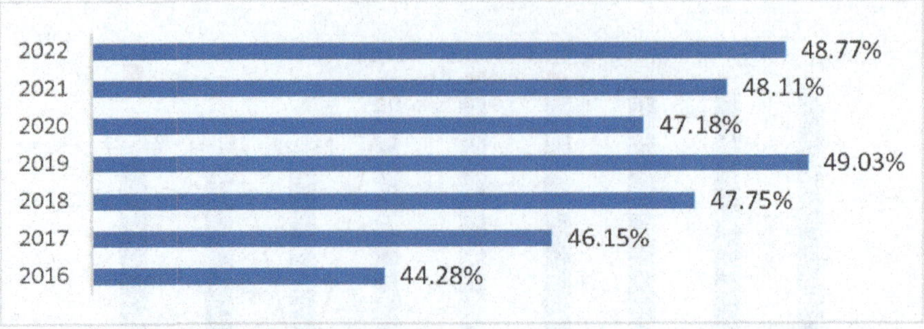

Figure 5-4 Urbanization rate of Huaihua City, 2016-2022

Urbanization and Population Mobility in the Southwestern Hunan Area

As an inland city, Huaihua is committed to developing the port economy, shipping logistics, e-commerce and new-generation information technology industries with its geographical advantages and policy support. It has become a logistics center for the Wuling area and the five bordering provinces of Hunan, Hubei, Chongqing, Guizhou, and Guangxi, as well as a demonstration zone for the inland port economy. Thus, it boosts the economic prosperity of the project's impact area and brings new vitality to the region's development. Since 2019, the level of urbanization has been rising. However, the city's population has declined, and the deceleration has shown a steady trend. As shown in Figure 5-5, the total population of Huaihua City is decreasing, but the rural and urban people present opposite directions. The rural population continues to decline while the urban population continues to rise.

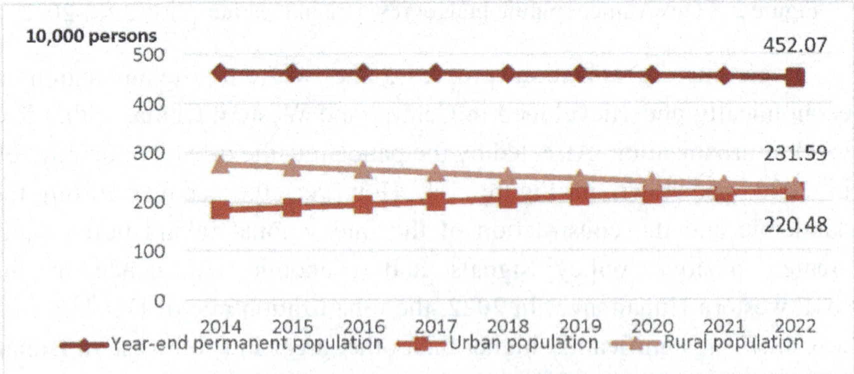

Figure 5-5 Population change in Huaihua City, 2014-2022

Huaihua and the surrounding five provinces are populous and have abundant labor resources. Due to the economic disadvantages, the western Hunan region has long seen massive population outflows, with the urbanization rate significantly lower than the national level. The construction of Huaihua International Inland Port will guide the industrial restructuring and arrangement adjustment of Huaihua City. It will promote trade circulation and drive the rapid development of commerce, logistics and transportation industries. As a result, it will drive population and economic growth in the local and radiating areas. However, the construction of the international inland port remains at an initial stage. Due to the high population outflows, the floating population has no significant growth. Local urbanization and population mobility may change in settings.

The information in Table 5-1 regarding population structure can be analyzed. Regarding the sex ratio, the ratio of males to females in 2022 was 51:48; there is no significant difference between males and females, with males slightly outnumbering females. Regarding age structure, 13% of the population is over 65, 18.6% is under 15, and 49.7% is between 16 and 59. The old-age dependency ratio is 20%, the child dependency ratio is 27%, and the total dependency ratio is below 50%. Therefore, there is some room for a demographic dividend.

Table 5-1 Population Structure of Huaihua City in 2022

Category	Age				Gender	
	0-15	16-59	60-65	Over 65	Male	Female
Population (10,000 persons)	96.79	260.09	95.19	71.19	233.8	218.27

Generally speaking, the southwestern Hunan area is characterized by hollow cities with high dependency ratios due to the massive population outflow. However, due to Huaihua's unique geographical location and the international inland port project, the population structure is reasonable, and the dependency ratio is less than 50%. There is still room to utilize the demographic advantage. With the continuous improvement of the inland port project, more human resources will be introduced, and the population structure will be rationalized.

Expected Changes in Urban Residents' Housing Demand in Southwest Hunan

The change in the population flow structure will affect urban residents' housing demand and the local housing market. Currently, the housing prices in Huaihua are low and stable, and residents have strong affordability and high accessibility to housing. The construction of the international inland port brings population siphoning power to Huaihua. In the future, with the continuous inflow of population, urban residents' demand for housing will shift from satisfying primary living conditions to upgraded, family-style housing. The government and related industries should accelerate the housing market's improvement and integrate the development of affordable, commercial, and rented housing markets.

Housing Status Analysis of Huaihua

The southwestern Hunan area is a typical region of population outflow due to its economic underdevelopment and severe brain drain. With convenient transportation facilities and the opportunity to build an international inland port in recent years, Huaihua's population outflow has been alleviated. The urban population is increasing continuously, and its urbanization has accelerated. With the progress of the international inland port project, Huaihua promotes the import and export trade of unique industries by relying on the global inland port platform. It facilitates the formation of industrial clusters, the cultivation of new trade patterns, the expansion of investment promotion, and the attraction of corporate investment in Huaihua.

Moreover, it can contribute to the high-quality development of Huaihua's open economy. The high-quality development of the regional economy will fuel its urbanization. Population agglomeration will inevitably lead to rising housing demand. The local government and industry practitioners should plan on how to cope with the housing problem arising from the population inflow and how to address the housing demand of the residents in phases.

According to the statistics provided by the Huaihua Municipal Bureau of Statistics, the construction area of housing buildings in Huaihua in 2022 was 21.97 million square meters, of which 3.92 million square meters were new starts. The housing market has been developing steadily. In recent years, housing prices have fallen due to the pandemic and the policy that housing is for living in, not for speculation. Since last year, housing stimulus policies such as mortgage rate adjustments and removal of purchase restrictions have been introduced. The price of new commercial housing in Huaihua has increased but stabilized at around RMB 4,700/m^2, as shown in Figure 5-6. Huaihua has been subject to population outflows for many years, with oversupply in the housing market. Commercial housing prices are low, and housing accessibility is high. It is desirable for the inflow of talent in the region.

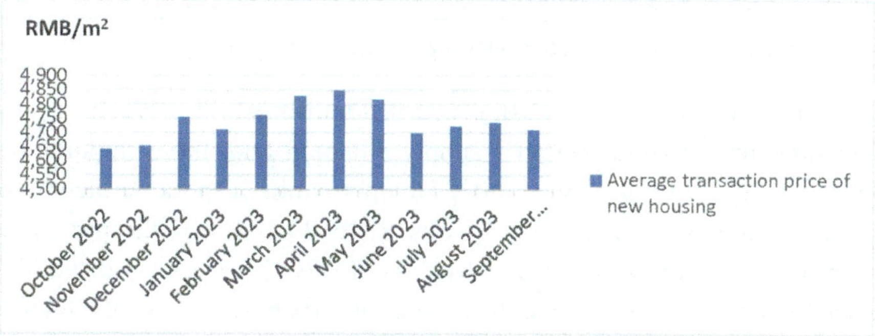

Figure 5-6 Average prices of new housing transactions in Huaihua, 2022-2023

The per capita urban living space in Huaihua is higher than the national level, indicating high redundancy in the current housing market in Huaihua. With the continuous improvement of affordable housing policies, the demand for upgraded housing in the future will be dominated by commercial housing. In small and medium-sized cities with rapid development and low house prices, residents' need for upgraded housing can be easily satisfied, which will also become one of the attractions for the inflow of people from neighboring regions (Figure 5-7).

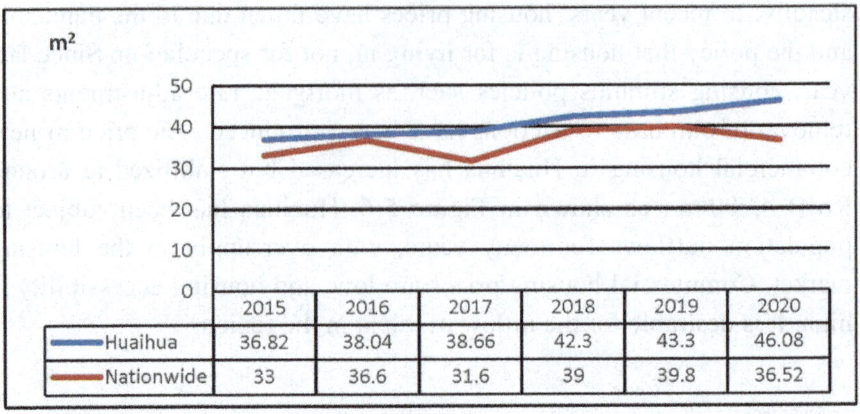

	2015	2016	2017	2018	2019	2020
Huaihua	36.82	38.04	38.66	42.3	43.3	46.08
Nationwide	33	36.6	31.6	39	39.8	36.52

Figure 5-7 Comparison of urban per capita living space, 2015-2020

The accessibility of housing lies in its affordability. We must also consider the housing market's supply situation and, more importantly, consumers' ability to pay. In 2022, the per capita disposable income of urban residents in Huaihua City was RMB 34,168, and the per capita consumption expenditure was RMB 24,543. Both per capita disposable income and consumption expenditure of urban residents in Huaihua show a rising trend. Since 2019, the per capita disposable income growth rate has been significantly higher than per capita consumption expenditure. It shows that urban residents in Huaihua can pay for their housing, and their ability to pay will continue to rise. From the perspective of the housing-price-to-income ratio (calculated for an 80-square-meter house for a family of two), the ratio is 5.5, within a reasonable range. It suggests low housing prices and high accessibility in Huaihua (Figure 5-8).

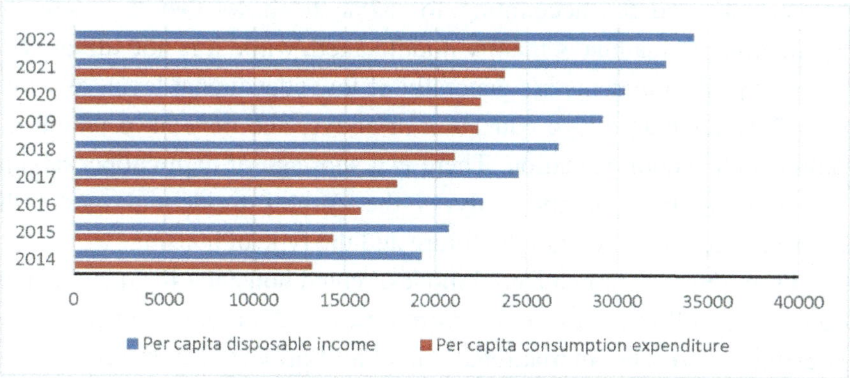

Figure 5-8 Disposable income and consumption expenditure of urban residents in Huaihua, 2014-2022

The housing market in Huaihua is developing healthily by considering housing prices, urban per capita consumption and disposable income, and urban per capita living space. Housing prices are low and stabilized, and there is sufficient supply in the housing market. The living area of urban residents is higher than the national level. The comparison of consumption expenditures shows that Huaihua residents have a solid ability to pay for their housing, and the accessibility of housing is high.

Population Mobility and Residents' Housing Demand in Southwest Hunan

Population inflow leads to higher housing demand, but housing demand varies among phases of population inflow. The research group conducted a field study in October 2023 at the Huaihua International Inland Port Project to better understand the change in housing demand by population inflow. The project is located in the Economic Development Zone. The study aims to investigate the impact of population inflow driven by the International Inland Port Project on residents' housing demand in the region. The research group selected the service companies most affected by the project, such as logistics, catering, and retail. Sampling was conducted to control the gender ratio of the permanent population in Huaihua City in 2022. An anthropological fieldwork method was applied, and one-to-one long-duration interviews were conducted. A total of 224 valid questionnaires were collected. The respondents were mostly aged between 45 and 55, accounting for 52%. It shows that the incoming population of Huaihua is mainly middle-aged, while it is not attractive to the young. Respondents are generally of low educational level, of which only 23% have a college education or above, and 66% have junior and senior high school education. There is a shortage of high-caliber talents. The investigation mainly analyzes the current residential mode, the desired residential mode in the future and the type of housing.

From the current residential modes, rented housing (48%) is the most dominant, followed by unit dormitories (32%) and self-purchased housing (13%). The international inland port project is at an initial stage, and the talent attraction effect is gradually visible. The incoming people need to adapt to the work and environment in the areas they are coming into before deciding whether to settle down or move with their families. Therefore, the leading residential modes are rented housing or dormitories (Figure 5- 9).

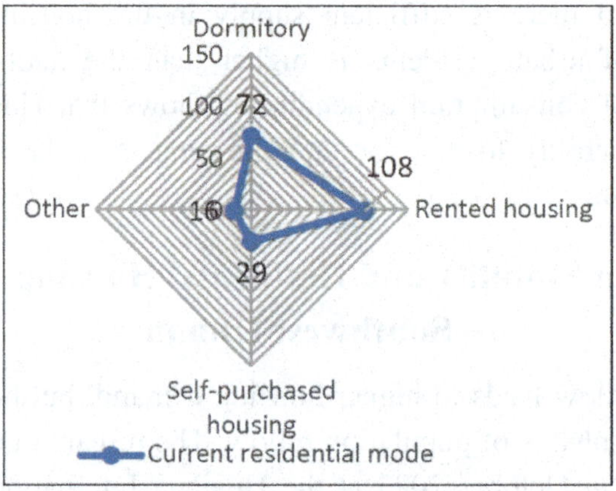

Figure 5-9 Current residential modes

For future residential modes, the desired residential way in three to five years will be dominated by self-purchased housing, accounting for 63% of the total. The proportion of rented accommodation decreases compared to the current residential mode, at 23%. In the medium to long term, most residents opted for self-purchased housing, intending to settle down. Some chose affordable housing. Due to the impact of the recent affordable housing policy, 21% of respondents mainly satisfied their housing demand by resolving the primary housing demand. 42% were willing to buy a better-quality commercial property to determine their housing demand. As the policy of equal treatment between residents who rent and buy properties continues to improve, a few who choose to rent want to settle down in the area (Figure 5-10).

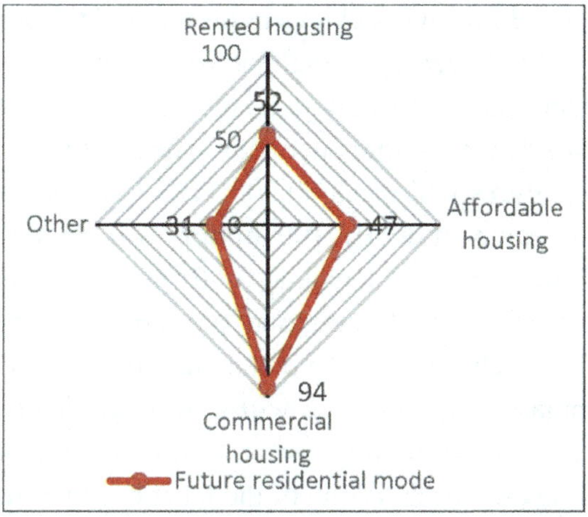

Figure 5-10 Residential mode prediction of future residents

Regarding future housing types, after determining that they will settle down in the city, 47% choose family-style apartments, 39% select single apartments, and 14% choose collective dormitories. In the long run, 47% of respondents preferred to move to large properties with their family members. 39% chose small units or preferred not to get married. It is consistent with young people's view of not marrying or having children. However, there is also an error caused by the age structure of the sample.

As the international inland port project develops, its impact will gradually be magnified. The population inflow will stabilize progressively and attract more high-caliber talents. Demand for housing is expected to rise as the population grows. Residents tend to rent in the short term and purchase their own homes in the medium to long term. In the long run, they will mainly purchase upgraded units.

Response to Population Mobility and Residents' New Housing Demand

Huaihua International Inland Port has been developing rapidly since its construction. The research group anticipates that by 2026, Huaihua International Inland Port will achieve a foreign trade dependency of more than 10%. The annual cargo throughput will reach 10 million tons, and the rail-sea intermodal transportation and cross-border trains will run daily, with more than 500 trains per year. The total volume of container arrivals and departures will reach 50,000 TEUs. The port industry cluster with an output value of RMB 100 billion will be formed. With the deepening of the project, Huaihua will develop into a first-class international inland port in Central and Western China and a significant engine for the high-quality development of the surrounding five provinces. Population siphon force will also be gradually demonstrated. The housing demand from population inflow should be addressed in phases depending on the status quo of the local housing market.

In the short term, when the population first flows in, it is also the beginning of the international inland port. The low population inflow cannot cover the population outflow. Since Huaihua has always been a city of population outflow, a small influx of people does not affect the housing market supply. Most of the incoming people rent houses to meet their housing demands. On the one hand, the government should revitalize the local housing market and provide multi-level and diversified housing to meet residents' housing demand.

On the other hand, it should improve the rental market by building a high-quality and compliant rental platform so that residents can rent their homes properly. In the medium and long term, the effect of population inflow has emerged, and the international inland port project has taken shape and is developing rapidly. The considerable increase in population inflow can cover the population outflow, and the local housing stock cannot meet the housing demand from the population increase. Affordable and commercial housing will become the leading residential modes in this stage. The government should speed up the construction of affordable housing, improve the procedures for access and transfer, and solve fundamental housing problems. Real estate enterprises should develop family-type and upgraded housing units as their primary products and promote the trading of residential commodities. In the long run, industrial clusters will be formed in Huaihua based on the development of the international inland port project and will influence the surrounding areas. Population inflows will continue and stabilize, with high-quality professionals dominating the influx, creating higher demands on the local housing market. Their housing needs shift from basic residential needs to upgraded, high-quality, and unique properties. The government should continue to improve the policy of equal treatment for residents who rent and buy homes and integrate the rental and purchase markets. Real estate companies should adopt a consumer demand-oriented approach to develop high-quality properties and emphasize after-sales services like property management.

Conclusion

The development of the Huaihua International Inland Port has generated positive policy signals and economic confidence in the southwestern Hunan area. It is effectively promoting the economic and social development of Huaihua City. In 2022, the annual GDP of Huaihua City grew by 3.8%, the total imports and exports rose by 135.6%, the employed population increased by 1.67%, and the urbanization rate reached 48.77%. The effect of population inflow will generate new housing demand, and the current housing market in Huaihua is healthy, with sufficient supply and low and stable prices. Key real estate indicators have performed well: urban per capita consumption and disposable income, urban per capita living space, and housing-price-to-income ratio. It reflects residents' strong ability to pay for housing and the high accessibility of housing in Huaihua. It is found that with the continuous progress of the project, the incoming population will increase significantly and gradually cover the outgoing. Residents' housing demand will also change in phases. In the short term, the population inflow is low and does not cover the population outflow. The incoming people tend to satisfy their housing needs by renting apartments. The population inflow is large enough to cover the population outflow in the medium to long term. The local housing stock cannot meet the housing demand due to the population increase. Affordable and commercial housing will become the primary residential modes in this stage. In the long run, the population inflow will continue and stabilize and be dominated by the influx of high-quality talents. Their demand for housing will shift from basic housing needs to upgraded, high-quality, featured properties.

The government and the industry should respond to the new housing demand in different stages. In the near and short term, the government should revitalize the local housing market and provide multi-level and diversified housing to meet residents' housing demand. On the other hand, it should improve the rental market and build a high-quality and compliant rental platform so that residents can rent their homes properly. In the medium and long term, the government should speed up the construction of affordable housing, improve the procedures for access and transfer, and solve the fundamental housing problems. Real estate enterprises should develop family-type and upgraded housing units as their primary products and promote the trading of residential commodities. In the long run, the government should continue to improve the policy of equal treatment for residents who rent and buy homes and integrate the rental and purchase markets. Real estate companies should adopt a consumer demand-oriented approach to develop high-quality properties and emphasize after-sales services like property management.

This study aims to clarify the impact of the Huaihua International Inland Port on local urbanization and the changes in housing demand caused by population mobility. It provides planning and development ideas for the local government and related industries, which is significant to the local economy and people's livelihood. At the same time, this study also has some theoretical implications for developing the real estate industry in the urbanization of small and medium-sized cities. Since the Huaihua International Inland Port project is still in the initial stage of development, the data has not been collected sufficiently. In the future, the scope of the survey can be increased. It is also feasible to observe the changes in housing demand from different perspectives (consumers or producers) and summarize the relevant rules more comprehensively and systematically.

Chapter 6
Integrated Supervision Center

Building an integrated supervision center in Huaihua is feasible and essential because Huaihua City is at the center of the border regions of Hunan, Hubei, Chongqing, Guizhou, and Guangxi. In addition, it is a national transportation hub in China because of its distinctive geographic location, abundant resources and labor force. Due to the development of Huaihua International Inland Port, Huaihua has an excellent opportunity to be a logistics and trade center for inland areas in Central China. Food security, economic development and other factors Given considerations in national strategies, an integrated supervision center can be built in Huaihua, as it can promote the connectivity of the Wuling Mountain area and the neighboring provinces, contribute to regional economic development, and enhance China's national security and supervisory capacity. The development of Huaihua as an integrated supervision center facilitates the processing, bonded warehousing and logistics distribution of high-quality imported commodities from neighboring countries, especially ASEAN countries.

Introduction

Located in western Hunan, Huaihua is at the center of the border regions of Hunan, Hubei, Chongqing, Guizhou, and Guangxi. It is a significant node in the Guiyang-Chongqing-Yichang-Changsha-Guilin circle, with no metropolitan cities within a radius of 350 kilometers. It can promote the development of the surrounding 71 counties, with 90,000 square kilometers and a population of 40 million people. Huaihua is an essential node for China's Belt and Road Initiative to connect other Asian countries and Europe to the north and ASEAN to the south. It is a significant node city on the "Guangdong-Hong Kong-Macao-Chengdu-Chongqing Axis," the "Shanghai-Kunming Corridor," and the "Erenhot-Zhanjiang Channel" in the national comprehensive three-dimensional transportation network. The national comprehensive three-dimensional transport network comprises 6 Axes, 7 Corridors and 8 Channels.

Moreover, it is the bridgehead of East-Central to Southwest China and the national integrated hub city. It has formed a three-dimensional transportation network of one airport, three high-speed railroads, four general railroads and five expressways. Huaihua is the only high-speed railway hub in China that is not a provincial capital city, and it is the first city in Hunan Province in terms of expressway mileage. Huaihua Railway Marshalling Station is the ninth-largest marshaling station in China and the largest in Southwest China, with a daily marshaling capacity of more than 12,000 trains and an annual throughput of 200 million tons. The station undertakes more than 70% of the cargo capacity of the New International Land-Sea Trade Corridor in Western China. Huaihua West Railway Marshalling Station is a leader in intelligent technology in China. The applications of the 5G+Beidou millimeter positioning system and other advanced technologies have made intelligent traffic management, train pickup and dispatching, and shunting operations possible.

Historically, during the Chinese People's War of Resistance Against Japan, Huaihua was a rear area and a strategic gateway from North, Central and East China to Southwest China. Huaihua was the military, political, economic and cultural center with its unique geographic location and strategic importance. The Battle of Xiangxi, the last battle of the Chinese People's War of Resistance Against Japan, marked the complete victory of the Chinese nation. Zhijiang Dong Autonomous County in Huaihua City is an important military fortress and the center of the war of resistance. In Zhijiang, the Chinese people accepted the surrender of the Japanese invaders. Since the late 1960s, Huaihua has been one of the critical areas for large-scale infrastructure development in national defense, science and technology, industry and transportation. It is a strategically important rear industrial base in China. However, Huaihua is part of the economically underdeveloped Wuling Mountain area (a national demonstration area for poverty alleviation). The area is economically backward, and its rural revitalization efforts remain ineffective. The people are eager to develop their economy and improve their living standards.

Under The Belt and Road Initiative, in August 2019, China's National Development and Reform Commission (NDRC) released the Master Plan of the New Western Land-Sea Corridor. The plan positions Huaihua as a vital node city on the main "Chongqing-Huaihua-Liuzhou-Beibu Gulf" corridor. It is the only node city in Hunan Province included in the New International Land-Sea Trade Corridor in Western China. Thus, Huaihua can connect to the Chengdu-Chongqing Economic Circle to the West and Central Asia, the Middle East, and Europe via the China-European Railway Express to the north. Also, it can be linked to ASEAN, the South China Sea and the whole world via the Beibu Gulf of Guangxi to the south. It is the most convenient international channel from Central China to ASEAN. On September 13, 2021, the Huaihua International Inland Port officially commenced construction. On May 9, 2022, Hunan adopted the Implementation Plan on Supporting the Construction of Huaihua International Inland Port for Further Integration into The Belt and Road Initiative.

The land port is set to achieve 2026 an annual cargo throughput of 10 million metric tons, an annual number of more than 1,000 scheduled trains, and a 100-billion-yuan port-related industry. Huaihua International Inland Port will be built into a first-class international port in Central and Western China. It will become one of China's top platforms for connecting to ASEAN. At present, three major international logistics channels have been opened. They are the rail-sea intermodal transport service linking the Beibu Gulf Port, Zhanjiang Port, and Guangzhou Port; the China-Laos Railway connecting Huaihua, Mohan, Yunnan-Vientiane, Laos; and the China-Vietnam Railway linking Huaihua, Pingxiang, Guangxi, and Hanoi, Vietnam. Huaihua became the first city in Central China to realize the two-way operation of international trains between China and Laos and China and Vietnam.

On the morning of April 17, 2023, the opening ceremony of Guangzhou Port stationed in Huaihua International Inland Port was held. It actively promotes Huaihua International Inland Port and coastal ports to gradually fulfill the goal of offering the same fare and efficiency in one port. In 2022, Huaihua International Inland Port ran 151 international express trains, completing 151% of the scheduled tasks. In 1H23, 209 trains were operated, completing this year's tasks planned. It is about to achieve the goal of taking shape in two years, gaining momentum in three years, and becoming a benchmark in five years. Opening up to the West has become the most powerful call of the times.

Figure 6-1 Huaihua Sea Voyage Map

Table 6-1 Detailed Information Contained in Figure 6-1

1	Yekaterinburg	2	Novosibirsk
3	Ust-Kut	4	Bodaybo
5	Aldan	6	Magadan
7	Sea of Okhotsk	8	Ural River
9	Kazakhstan	10	Silk Road Economic Belt
11	Alataw Pass	12	Mongolia
13	Manzhouli	14	Amur River
15	Erenhot	16	Horgos

17	Urumqi	18	Guiyang
19	Liuzhou	20	Beibu Gulf Port
21	Huaihua	22	Nanning
23	Kunming	24	Beijing
25	North Korea	26	Sea of Japan
27	Japan	28	South Korea
29	Iran	30	Uzbekistan
31	Afghanistan	32	Pakistan
33	India	34	Indus River
35	Ganges	36	Bhutan
37	Nepal	38	Bangladesh
39	Vientiane	40	Bangkok
41	Malaysia	42	Yellow Sea
43	East China Sea	44	Myanmar
45	Thailand	46	Bay of Bengal
47	Arabian Sea	48	Mekong River
49	South China Sea	50	Caspian Sea
51	Sri Lanka	52	Singapore
53	Philippines	54	Laos
55	Cambodia	56	Maldives
57	Indonesia	58	Papua New Guinea
59	Major channel for intermodal transport of international cross-border trains: Huaihua-Chongqing-Alataw Pass/Horgos-Europe	60	Major channel for sea-rail intermodal transport: Huaihua-Beibu Gulf Port/Zhanjiang Port-ASEAN countries-Africa
61	Major channel for railway and road transport: Huaihua-Hengyang-Guangzhou	62	Major channel for intermodal transport of cross-border trains: Huaihua-Pingxiang Port-Vietnam (Hanoi)
63	Huaihua-Tehran (China-Central Asia	64	Huaihua-Hamburg (China-Europe

	trains)		trains)
65	To America	66	To Oceania
67	To Africa	68	Turkmenistan
69	21st Century Maritime Silk Road	70	Tajikistan

Following President Xi Jinping's concept of building a new development paradigm, the Hunan Provincial Government has tried to faithfully study and implement the guiding principles of Xi's important speech and instruction on the development of Hunan. With the opportunity of the rapid growth of economic and trade cooperation between China and ASEAN and the location advantage of the Belt and Road, it creates a strategic platform for integrating into The Belt and Road and an essential hub for connecting Central and Western China to ASEAN.

Moreover, Huaihua International Inland Port will be built into a first-class international inland port in Central and Western China. By integrating the port and the city and developing the city by port, Huaihua will become a demonstration node city of a double-cycle economy, a new engine for developing the Wuling Mountain area, and a new high ground for reform and opening up the inland region. However, the railway port in Huaihua has too few functions, and imported fruits, grains and meat can only be declared, inspected and cleared at the port of entry. It has become a significant obstacle to the construction of international inland ports.

Necessity Analysis

Implementing President Xi Jinping's Plan to Build a New High Ground for Reform and Opening Up in the Inland Areas

President Xi Jinping stated, "Reform and opening up is crucial to the fate of contemporary China, and the realization of the Two Centenary Goals and the great rejuvenation of the Chinese nation." Xi attaches great importance to the reform and opening up of landlocked Hunan and has positioned Hunan as a high ground for reform and opening up in the inland region. Huaihua International Inland Port was established at the right time. The Hunan Provincial Government needs to build a first-class international inland port in the mountainous areas with weak industries and backward development. Then, it can gather industries and develop the city with the port, building Huaihua into an internationalized city in the central-western part of China. For this, it should implement President Xi's policy of creating a new high ground for reform and opening up in the inland areas. Huaihua's application for establishing a dedicated comprehensive supervision center is essential for opening up.

National Strategic Security and Strategic Grain Reserves in a Complex International Situation

The report of the 20th CPC National Congress points out that "China has entered a period of development in which strategic opportunities, risks, and challenges are concurrent, and uncertainties and unforeseen factors are rising. Various "black swan" and "gray rhino" events may occur at any time. "Many major issues must be resolved to guard against financial risks and ensure that food, energy, and industrial and supply chains are secure and reliable." Huaihua is located in the central node of the Indian Ocean Economic Circle and the Pacific Economic Circle. With the opening of the China-Vietnam and China-Laos railway lines, it has become an important node city of the Trans-Asian Railway connecting Central and Eastern China.

At present, Russia announced that it was terminating participation in the Black Sea Grain Initiative after the outbreak of the Russia-Ukraine war. The U.S. and Europe jointly suppressed China and interfered in Taiwan. Under such a complicated and severe international environment, China and ASEAN's economic and trade cooperation has been multiplying. At the Special Summit to Commemorate The 30th Anniversary of China-ASEAN Dialogue Relations on November 22, 2021, President Xi Jinping pledged to buy up to US$150 billion of agricultural products from ASEAN in the next five years. On the occasion of the entry into force of the Regional Comprehensive Economic Partnership (RCEP) in 2022, the leaders of China and ASEAN member states designated 2023 as the ASEAN-China Year of Agricultural Development and Food Security Cooperation at the 25th China-ASEAN Summit.

Also, the ASEAN-China Joint Statement on Food Security Cooperation was adopted. Huaihua is the birthplace of hybrid rice. With the efforts of Academician Yuan Longping's team, a seed, moving from Huaihua to the outside world, began to change the world. It is one of the critical areas for developing large-scale infrastructure for national defense, science and technology, industry, and transportation. With national strategic security and grain reserve functions, it is a crucial node city to ensure China's national, rear supply chain and strategic grain reserve security.

Moreover, it can help avoid the over-concentration of critical industries in coastal areas and reduce the risk of potential threats and attacks. In addition, it can promote coordinated regional development, strengthen internal and external trade links, facilitate economic transformation and enhance China's comprehensive strength. Therefore, setting up a dedicated comprehensive supervision center in Huaihua is urgent.

Construction of the Important Node of the New International Land-Sea Trade Corridor in Western China under the Belt and Road Initiative

According to the report of the 20th CPC National Congress, China will accelerate the construction of the New International Land-Sea Trade Corridor in Western China. The new journey of the new era has brought the construction of the New International Land-Sea Trade Corridor in Western China to an unprecedented level. In the document "Key Measures of Customs to Support the New International Land-Sea Trade Corridor in Western China" (No. 74 [2023] of General Administration of Customs), it is explicitly stated that it will support the construction of open platforms along the new corridor. Huaihua is a vital node city on the eastern route of the New International Land-Sea Trade Corridor in Western China, and it is the only node city in Central China. It is also the strategic gateway city of Hunan Province for interfacing with ASEAN and integrating into the New International Land-Sea Trade Corridor in Western China.

In 2022, Huaihua City in Hunan Province was incorporated into the New International Land-Sea Trade Corridor's inter-provincial consultation and cooperation mechanism in Western China. It has formed a "13+2" cooperation pattern between 12 western provinces, autonomous regions and municipalities with Hainan Province, Zhanjiang City, Guangdong Province and Huaihua City. Currently, the eastern route of the New International Land-Sea Trade Corridor in Western China, where Huaihua is based, is responsible for 70% of the logistics of rail-sea intermodal transportation. To the West, Huaihua operates two-way China-Laos and China-Vietnam freight train services. To the north, it travels to Central Asia, the Middle East, and Europe through the China-Europe Railway Express.

In the long run, it is strategically crucial for promoting regional economic integration, facilitating the implementation of The Belt and Road Initiative, and enhancing China's status and influence in the international arena. From 2013 to 2022, China's bilateral trade in goods with ASEAN increased from US$443.6 billion to US$975.3 billion, with an average annual growth rate of 9.1%. It was higher than the growth rate of China's imports and exports of 4.7%, and its share in China's imports and exports increased from 10.7% to 15.5%. Huaihua's application to establish a dedicated comprehensive supervision center will further strengthen cooperation between Huaihua, Hunan Province, and even the central region of China and ASEAN countries. Moreover, it will promote regional connectivity and economic integration and facilitate shared prosperity and development.

Connecting with the China-Laos Railway in the Trans-Asian Railway to Build a Central Node City

The 20th CPC National Congress report proposes that the CPC promote high-standard opening. China will steadily expand its institutional opening regarding rules, regulations, management, and standards to accelerate its transformation into a trader of quality. Also, China will promote the high-quality development of the Belt and Road Initiative and preserve the diversity and stability of the international economic landscape and economic and trade relations. China-Laos Railway, an integral part of the Trans-Asian Railway, is the first international railroad that adopts Chinese standards, constructed and operated jointly by China and Laos.

It is directly connected to China's railroad network. It is a landmark project for China's Belt and Road Initiative, essential infrastructure for promoting the China-ASEAN Free Trade Area, and a "Golden Corridor" from Hunan to ASEAN. On December 3, 2021, President Xi Jinping held a video meeting with Thongloun Sisoulith, general secretary of the Lao People's Revolutionary Party Central Committee and Lao president. Moreover, they also attended a virtual ceremony to jointly witness the opening of the China-Laos Railway by video link.

President Xi Jinping said, "The China-Laos Railway is a landmark project for the high-quality Belt and Road cooperation. With the railway, the mountain from Kunming to Vientiane is no longer high and the road no longer long." Also, Xi called on both sides to make persistent efforts, maintain and operate the railway well, develop and construct well the areas along the line, and create a golden line for the benefit of the people of both countries. Since the opening of the China-Laos Railway, it has transported more than 20 million passengers and 24 million tons of goods, and cross-border cargo transportation has covered more than ten countries and regions.

China-Laos-Thailand cold chain transportation of fruits and vegetables made a breakthrough, with the cumulative transportation of imported tropical fruits exceeding 60,000 tons and the value of goods exceeding 1.5 billion yuan. Located at the central intersection of the Indian Ocean Economic Circle and the Pacific Ocean Economic Circle, Huaihua is the only node city of Hunan in the New International Land-Sea Trade Corridor in Western China and the hub of freight transportation to ASEAN. Huaihua led the two-way operation of China-Vietnam (Huaihua-Hanoi) and China-Laos (Huaihua-Vientiane) international freight trains. The China-Laos Railway has made Huaihua a critical node city in Central and Eastern China for trade between China and Southeast Asian countries. Establishing a dedicated comprehensive supervision center in Huaihua will significantly promote the entry of tropical agricultural products, such as fruits and grains from Southeast Asia, into large markets in Central China.

Linking the Yangtze River Economic Belt and Promoting Dual-Cycle Development of Chinese and Foreign Economies

The report of the 20th CPC National Congress emphasized the need to promote the development of the Yangtze Economic Belt and drive forward the development of the Chengdu-Chongqing economic zone. Huaihua is connected to the Chengdu-Chongqing economic zone in the West and backed by the Yangtze Economic Belt. In 2022, an agreement was signed between Hunan, Hubei and Jiangxi provinces. The agreement clarifies that it will rely on the advantages of Huaihua International Inland Port's external channel and its connection with ASEAN brands. Then, the three provinces will jointly gather cargo sources of cities on the Jiaozuo-Liuzhou Railway and Shanghai-Kunming Railway in Huaihua. Moreover, Huaihua will become the hub of freight transportation for ASEAN, led by Hunan, Hubei, and Jiangxi provinces, and will be a significant platform for high-standard opening up in Central China.

In the 20th CPC National Congress report, President Xi Jinping stated that China will accelerate efforts to foster a new development pattern. The pattern is focused on the Chinese economy and features a positive interplay between Chinese and international economic flows. Based on this, Huaihua strives to connect all the elements and smooth the information flow channel through the unified intelligent port platform. Regional distribution centers will be established to facilitate the smooth internal circulation of the logistics channels. The three-dimensional transportation system will be improved to facilitate efficient transportation routes in the Chinese market.

Also, it will join the multimodal transportation alliance to connect the logistics channels for Chinese and foreign markets. At the same time, it will join the international freight forwarding alliance, unblocking the trade channels between China and other countries. Eventually, Huaihua will become a model node city for positive interplay between Chinese and international economic flows. By setting up a dedicated comprehensive supervision center in Huaihua, the Chinese and international economic flows will be unimpeded, and new progress will be made.

Revitalizing the Countryside in the Wuling Mountain Area, Ethnic Areas and Old Revolutionary Base Areas

The 20th CPC National Congress report underlines that China will support old revolutionary base areas and areas with large ethnic minority populations in speeding up development. There are 46 ethnic minorities in Huaihua, accounting for 41.91% of the city's total population. The numerous minority villages have nurtured the colorful and mysterious Wuxi ethnic culture. Huaihua boasts rich ICH items, represented by Chenhe Gaoqiang opera, folk songs of the Miao ethnic group, the Grand Song of the Dong ethnic group, cross-stitch skills of Huayao people, and Yuanzhou Stone Carving. It will be helpful for the export of its ICH products.

Huaihua is in the Wuling Mountain area and is known for numerous revolutionary stories about the CPC. In Zhijiang, the Chinese People accepted the surrender of the Japanese invaders at the victory of the War of Resistance Against Japan. In Tongdao Dong Autonomous County, the famous "Tongdao Meeting" was held to carry out the strategic transfer that saved the Chinese revolution, the strategic "Transfer in Tongdao" in history. There is the Hunan-Hubei-Sichuan-Guizhou revolutionary base area. In Shibadong Village, Huayuan County, Hunan Province, Xi Jinping proposed the concept of targeted poverty alleviation in line with local conditions for the first time.

The Wuling Mountain area is one of the 14 national contiguous poor areas. Therefore, it is a long way to consolidate the results of targeted poverty alleviation and realize rural revitalization. The construction of Huaihua International Inland Port has fueled the area's development and brought about unlimited opportunities. The government should implement President Xi Jinping's critical exposition on the work of agriculture, rural areas, and rural residents.

With Huaihua International Inland Port as a link, it will promote the development of export-oriented agriculture and the export of unique agricultural products in the area and drive comprehensive rural revitalization by boosting port-related industries. It will facilitate the economic development of Huaihua and the five neighboring provinces and further serve the whole country by demonstrating the effect of Huaihua International Inland Port for rural revitalization. Huaihua will take the lead on the road to shared prosperity. Therefore, Huaihua is duty-bound to set up a dedicated comprehensive supervision center.

Building a Green Railway Port with Carbon Neutrality and Peak Carbon Emission Goals

China will work actively and prudently toward reaching peak carbon emissions and carbon neutrality, according to the 20th CPC National Congress report. It is a decision made by the CPC Central Committee with Comrade Xi Jinping at its core after integrating the balance between domestic and international situations. It is of great significance to build China into a modern socialist country in an all-around way, promoting the sustainable development of the Chinese nation and building a global community with a shared future. President Xi Jinping emphasized: "We must protect natural resources while pursuing economic development. Improving the ecological environment is increasing productivity." Huaihua has a forest cover of 71%. Huaihua and the whole Wuling Mountain area are national ecological function areas, green ecological barrier areas of Hunan Province, and the Yangtze River Economic Zone. It is one of the nine regions with healthy ecosystems in China. A good ecological environment and beautiful scenery are the most significant advantages of Huaihua.

Based on its resource endowment, it adheres to ecology priority and green development and transforms Huaihua into a pilot city of the national ecological product realization mechanism. With the principle of green and intelligent transformation and development, Huaihua International Inland Port will be built as a green inland port by strengthening the prevention and control of pollution, energy saving and emission reduction. First, it will uphold the concept of green development and incorporate biodiversity, wetland environment, soil quality and noise pollution into the criteria for green port construction. It will comprehensively upgrade the system and standards of international inland port development.

Secondly, it will intensify technological drive, create low-carbon collection and distribution modes, and vigorously promote the development of multimodal transportation. It will also increase the proportion of low-carbon transportation modes for cargo collection and distribution at the inland port. It will stimulate the low-carbon development of the entire life cycle of the international inland port.

Thirdly, the government will step up its policy support by introducing incentives and supporting measures. The government will offer preferential policies such as financial subsidies and procedural priorities for using clean energy on inbound freight trains. It will organize and research ecological pollutant detection technology for the trains and establish a supervision, inspection and management mechanism. It will advance the development of testing equipment and capacity and establish a sound system for monitoring the ecological environment. Huaihua International Inland Port will become a world-class green ecological port. Establishing a dedicated comprehensive supervision center in Huaihua is crucial in completing this process.

Filling the Vacancy of Railway Ports in Central and South China for Regional Coordinated and Balanced Development

As the 20th CPC National Congress report emphasizes, China will thoroughly implement the coordinated regional development strategy, major regional strategies, functional zoning strategy, and new urbanization strategy. China will also improve the distribution of the primary productive forces, develop a regional economic layout and a territorial space system to complement each other's strengths and promote high-quality development. Railroad port construction has become the main focus to fulfill the instruction of President Xi Jinping to build a new high ground for reform and opening up in the inland area. From the current layout of railway ports, there are no railway ports in Hunan Province or Central and Southern China. In line with the region's need for coordinated and balanced development, it is a perfect choice to set up a dedicated comprehensive supervision center in Huaihua.

Figure 6-2 Map of national (temporary) railway ports

Table 6-2 Detailed Information Contained in Figure 6-2

Railway ports: Harbin Beijing Zhengzhou Shanghai Dongguan	Temporary ports: Chengdu Chongqing Xi'an Ganzhou Yiwu
Huaihua	

In the keynote speech at the opening ceremony of the Second Belt and Road Forum for International Cooperation, President Xi Jinping said that China does not seek a trade surplus and wants to import more competitive quality agricultural products, manufactured goods and services to promote balanced trade. Huaihua International Inland Port must be connected to China's domestic market to develop high-quality foreign trade by promoting balanced trade. It must fully seize the opportunity to fulfill President Xi Jinping's pledge to buy up to US$150 billion of agricultural products from ASEAN from 2021 to 2026.

The pledge was made at the Special Summit to Commemorate The 30th Anniversary of China-ASEAN Dialogue Relations. Based on this, it needs to import more quality agricultural products from ASEAN to realize the balanced development of import and export trade. A dedicated comprehensive supervision center can be set up to enable Huaihua Customs to import fruits, grains, meat and other major agricultural products from ASEAN. It is fundamental to realize the strategic intention and achieve balanced trade.

Feasibility Analysis

Foundation and Achievements

At present, through one and a half years of construction, the main functional area of Huaihua International Inland Port is being completed with high quality. It has accelerated the construction of the main functional zones, such as the port logistics, international trade, and port industrial zones. Moreover, it has expedited the construction of multiple projects (the multimodal transportation center, modern logistics distribution center, bonded logistics center, ASEAN integrated service center, cross-border e-commerce incubator, RCEP cross-border trading exhibition center, and HUB warehouse center).

At the same time, it has made every effort to promote the construction of "The RCEP Peninsula International Reception Room." It integrates the complementary functions of the Xianrenqiao High-end Business District and the main functional zones of the inland port, complemented by commercial and residential areas, education facilities, and recreational and tourism zones in a Southeast Asian style. ASEAN Town has been built to gather the headquarters of ASEAN multinational companies and financial institutions to form a cross-border trade business circle. Based on this, it has become the business "center" of Huaihua International Inland Port and the "platform" for integrating into RCEP international exchange. Moreover, it is the "living room" of the strategic gateway city for Western China's New International Land-Sea Trade Corridor. Thus, it realizes the seamless connection between urban development and the inland port, integrating the port, industry and city.

Huaihua International Inland Port has built a base to open the inland area to the outside world. Its pivotal role of connecting to and integrating into The Belt and Road has been further highlighted, and its synergy with the strategy of strengthening the provincial capital has become more powerful and efficient. Relying on Huaihua International Inland Port, the industry and trade synergies between Huaihua and Changsha are closer, and its development synergies with China (Hunan) Pilot Free Trade Zone are prominent. Moreover, it contributes more to trade development in the neighboring regions. Overseas warehouses for ASEAN countries have been fully arranged, and distribution channels have been primarily established. Cross-border e-commerce and other new foreign trade business models have taken shape.

Scale in the Port-related Industries

Huaihua International Inland Port fully grasps the development characteristics of international inland ports. It has constructed an industrial system with processing and manufacturing industries as the main body and modern logistics and trade service industries as the two wings. It actively cultivates the port manufacturing industry and performs targeted investment promotion campaigns around the actual economy of the port processing and manufacturing industries. It has attracted affiliates, foreign trade companies, and financial companies to settle in the port and introduced many enterprises and high-quality projects, giving full play to its leading role.

It has actively incubated port-related manufacturing projects. They primarily produce and process electronic components, energy storage equipment, agricultural machinery products, crushed rice, Chinese herbal medicine, green food, and light industries. Fruits, cassava, rubber, spices and other port-friendly industries with comparative advantages have been initially developed. Four projects have been completed, i.e., the packaging and processing base of port processing and manufacturing products, the production line of special light industrial processing of Zhushui Sculpture, Sinopharm Huaihua Pharmaceutical Logistics Zone, and Western New Special Drug Logistics Zone. Nine industrial projects have started construction, including the Smart Cold Chain Logistics Center, Central Kitchen, Huaihua ASEAN International Trade and Warehousing Expo Center, and Jia Tian Tian Rice Noodle Packaging and Processing Center. Twenty-five industrial projects have been carried out, with a total investment of 8.289 billion yuan.

Rapid Development of Business and Trade Services

Relying on the advantage of the logistics channel of Huaihua International Inland Port, it fully utilizes modern information technology to develop international trade, cross-border e-commerce, platform economy, modern finance, professional services and other international business and trade services. Thus, it drives traditional business, trade, and services, forming new platforms, business forms, and modes through innovation, transformation, and upgrading. Cross-border e-commerce will be developed into a mainstay industry in central and western China, supporting the export-oriented real industry.

Thirty-five new foreign trade companies were registered, and 32 new freight forwarders and cross-border e-commerce enterprises for import and export services were added. Vietnam Overseas Warehouse was put into operation. The Collaborative Linkage Zone of the China Hunan (Huaihua) Pilot Free Trade Zone has been formally established, and the Cross-border E-commerce Supervision Center has been implemented. Also, the Bonded Logistics Center (Type B) has progressed fully and orderly. It has laid out warehousing and logistics facilities in China and abroad and promoted the industry's transformation.

At the same time, the cross-border e-commerce industry chain and ecological chain will be built, and the cross-border e-commerce service system of Huaihua will be constructed. Thus, it can stimulate the international railroad container transportation business of cross-border e-commerce. Also, efforts can be made to boost the cross-border e-commerce business in Huaihua and Hunan to explore the ASEAN market. Ultimately, it can diversify cargo sources for freight trains in Huaihua International Inland Port to ASEAN.

Rapid Development of the Modern Logistics Industry

Huaihua Railway Marshalling Station undertakes more than 70% of the southward cargo transportation of the New International Land-Sea Trade Corridor in Western China. Its daily unmarshalling capacity reaches over 12,000 trains, and its annual throughput reaches 200 million tons. Huaihua is a national comprehensive logistics hub and critical cold chain logistics base. With the rapid development of the logistics industry, Huaihua is comprehensively promoting international logistics, specialized logistics, supply chain management platforms, intelligent and bonded warehousing and other forms of business.

Besides, it accelerates the development of overseas markets, extends the international service network, and creates the logistics system of the inland port with low-cost and high-quality services. Huaihua International Railway Port mainly undertakes the functions of international logistics, cross-border logistics services, international integrated port and supporting services for the supply chain. The Chinese Logistics Park primarily develops supply chain logistics, recycling logistics, emergency logistics and other professional logistics functions, realizing the professional division of labor in logistics. In 2023, the construction of the intelligent cold chain logistics center project of Huaihua International Inland Port was fully completed. Due to the establishment of secondary distribution centers such as S.F. Express branches, the import and export of agricultural products like fruits, grains, and meat are facilitated smoothly and efficiently.

Hunan (Huaihua) RCEP Economic and Trade Expo as A Charming Business Card of Huaihua's Opening Up to the World

RCEP, the Regional Comprehensive Economic Partnership Agreement, came into effect on January 1, 2022, and Hunan is accelerating its integration into the world's largest network of free trade partners. In 2022, Hunan's imports from and exports to other RCEP member countries amounted to 229.68 billion yuan, topping the list and accounting for nearly one-third of Hunan's total foreign trade value. As the only strategic platform for Hunan to connect with ASEAN, the Hunan RCEP Economic and Trade Expo was permanently held in Huaihua, and the first Hunan (Huaihua) RCEP Economic and Trade Expo was successfully held on May 4-7, 2023.

The Expo invited more than 1,200 guests, including envoys to China from RCEP member countries, enterprise representatives, representatives of business associations, experts and scholars. It attracted more than 600 renowned enterprises and 1,000 buyers from China and abroad, including 112 enterprises from 14 RCEP member countries like Australia, New Zealand, Thailand, and Laos. One hundred and thirteen cooperative projects were signed, with a total investment of 75 billion yuan. Hunan (Huaihua) RCEP Economic and Trade Expo has become a splendid name card of Huaihua's opening up to the outside world.

Concerted Efforts to Build a New High Ground for Reform and Opening Up in the Inland Area

Huaihua International Inland Port is constructed following the strategies of China's Belt and Road Initiative and the New International Land-Sea Trade Corridor in Western China. Moreover, the Hunan Provincial CPC Committee and Provincial Government have broken the bottleneck of policies and mechanisms to promote the project, and the Huaihua Municipal CPC Committee and Municipal People's Government have made scientific plans and innovations. It embodies the great spirit of struggle in the new era, where people with one mind will remove Mount Tai.

On May 23, 2022, the Hunan Provincial Government issued the Implementation Plan on Supporting the Construction of Huaihua International Inland Port for Deep Integration into The Belt and Road Initiative. It issued specific policies to support the construction of Huaihua International Inland Port and even the economic and social development of Huaihua City. On July 26, 2022, the Third Plenary Session of the Sixth CPC Huaihua Municipal Committee adopted the Decision on Accelerating the Construction of Huaihua International Inland Port and Fully Promoting the High-Level Openness and High-Quality Development. It represents the struggle for a new reform chapter and opening up, setting off a new tide of inland port construction. On May 23, 2023, the Standing Committee of Huaihua Municipal People's Congress conducted several legislative debates and widely solicited opinions and suggestions on the Regulations on Accelerating the Construction of International Inland Port in Huaihua City (Draft).

The regulations are the first local regulations in Huaihua City drafted by a working group under the leadership of the Standing Committee of the Municipal People's Congress. Moreover, it accelerates the promotion of international inland port legislation, builds Huaihua into a city driven by the inland port, and pioneers legislation for international inland port development in China. It is a strong guarantee that establishing a dedicated comprehensive supervision center in Huaihua is feasible and practicable.

Comparative Advantages of a Dedicated Comprehensive Supervision Center in Huaihua

Location and Transportation Advantages

Huaihua is a node city connecting the Silk Road Economic Belt and the Maritime Silk Road under China's Belt and Road Initiative. The core area connects the Guangdong-Hong Kong-Macao Greater Bay Area, Hanzhong City Cluster, Qianzhong City Cluster, Chengdu-Chongqing Economic Circle, Yangtze River Delta Economic Zone, and Beibu Gulf Economic Zone. More importantly, Huaihua is an essential node of the eastern route of the New International Land-Sea Trade Corridor in Western China. It is the only city in Central China to be included in the Corridor, a node city of the "South Wing" of the Yangtze River Economic Belt, a city of ecological innovation, and a center city of the border area between Hunan, Hubei, Chongqing, Guizhou, and Guangxi. Moreover, it is a vital node of the main framework identified in the Outline of the National Comprehensive Three-dimensional Transportation Network Plan.

Huaihua has been approved as a national pilot demonstration city for logistics and cold-chain circulation standardization of agricultural products. It has been approved as a demonstration project of multimodal transportation, urban green freight distribution, and a demonstration city to promote e-commerce in rural areas. At the same time, it is also the demonstration zone for undertaking industrial transfer in southern and western Hunan and a national logistics hub city for business and trade services.

On the one hand, exports from central provinces to ASEAN can be quickly consolidated and transported in Huaihua. On the other hand, products with comparative advantages can be imported from ASEAN, especially agricultural products such as fruits, grains, and fresh meat, which are suitable for railroad transportation. A national collection center can be set up in Huaihua. As a result, these products can be quickly distributed to Hunan, Hubei, Jiangxi, and even the whole country through cold chain logistics.

Huaihua is a national comprehensive transportation and logistics hub for business and trade services. In February 2021, China launched a national comprehensive three-dimensional transportation network of “6 axes, seven corridors and eight channels.” The Guangdong - Hong Kong - Macau - Chengdu-Chongqing axis, Shanghai-Kunming corridor, and Erenhot-Zhanjiang channel intersect in Huaihua, creating a unique advantage of Huaihua’s transportation location. Huaihua has a prominent position as a railroad hub. The three ordinary railways (Shanghai-Kunming, Jiao Liu and Chongqing-Huaihua railways) and the three high-speed railways (Shanghai-Kunming, Zhangjiajie-Jishou-Huaihua and Huaihua-Shaoyang-Hengyang high-speed railways) converge in Huaihua. Huaihuaxi Railway Station is one of the nine largest marshaling yards in China.

Huaihua Railway Hub is one of the three major railroad hubs in Hunan Province. Huaihua has national highways such as Shanghai-Kunming, Hangzhou-Ruili, and Baotou-Maoming expressways and provincial highways such as Changsha-Zhijiang Expressway. The mileage of highways in Huaihua reaches 717 kilometers. In terms of water transportation, there is a high-grade waterway of Yuanshui River, and the mileage of the grade waterway reaches 570 kilometers. In terms of aviation, Zhijiang Airport has been constructed, and in 2019, the passenger throughput exceeded 600,000 passenger trips.

As of July 2, 2023, Huaihua Zhijiang Airport had a cumulative passenger throughput of 195,500 and safeguarded 2,204 transport takeoffs and landings. Passenger throughput and flights increased by 219.1% and 97.31% year-on-year. Huaihua is built as a new high ground for reform and opening up in the inland area. Hence, it has apparent transportation advantages for establishing a dedicated comprehensive supervision center.

Figure 6-3 Physical geography of Huaihua

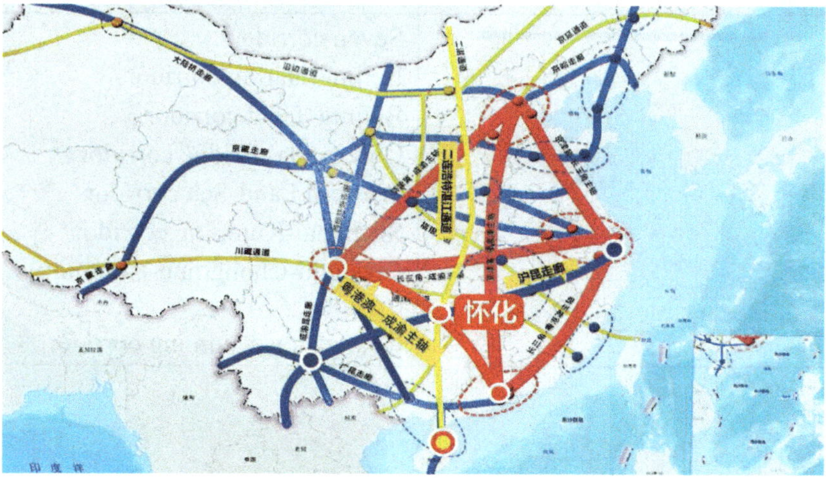

Figure 6-4 Huaihua's position in the national three-dimensional transport network

Table 6-4 Detailed Information Contained in Figure 6-4

(yellow line)	Eight channels: Suifeng River-Manzhouli channel Beijing-Hunchun channel Border channel Fuzhou-Yinchuan channel Erenhot-Zhanjiang channel Sichuan-Tibet channel Changsha-Pingxiang channel Xiamen-Chengdu channel
(red line)	Six axes: Beijing-Tianjin-Hebei-Yangtze River Delta axis Beijing-Tianjin-Hebei-Guangdong-Hong Kong-Macau axis Beijing-Tianjin-Hebei-Chengdu-Chongqing axis Yangtze River Delta - Guangdong-Hong Kong- Macao axis Yangtze River Delta-Chengdu-Chongqing axis Guangdong - Hong Kong - Macau - Chengdu-Chongqing axis
(blue line)	Seven corridors: Beijing-Harbin corridor Beijing-Tibet corridor Continental Bridge corridor Western Land-Sea corridor Shanghai-Kunming corridor Chengdu-Chongqing-Kunming corridor Guangzhou-Kunming corridor

Policy Advantages

(1) Increasing support of port policies

The policy support system of Huaihua International Inland Port has been gradually improved. On April 19, 2022, Hunan Provincial CPC Committee and Changsha Municipal People's Government issued Several Opinions on Implementing the Strategy of Strengthening the Provincial Capital and Supporting the High-Quality Development of Changsha Municipality and the list of policies. It supports Huaihua's integration into the strategy of strengthening the provincial capital by relying on the inland port.

On May 12, the Hunan Provincial Government officially issued the Implementation Plan on Deeply Integrating into The Belt and Road and Supporting the Development of Huaihua International Inland Port (No. 24 [2023] of the General Office of Hunan Provincial People's Government). For five consecutive years, 300 million yuan per year would be allocated, with 100 million yuan of financial funds and 200 million yuan of special local bonds, to support the construction of the inland port. The Third Plenary Session of the Sixth CPC Huaihua Municipal Committee requested to accelerate the construction of Huaihua International Inland Port and make every effort to promote the high-level opening and high-quality development of Huaihua.

The Decision of the CPC Huaihua Municipal Committee on Accelerating the Construction of Huaihua International Inland Port and Fully Promoting High-Level Opening and High-Quality Development was deliberated and adopted. Huaihua will accelerate the construction of Huaihua International Inland Port with concerted efforts of the whole city and strive to realize the goal of building the port in two years, gaining momentum in three years, and becoming a benchmark in five years.

Huaihua has secured a 52% freight rate reduction within China Railway Guangzhou Group Co., Ltd. and a 30% reduction across bureaus from China Railway Nanchang Group Co., Ltd. Moreover, it has secured a 30% freight reduction for 20-foot containers and a 15% for 40-foot containers from Qinzhou Port to Huaihua West Railway Station. A support policy for freight transportation between ASEAN and Huaihua has been formulated, and the train platform company has included the subsidy directly in the offer. Enterprises do not need to pay the freight rates before being subsidized. Subsidies are granted to the everyday freight trains between Huaihua and Changsha. Through the superposition of policies, goods imported and exported can have zero transportation cost from the inland port to the border port.

According to Several Measures for Promoting High-Quality Development of Foreign Trade and Export Economy in Huaihua City, imports and exports are encouraged. Twenty Measures to Accelerate the Development of the Modern Logistics Industry in Huaihua City were introduced. The government supports the construction of logistics parks (including land use, construction of standard warehouses and leasing, and interest rate subsidies).

Also, it supports the development of logistics (courier) enterprises, cold-chain logistics, road-to-rail transportation, online cargo transportation, and trucking. These include a maximum subsidy of 2 million yuan for the construction of standard warehouses, a maximum award of 1 million yuan for the construction of branded logistics enterprises, and 1 million yuan per year for the construction of logistics standardization. Since September 1, 2022, the tolls for international TEU vehicles arriving at and departing from Huaihua International Inland Port on the Hunan Expressway have been reduced by half for the highway sections within Hunan Province. The policy advantage is desirable for Huaihua to build a new high ground for reform, open up the inland area, and set up a dedicated comprehensive supervision center.

(2) The optimized business environment of Huaihua International Inland Port

Following the requirements of the CPC Central Committee and the State Council, the CPC Huaihua Municipal Committee and Municipal People's Government have conscientiously deepened reforms to streamline administration and delegate power, improve regulation and upgrade services. In addition, the business environment at the port has been constantly optimized. The port office of Huaihua Municipal People's Government has thoroughly sorted out port charges, lowered the cost of compliance, resolutely banned unreasonable charges, and implemented a fee disclosure system. Moreover, it has accelerated the promotion and use of a single window for handling international trade affairs and personnel training.

Changsha Customs issued 18 Measures to Support the Construction of Huaihua International Inland Port. It supports Huaihua in improving the efficiency of inspection operations and customs clearance, establishing a green channel and the mechanism of on-demand declaration, inspection and clearance. In addition, it applies an appointment system for customs declaration and provides 24/7 customs clearance services. It has implemented reforms to facilitate customs clearance, adopting modes such as customs integration and customs transfer for customs clearance procedures.

At the same time, it promotes reforms such as the two-step declaration and early declaration. China Railway Guangzhou Group Co., Ltd. has launched reforms of fast customs clearance for inbound and outbound goods and handling upon arrival of export cargoes. Based on this, the efficiency of customs clearance has been significantly improved. Huaihua Customs has signed a memorandum of cooperation with Pingxiang and three other customs branches to promote the seamless intermodal transport of goods between Hunan, Hubei and Jiangxi provinces. Therefore, there is a favorable business environment for Huaihua to build a new high ground for reform, the opening up of the inland area, and a dedicated comprehensive supervision center.

Advantages of Economic Carrying Capacity of the Port

(1) A solid economic foundation

Huaihua vigorously develops port-related industries around the inland port. The construction of the integrated trade and processing zone and industrial bases has been accelerated. Fruit, cassava, rubber, spices and other port-friendly industries have taken initial shape. Eight critical industrial projects, including Hurricane Intelligent Cold Chain Logistics Center, started construction. Thirty-five new foreign trade companies were registered, and 32 new freight forwarders and cross-border e-commerce enterprises for import and export services were added. Vietnam Overseas Warehouse was put into operation. By 2026, the output value of port-related industries will reach 100 billion yuan. Huaihua International Inland Port will be built into a national logistics hub with business and trade services, an ASEAN cargo consolidation center and a demonstration base for international production capacity cooperation. It will drive the development and growth of exceptional and competitive industries, and the comprehensive economic strength of Huaihua City will be significantly enhanced.

Relying on the New International Land-Sea Trade Corridor strategy in Western China, the port will promote the integrated development of business, trade and logistics. It will primarily support the trade of cassava, rice, fruits, timber, frozen seafood, spices, medicinal herbs and other products. Given this, the port will actively develop the functions of international business and trade expo, intelligent logistics, trading and settlement, financial services, information services, and e-commerce. Moreover, it will integrate the new sales model with cultural exchange, trading with science and technology, domestic trade with foreign trade, offline with online, and commodity trading with city travel and shopping.

It will promote the integrated development of business, people, logistics, and information flows and upgrade the traditional business and trade system to a diversified and intelligent one. It will jointly form a functional pattern combining offline and online services of international business and trade, intelligent logistics, specialized consumption and extended services. Therefore, establishing a dedicated comprehensive supervision center allows for the rapid realization of the flow of various elements and the formation of productivity.

(2) Continuous improvement of port infrastructure

In 2022, the total investment of the Huaihua International Inland Port project was 9.8 billion yuan. Ten projects have been completed, including the first phase of the customs supervision center. The construction of 15 projects, such as comprehensive upgrading and renovation of the port front and container consolidation center, started. The new area of logistics warehousing is 52,300 square meters. In addition, the functions of international freight transport document processing, loading and unloading inspection, storage and distribution have been continuously improved. Since 2023, several port facilities will be constructed.

A multimodal transportation zone and integrated urban and rural distribution will be built in the first year, with the West Freight Yard as the core. The works include a dedicated railroad line, a steel logistics area (trading center), a spice trading center, a transit and distribution zone, and a grain logistics area (trading center). It will also build the east gate of the international inland port, a container consolidation center, a bonded logistics center (type B), a distribution area for urban and rural integration, and the first phase of the inland port service center. The particular research and design of the railroad line at the Xiping Freight Depot will be carried out. In the second year, the second phase of the transit and distribution area, the second phase for urban and rural integration, the highway logistics port, the transshipment area for break-bulk cargoes, and the container transfer center will be improved.

Furthermore, the preliminary study and design of the water transportation terminal will be initiated. In the third year, the multimodal transportation function will be improved, and the construction of the first batch of storage areas of Xiping Freight Depot will be advanced. Meanwhile, the construction of six berths of the first phase of the water transportation terminal will be launched. Thus, the infrastructure for establishing a dedicated comprehensive supervision center is entirely feasible.

Advantages of Regional Economic Development

(1) Prominent driving effect of Huaihua Port on foreign trade

In recent years, the CPC Huaihua Municipal Committee and the Huaihua Municipal People's Government have attached great importance to developing foreign trade. Huaihua is a vital node city of Western China's New International Land-Sea Trade Corridor and an ASEAN freight collection center in Hunan Province. Based on this, Huaihua accelerates the construction of the open platform centered on Huaihua International Inland Port. Besides, it actively builds smooth and efficient international logistics channels and drives the rapid development of foreign trade.

In 2022, 151 trains were operated, including international freight trains to Vientiane, Laos and Hanoi, Vietnam, and rail-sea intermodal trains to Beibu Gulf Port. The import and export volume of Huaihua City was 4.67 billion yuan, a year-on-year increase of 135.6%, ranking first in the province in terms of growth rate. One hundred twenty enterprises achieved positive results in foreign trade, a year-on-year increase of 54%. Foreign trade partner countries reached 168, of which the import and export volume with ASEAN was 1.06 billion yuan.

ASEAN has become Huaihua's largest trading partner. Electronic information, apparel and clothing, bamboo and wood products have become the preferred products for foreign trade. It is planned that by 2026, the import and export volume of Huaihua will reach 26 billion yuan. Also, it will prioritize forming leading industries for foreign trade, such as electronic information, green agricultural products and their processing, garments and apparel, and chemical industries.

(2) Opportunities for regional cooperation

In 2013, the U.N. Economic and Social Commission for Asia and the Pacific (ESCAP) developed the Intergovernmental Agreement on the Asian Highway Network and the Intergovernmental Agreement on the Trans-Asian Railway to promote connectivity among countries in the Asia-Pacific region. It wants to make greater use of the Asian Highway and Trans-Asian Railway networks and other infrastructure. As such, it can further accelerate the construction of logistics and multimodal transport systems in the Asia-Pacific region. To this end, ESCAP has proposed establishing an Asia-Pacific network of inland ports. Inland ports are defined as modern logistics centers with port services such as customs clearance, inspection, and bill of lading in inland areas, which are linked to ports through the transport network.

The agreement will enable member countries to recognize inland ports in other countries (for business and investment opportunities). The agreement will provide valuable guidelines for countries to clarify the minimum requirements for inland ports and formulate policies to promote strategically essential ports. As the construction of inland ports has been in full swing in recent years, it is possible to establish a dedicated comprehensive supervision center in Huaihua to join the Asia-Pacific circle of inland ports and boost regional cooperation and trade facilitation. In that case, more business opportunities may come to Huaihua International Inland Port.

In addition, by establishing a dedicated comprehensive supervision center in Huaihua, Huaihua will cooperate with the ASEAN Chambers of Commerce for trade and investment development. Such a partnership will bring more business opportunities and international cooperation platforms to Huaihua International Inland Port.

Feasibility Analysis of a Dedicated Comprehensive Supervision Center in Huaihua (Fruits)

In Hunan, Changsha Huanghua Airport and Zhangjiajie Hehua Airport are designated supervisory centers for imported fruits, mainly high-grade ones. With a CAGR of 2%, China's fruit market will reach 3.24 trillion yuan in 2024 (Fig. 5). Fruit consumption has a considerable development space. Fruits are mainly imported from ASEAN countries (Fig. 6). In establishing a dedicated comprehensive supervision center in Huaihua, it is planned to build a designated supervision center for imported low- and medium-grade fruits, mainly through railroads, to complement the existing port. Low- and medium-grade fruits are imported into Hunan to supply urban and rural wholesale markets through various means.

The cost of importing fruits into Hunan consists of fruit prices, tariffs, customs clearance fees and logistics fees. Among them, the fruit price is transparent and fixed. Tariffs and customs clearance fees vary depending on the customs regulations of the place of entry. Logistics costs, comprising transportation costs and labor costs, are affected by the distance of air routes and land distances. Huaihua mainly purchases imported fruits from Nanning and Changsha and occasionally imports fruits in LTL from Vietnam and Thailand. In the case of imported fruits from Vietnam, the total logistics cost is about 23,000 yuan, and railroad or rail-sea intermodal transportation can be used to reduce the cost and time.

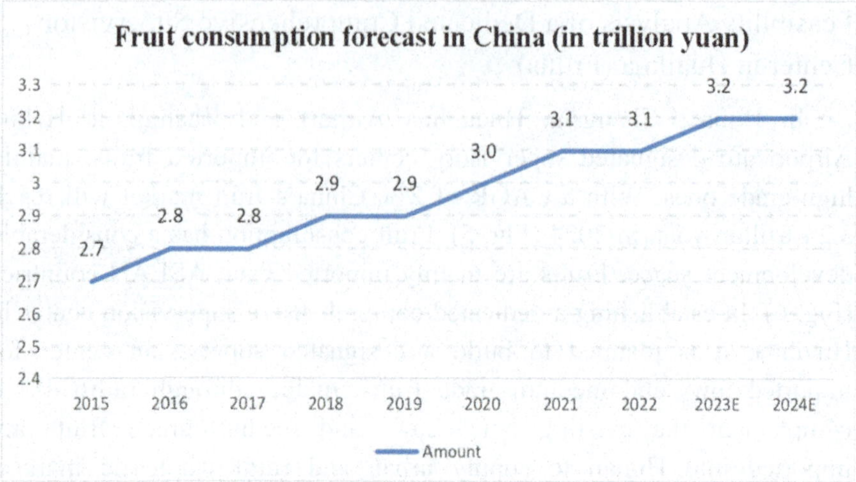

Figure 6-5 Fruit consumption in China

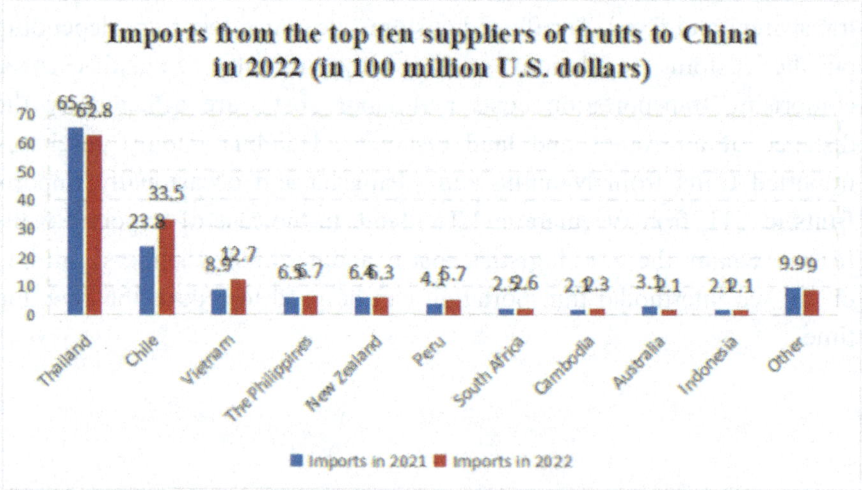

Figure 6-6 Top suppliers of imported fruits to China in 2022

In the middle of Hunan Province, Huaihua boasts convenient transportation, relatively close to China's main ports and border crossings. It provides favorable conditions for Huaihua to establish a dedicated comprehensive supervision center, as it facilitates the land transportation of fruits and shortens the transportation time. Next, the demand for fruits is stable and has excellent potential in the surrounding areas of Huaihua and even in Hunan, Hubei, and Jiangxi provinces. With the improvement of people's living standards and health consciousness, consumers' demand for high-quality fruits is increasing. By establishing a dedicated comprehensive supervision center, diversified fruit products can be introduced more conveniently to meet the market demand and expand the consumer market.

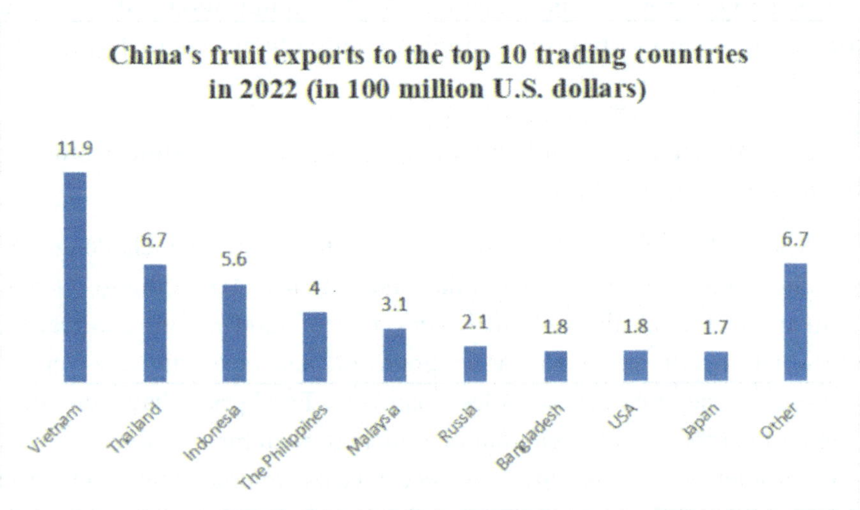

Figure 6-7 China's major export markets for fruits in 2022 (in 100 million U.S. dollars)

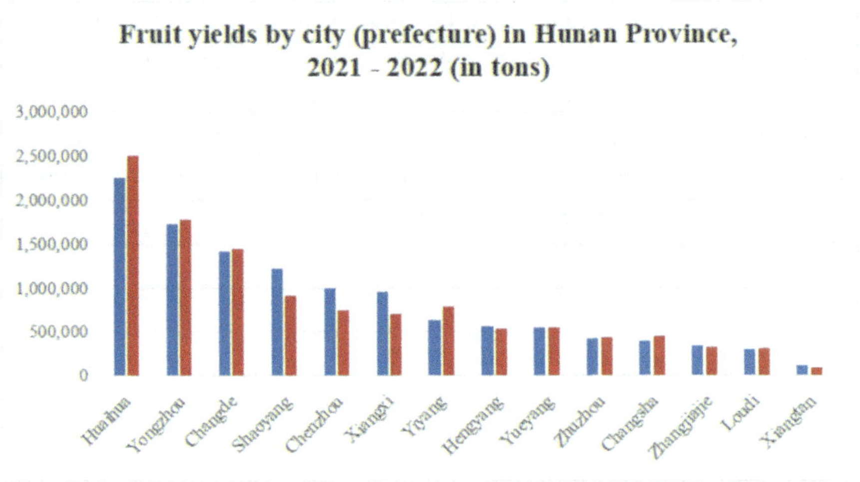

Figure 6-8 Comparison of fruit yields by city (prefecture) in Hunan Province

In addition, China's leading fruit exporters are ASEAN countries (Fig. 7). As a significant agricultural base, Huaihua boasts rich fruit cultivation resources (Fig. 8). A dedicated comprehensive supervision center can realize the fast export of fruits and improve the marketing efficiency and competitiveness of agricultural products. At the same time, introducing imported fruits can stimulate the optimization and upgrading of China's fruit industry, driving agricultural restructuring and development.

Feasibility Analysis of a Dedicated Comprehensive Supervision Center in Huaihua (Grain)

Currently, China's food security has turned to the challenges of production and prices of feed grains and proteins. According to relevant statistics, although the self-sufficiency rate of food rations has reached 99%, China still needs to import grain, oil and meat, and the implicit self-sufficiency rate of food is less than 70%. Food prices have long been higher than those on the international market, with high production costs, low efficiency and insecurity. In recent years, international food prices have risen, and the international supply chain is at risk of disruption.

According to China Customs data, China's total grain imports exceeded total exports in 2016-2022, with the volume of imports peaking in 2021 (Fig. 9). In recent years, the amount of China's grain imports is more than that of its exports, represented by a trade deficit. China is facing a new situation of food imports, in which the cost of imports has increased despite the decrease in import volume. With food security and price stability challenges, the rational introduction of imported grain is crucial for guaranteeing China's food supply.

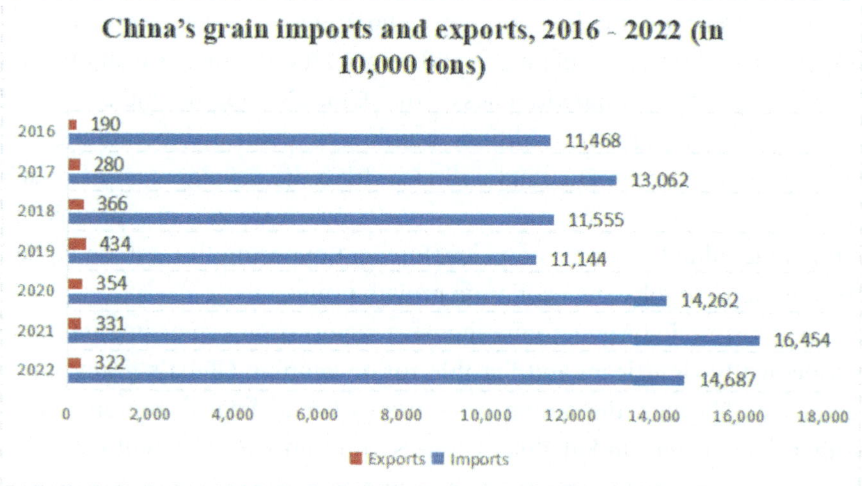

Figure 6-9 China's grain imports and exports, 2016-2022

Hunan's grain production continues to grow, exceeding the planned area and producing more than 60 billion kilograms for three consecutive years. However, the structure of grain cultivation favors rice, and the per capita grain possession is lower than the national average. Hunan suffers from diverse natural disasters and environmental pollution challenges. The Russian-Ukrainian conflict and international market pressure have intensified the pressure on Hunan's grain supply and market. Hunan's grain and oil processing industries are developing rapidly, but it is still necessary to deepen the industrial development model and create a modern grain and oil industry system. It is also a pressing issue to open up external import channels and improve the capacity of grain supply.

Huaihua has significant geographical advantages in the middle of Hunan Province. Firstly, a dedicated comprehensive supervision center in Huaihua will effectively open the logistics channel between inland areas and the port and optimize the supply chain of grain import trade. Moreover, it can improve the efficiency and stability of grain imports and ensure the security of China's grain supply. Secondly, Huaihua's neighboring areas have abundant farmland resources and excellent agricultural product processing capacity.

Through a dedicated comprehensive supervision center, more high-quality imported grains can be introduced to enhance the quality and variety of grains in China and meet the demand for high-quality grains in

China's domestic market. At the same time, it is also conducive to promoting farmers' income and agricultural modernization and enhancing the competitiveness of China's grain industry and international image. In addition, building a dedicated comprehensive supervision center in Huaihua will also drive the development of related industries. In grain logistics, transportation, warehousing, processing, and value-added services, new development opportunities will be gained. It will increase jobs and economic growth points.

In short, a dedicated comprehensive supervision center in Huaihua is strategically significant and feasible for developing China's grain import industry. Through the active promotion of a dedicated comprehensive supervision center in Huaihua, China's grain import trade will usher in a broader development space. At the same time, it will also contribute to agricultural modernization and food security.

Market Demand for a Dedicated Comprehensive Supervision Center in Huaihua (Meat)

Hunan Province is a large meat consumer in China, and imported meat products are in great demand in urban and rural households and the meat processing and catering industries. In Hunan Province, there are four designated meat supervision and control centers in Changsha, Xiangtan, Chenzhou and Yueyang, all of which are in eastern Hunan. Huaihua, located in southwestern Hunan with an international inland port, is at the intersections of five southwestern provinces. With its favorable geographical location, Huaihua is close to economically developed regions such as Guangdong and Guangxi.

The construction of a designated meat supervision site in Huaihua will further promote the facilitation and development of meat imports and exports. Besides, it will attract more traders and investors, drive Huaihua's and its neighboring areas' economic development, and satisfy the tourism market's demand. In this way, it can further contribute to the economic prosperity and social progress of ethnic regions. The operation of the designated supervisory site for imported meat can significantly improve the efficiency of meat customs clearance, reduce logistics costs, and support the development of meat industry aggregation.

Moreover, it plays a positive role in building a complete industrial chain integrating meat import, deep processing, cold storage and transportation, transit and express transportation. It helps to increase the scale and modernize the meat industry in Huaihua and the Wuling Mountain area. It can better serve the strategy of "Three Highlands and Four New Missions[2]." Building a center for meat import, export, warehousing, logistics, and distribution in the Wuling Mountain area is vital.

China's meat consumption shows sustained growth along with economic development and the continuous improvement of people's standard of living. China has been the world's largest meat producer, consumer and importer for many years. Meat imports are an essential supplement to the supply and necessary for the trade balance between China and importing countries. In 2022, China's meat consumption was about 100 million tons, and the import volume was about 7.4 million tons.

The strong consumer demand in China's domestic meat market has led to the prosperity of the world meat trade market. It also propels China's meat import, processing, finance, cold chain logistics and other related industries to form a perfect industrial chain and supply chain. Also, it provides Chinese consumers with a more secure, sufficient, high-quality and convenient supply of imported meat. The Chinese government attaches great importance to the development of the meat industry.

It has formulated policies and measures, including the Opinions on Promoting the High-Quality Development of the Livestock Industry and the Opinions on Comprehensively Promoting the Priorities of Rural Revitalization for 2022. These measures stabilize the production of hogs, beef, mutton and related meat products, advance the transformation and upgrading of the animal husbandry industry, and boost the sustainable development of the meat industry.

---

[2] The Three Highlands refer to shaping a national advanced manufacturing industry, nurturing innovative technology with a competitive edge, and expanding opening-up and reform. The Four Missions mean realizing integrated development, assuming new responsibilities in promoting the development of China's central region and Yangzi River Economic Belt, striving to write a new chapter for Hunan to adhere to, and developing socialism with Chinese characteristics in the new era.

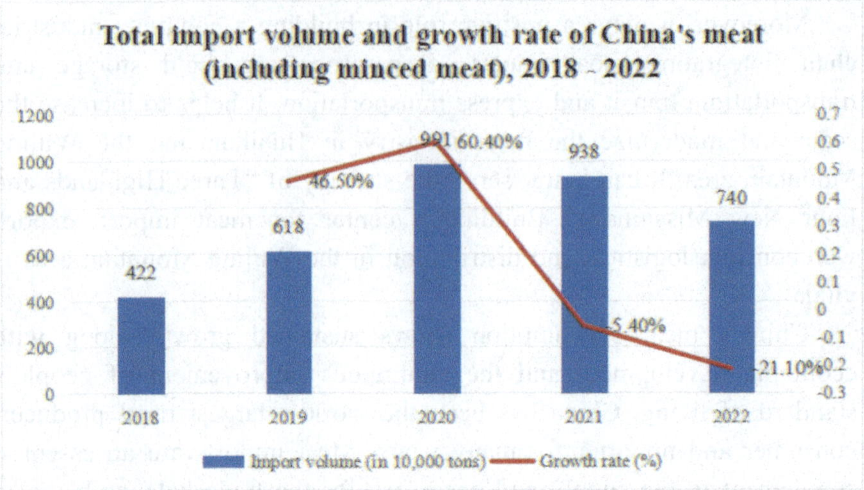

(Source: General Administration of Customs of the People's Republic of China, China Meat Association)

Figure 6-10 Total import volume and growth rate of China's meat (including minced meat), 2018 - 2022

The Chinese market has a high demand for high-quality imported beef, mutton and poultry meat. Based on China's meat imports in January-April 2023, beef had the highest share, amounting to 32.1%; pork and poultry also held shares of 26.2% and 18%, respectively. It is different from the structure of China's meat consumption (pork accounting for more than 60% of the total). Besides, it fully reflects Chinese consumers' high demand for imported beef. The import volume of related meat products is expected to keep growing.

Recently, meat imports and exports in Hunan Province have steadily grown. Hunan's meat production in 2021 ranked fourth in China, mainly due to the higher domestic market demand and the rising prices in the international market. The trade cooperation between Hunan and ASEAN countries has been strengthened, and the meat export market has expanded gradually.

However, imported meat requires long transportation and customs clearance procedures, resulting in high prices and unstable supply. Establishing a dedicated comprehensive supervision center in Huaihua can lower prices and increase supply to meet people's needs. At the same time, introducing more foreign commodities and technologies will help to enhance the opening-up level of Hunan, Hubei, Jiangxi, and Guizhou provinces. It can attract more investment and talented people and promote regional economic integration and development.

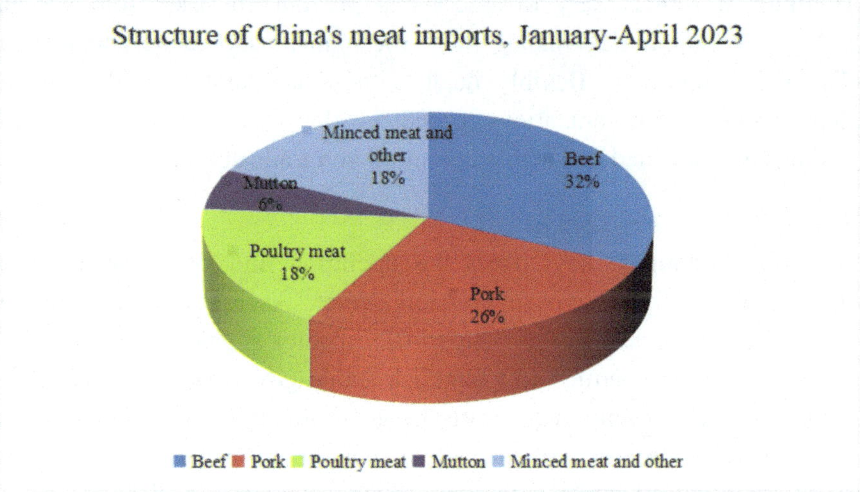

(Source: General Administration of Customs of the People's Republic of China)
Figure 6-11 Structure of China's meat imports, January-April 2023

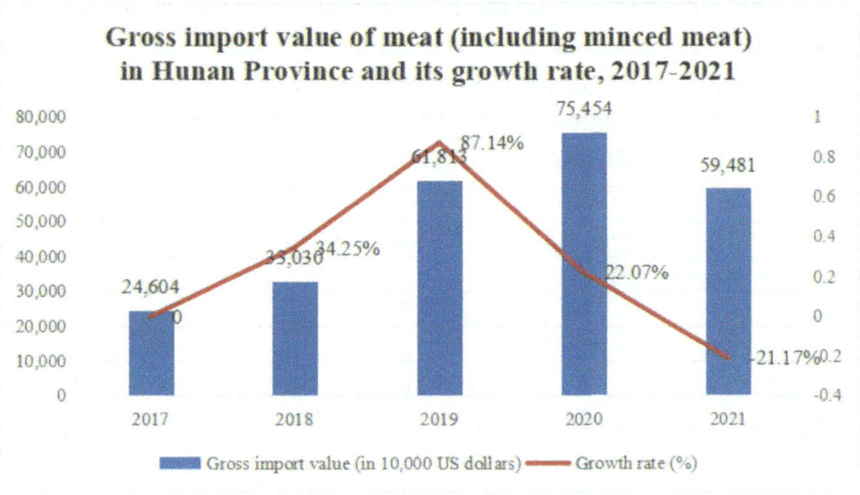

(Source: Hunan Statistical Yearbook)
Figure. 6-12 Gross import value of meat (including minced meat) in Hunan Province and its growth rate, 2017-2021

Risks and Prevention

While developing the dedicated comprehensive supervision center in Huaihua, it is necessary to assess and prevent all risks from various aspects. A sound risk management mechanism should be established. The risks should be flexibly dealt with in cooperation with relevant departments and organizations to achieve the development goals better and ensure sustained and stable operation and trade activities.

Policy Risk and Prevention

Policy changes may affect the operation and development of a dedicated comprehensive supervision center. As a response to policy risks, the management of the supervision center should keep abreast of relevant policy dynamics and establish stable governmental relations. It should actively communicate with the government and participate in the policy-making process. Policy risks can also be mitigated by diversifying trade channels and reducing the dependence on a single policy.

Competitive Risk and Prevention

Other dedicated comprehensive supervision centers or regions may have similar development plans and competitive advantages. In the face of competition, the dedicated comprehensive supervision center in Huaihua needs to enhance its competitiveness by improving service quality, reducing costs and expanding markets. Establishing cooperative relationships with other dedicated comprehensive supervision centers or regions for mutual benefit and win-win cooperation is also an option for preventing competitive risks.

Environmental Risk and Prevention

The development of the dedicated comprehensive supervision center may affect the environment in areas such as water sources, land use, and ecosystems. To prevent environmental risk, it is necessary to conduct environmental assessment and monitoring and take environmental protection measures to ensure the sustainable development and ecological protection of the dedicated comprehensive supervision center.

Economic Risk and Prevention

Uncertainty in the global economic environment may impact trade and investment in Huaihua International Inland Port. In the face of economic risks, the dedicated comprehensive supervision center in Huaihua should adopt a diversified market strategy, look for new trading partners, and reduce dependence on a specific market. At the same time, the stable development of trade should be facilitated by providing flexible trade financial services and reducing trade barriers.

Ecological Risk and Prevention

On April 15, 2021, the Biosecurity Law of the People's Republic of China came into force. The law makes explicit provisions on the unauthorized introduction, release or disposal of alien species. For possible ecological risks, on the one hand, the dedicated comprehensive supervision center will strictly implement closed-loop container management. Inbound goods will be stored at designated closed places through dedicated containers.

On the other hand, Huaihua Customs will synchronize the prevention and control of major animal and plant epidemics and diseases, prevention and control of invasive alien species, animal and plant pests monitoring and other quarantine work of inbound and outbound animals and plants. An overall outlook on national security will be established, and ecological security barriers will be built. It will set up a special team to prevent and control invasive alien species and strengthen the construction of risk prevention and control systems in conjunction with multiple departments.

Furthermore, it will promote joint prevention and control between customs and enterprises. The accuracy of the dedicated comprehensive supervision center in intercepting invasive alien species can be significantly improved. At the same time, an epidemic information team will be formed to strengthen the collection of information on overseas epidemics. Action programs and operational guidelines will be formulated to enhance monitoring and early warning.

Analysis of Expected Benefits

Social Benefits

Firstly, the project is essential for Hunan Province to respond to China's Belt and Road Initiative. As an inland city, Huaihua is committed to developing the port economy, shipping logistics, e-commerce and new-generation information technology industries with its geographical location and policy support. It will create a logistics center and inland port economy demonstration area in the Wuling area and five neighboring provinces.

Besides, it will become a powerful driver of the "Three Highlands and Four New Missions" strategy of the CPC Hunan Provincial Party Committee and Provincial People's Government. The project will guide the adjustment of the industrial structure and layout of Hunan Province, promote trade circulation, and facilitate the rapid development of commerce, logistics and transportation industries. As a result, it will boost the economic prosperity of the areas affected by the project. The project is also conducive to building an inland high ground of openness and logistics in Hunan Province, injecting new vitality into the regional development.

Secondly, the project will boost regional economic growth and create jobs, promote the rapid development of business, logistics and transportation industries, raise people's income levels and enhance social stability. In addition, the dedicated comprehensive supervision center will accelerate trade facilitation, simplify trade procedures, and attract more enterprises to engage in trade activities in Huaihua, stimulating regional development and economic prosperity.

The project will also facilitate trade cooperation between Hunan and ASEAN, enrich the cultural horizons of Huaihua residents, boost cultural industries, and enhance the city's international image. Finally, the project will strengthen the supervision and management of imported and exported goods, ensure their security and quality, and improve regional security and social stability. In sum, constructing a dedicated comprehensive supervision center in Huaihua will lead to positive changes and development opportunities for local economic prosperity and social benefits.

Economic Benefits

The construction of a dedicated comprehensive supervision center brings significant economic benefits to the government. First, it will provide efficient transportation modes, improve the logistics supply chain, and enhance the reliability and flexibility of the supply chain and market competitiveness. Second, constructing a dedicated comprehensive supervision center will drive trade growth and improve economic efficiency. It will simplify trade procedures, reduce time costs and promote regional economic integration. In addition, the international inland port as a modern transportation hub will attract investors, facilitate industrial development, create jobs, and optimize the industrial structure.

Meanwhile, efficient operation will reduce logistics costs and expand market scope. Finally, constructing a dedicated comprehensive supervision center will raise local financial income and tax contribution, support public services and infrastructure development, and facilitate the sustainable development of the local economy. In conclusion, a dedicated comprehensive supervision center in Huaihua will generate substantial economic benefits for the government, contributing to economic growth and regional development.

Environmental Benefits

It will actively guide and promote the development of green logistics and the transition to a sustainable and low-carbon economy. It can introduce eco-friendly technologies and equipment, optimize the organization and flow of cargo transportation, and popularize the use of clean energy. It will actively guide and promote the development of green logistics and advance sustainable development and low-carbon economic transformation. At the same time, it is committed to improving energy utilization efficiency. It can build intelligent and efficient port facilities and equipment and introduce intelligent management systems. In this way, energy consumption can be optimized, and energy waste can be decreased.

Also, advanced loading and unloading technologies and equipment can be adopted to reduce energy consumption and improve loading and unloading efficiency. It will enhance energy utilization efficiency and lead to a sustainable development path. It also emphasizes regional environmental protection. It will actively promote the management and protection of rivers and waters and strengthen water quality monitoring and environmental management. In addition, it will rationally plan and design natural ecosystems such as wetlands and vegetation to maintain ecological balance and contribute to regional sustainability.

The dedicated comprehensive supervision center will introduce advanced environmental management concepts and technologies to enhance the environmental awareness of port operators and participants. Through exchanges and cooperation with international ports, it will share and learn from environmental protection experiences and disseminate the concept of environmental protection. Besides, cultural exchanges can strengthen the collaboration between different regions and jointly achieve the goals of environmental protection and sustainable development. Huaihua International Inland Port will play an important role in green logistics, energy efficiency, regional environmental protection, and environmental awareness, and it will contribute positively to sustainable development.

Conclusion and Recommendations

Conclusion

With its distinctive geographic location, abundant resources and labor force, Huaihua has the potential to become a logistics and trade center for the inland region to open up to the outside world. Building a dedicated comprehensive supervision center in Huaihua is considered imperative and feasible. Furthermore, it can promote the connectivity of the Wuling Mountain area and the neighboring provinces, balance domestic and foreign trade, contribute to regional economic development, and enhance China's national security and supervisory capacity.

The application of Huaihua for a dedicated comprehensive supervision center will facilitate the processing, bonded warehousing and logistics distribution of high-quality imported commodities from neighboring countries in Huaihua. Thus, it can help to create industrial clusters in Huaihua, cultivate new trade patterns, attract enterprises to invest in Huaihua, and encourage job placement. It will give new impetus to the high-quality development of the open economy of Huaihua and the Wuling Mountain area. Further, it will be more supportive to serve the development of the Wuling Mountain area, Hunan Province and Central China.

Recommendations

Firstly, strict supervision should be strengthened when goods are transported to the dedicated comprehensive supervision center. Supported by intelligent supervision and based on the successful experience of advanced customs administrations, a "goods-in-transit supervision system" should be developed. Intelligent customs locks and satellite positioning monitoring subsystems should be used to monitor the goods in real time and analyze the trajectory of the vehicles. Inspection should also be intensified to reduce transportation risk.

Secondly, the consciousness of enterprises' responsibilities should be strengthened. Large-scale transportation companies with standardized management should be selected, and agreements should be signed to prohibit unauthorized actions such as unsealing or handling goods. At the same time, freight companies should communicate closely with customs brokers and the operating units of the specified supervisory sites to keep track of the vehicles' conditions and minimize their deviation from the designated routes.

Thirdly, a perfect contingency plan should be formulated to deal with epidemic outbreaks. An epidemic prevention and control system and a contingency plan should be formulated for the sudden outbreak of significant epidemics when imported goods are in transit or arrive at the dedicated comprehensive supervision center. Once found, a considerable epidemic outbreak should be reported, and the contact personnel should be isolated and pacified. The goods should be detained and sealed to avoid panic and cross-infection. Besides, the departments concerned should handle affairs properly after the epidemic is terminated.

Fourthly, relevant personnel should be regularly organized for emergency drills to enhance their emergency response capabilities. Customs staff, dedicated comprehensive supervision center employees, enterprise assistants and drivers should participate in the emergency drills by simulating unexpected situations. As a result, the staff can familiarize themselves with the emergency response process and enhance their response capabilities.

Fifthly, post-operational supervision should be strengthened, and special inspections should be carried out to prevent loopholes. Special assessments should be conducted on critical commodities and enterprises in the dedicated comprehensive supervision center to prevent unscrupulous enterprises from making profits, disrupting the implementation of policies and jeopardizing national interests. Within three years, the Customs may still inspect the import behavior, combat illegal smuggling practices, and make dynamic adjustments depending on the enterprises' credit standing.

References

Abdulaini, S., Guo, H., Feng, H. Z. (2022). Research the constraints and countermeasures of export-oriented economic development of Alashankou Port and inter-inland towns in Xinjiang. Practice in Foreign Economic Relations and Trade, 9: 49-56.

Ahmad, R., Gul, A. (2018). China-Laos Economic Corridor: Challenges for Regional and Policy Countermeasures. Global Economics Review, 3(2): 67-75.

Amon, A. (2019). Evaluation of Chen et al.: Overexpression of Protein Complexes and Aneuploidy. Cell Systems, 9(2): 107-108. doi: 10.1016/j.cels.2019.08.004. PMID: 31465727.

An, Z. Y., He, E. Q. (2022). Forecasting regional express demand based on SARIMA time series modeling: a case study of Jiangsu Province. Logistics Sci-Tech, 45(20): 63-6670

Bask, A., Roso, V., Andersson, D., Hämäläinen, E. (2014). Development of seaport-dry port dyads: Two cases from Northern Europe. Journal of Transport Geography, 39, 85 – 95.

Beresford, A., Pettit, S., Xu, Q. et al. (2012). A study of dry port development in China. Marit Econ Logist, 14, 73 – 98. https: //doi.org/10.1057/mel.2011.17

Beyene, Z., Nadeem, S., Jaleta, M. (2024). Developing a Measurement Framework for Ethiopian Dry Port Sustainability: An Empirical Study. Sustainability, 16, 3878. 10.3390/su16093878.

Chang, Z., Notteboom, T., Lu, J. (2015). A two-phase model for dry port location with an application to the port of Dalian in China. Transportation Planning and Technology, 38(4), 442 – 464.

Chansana, N. (2022). Study on the Bilateral Trade Potential between Laos and China. Hebei University. DOI: 10.27103/d.cnki.ghebu.2022.001870.

Che, W. (2015). A Study on Logistics Performance Evaluation and Dynamics Simulation of Kunming International Inland Port. Kunming University of Science and Technology.

Chen, J. H., Guo, F., Wu, Y. (2011). One Decade of Urban Housing Reform in China Urban Housing Price Dynamics and the Role of

Migration and Urbanization,1995-2002. Habitat International, 35, 1-8.

Chen, J. H., Huang, P. (2011). Competitiveness evaluation of international inland ports based on fuzzy-ANP. Systems Engineering, 29(12): 88-95.

Chen, J. H., Huang, P. (2011). Fuzzy-ANP-based evaluation of international inland ports’ competitiveness. Systems Engineering, 29(12):88-95.

Chen, L., Wang, Y. Z. (2003). Research on TOPSIS integrated evaluation and decision method based on entropy coefficient. Control and Decision, (04):456-459.

Chen, S. H. (2022). China’ s Hunan launches China-Laos international freight train service, Last updated on July 8, 2024,

Chen, Y. (2016). Analysis of population migration and its industrial structure effect in Taiwan. Journal of Minjiang University, 37(03).

Chen, Y. X. (2021). The quarterly GDP forecast for Guizhou Province is based on the SARIMA model. Management and Administration, (08): 170-175.

Cheng, Q. Y. (2010). Structure entropy weight method to confirm the weights of evaluation indexes. Systems Engineering-Theory & Practice, 30(07):1225-1228.

Cui, B. (2023). Accelerating the Construction of International Inland Ports to Create a New High Ground for Opening Along the Border-- A Case Study on the Construction of Manzhouli International Inland Port. Northern Economy, (10): 39-41.

Cullinane, K. P. B., Wilmsmeier, G. (2011). The Contribution of the Dry Port Concept to the Extension of Port Life Cycles. In J.W. Bose ed. Handbook of Terminal Planning, Operations Research Computer Science Interfaces Series, 49, Heidelberg, Germany: Springer, 359 - 380.

D'Andrea, E., Vinals, L., Patorno, E., Franklin, J. M., Bennett, D., Largent, J. A., Moga, D. C., Yuan, H., Wen, X., Zullo, A. R., Debray, T. P. A., Sarri, G. (2021). How well can we assess the validity of non-randomized studies of medications? A systematic review of assessment tools. BMJ Open, 11(3): e043961. doi: 10.1136/bmjopen-2020-043961. PMID: 33762237; PMCID: PMC7993210.

Dong, J. F., Gao, G. B. (2016). Strategies and Cases of Inland Port Planning in China under The Belt and Road. Planners, 32 (06): 129-136.

Dong, M., Lou, F. (2023). Prediction of shared bicycle user volume based on SARIMA and ARIMA-GARCH models: a case study of Hellobike. Modern Business, 17: 46-49.

Fazi, S. (2016). Routing containers in a dry port transport system//IEEE International Conference on Industrial Engineering & Engineering Management. IEEE. DOI: 10.1109/IEEM.2016.7797905.

Feng, H. L., Yang, M., Meng, G. Z., Yang, X., Tang, D. D., Zhao, X. P., Sun, Z. X., Feng, J. H. (2023). Optimization of the Extraction Process of Pneumonia Compound Based on AHP-Entropy Weight Method and Orthogonal Design. Special Wild Economic Animal and Plant Research, 1-7.

Feng, Y. D., Yuan, H. X., Liu, Y. B. (2023). Mechanisms for improving urban energy efficiency in new urbanization. China Population, Resources and Environment, 33(05):

Fu, X. J., Liao, G. Y. (2023). Opportunities, challenges, and countermeasures for developing Hainan’ s export-oriented economy in the context of constructing a free trade port. The New Orient, 1: 13-19.

Garriga, C., Hedlund, A., Tang, Y., et al. (2023). Rural-Urban Migration and House Prices in China. Social Science Electronic Publishing.

Geng, J. J., Ye, W. H. (2018). Empirical analysis and forecasting of consumer price index trend based on SARIMA model: a case study of Sichuan Province. Science & Technology Industry Parks, 1: 9.

Gong, Y., Yao, Y. (2021). Demographic changes and the housing market. Regional Science and Urban Economics, 12, 103734. DOI:10.1016/j.regsciurbeco.2021.103734.

Gou, C. N. (2011). A Study on the Linkage between International Inland Ports and Seaports Based on Gravity Modeling. Xi’ an: Chang’ an University.

Gujar, G. C., Ng, A. K. Y., Notteboom, T. (2019). The impacts of major government initiatives on the development of dry ports: A case study of the direct port delivery scheme in India. Journal of Transport Geography, 80, 102498. https: //doi.org/10.1016/j.jtrangeo.2019.102498.

Guo, H. T. (2023). Challenges and Countermeasures of China-Laos Railway in the Belt and Road Initiative Context. Journal of China People' s Police University, 39 (09): 71-77.

Guo, S. J., Xu, Y. D., Huang, J. Y. (2023). Evaluation of Green Development Level of Agriculture Based on Entropy Weighted TOPSIS Model--A Case Study of Henan Province. Journal of Zhejiang University (Agriculture & Life Sciences), (10): 1-10.

He, B. Y. (2019). Research on the Competitiveness Evaluation and Enhancement Countermeasures of Xi' an International Inland Port from the Perspective of Integrated Field. Chang' an University.

He, M., Wen, Y. Q., Deng, L., et al. (2024). Research Advances and Development Trends of China' s Inland Ports - A Knowledge Graph Visualization Analysis Based on Cite Space. China Logistics & Purchasing, (01): 84-87. DOI: 10.16079/j.cnki.issn1671-6663.2024.01.097.

He, X. D., He, X. Y. (2023). Research on countermeasures for high-quality development of Huaihai International Inland Port. Logistics Sci-Tech, 46(7): 26-28.

Henderson, J. V. (2009). Urbanization in China: Policy Issue and Options. China Economic Research and Advisory Programmer, Center for International Development at Harvard University, Cambridge, 11.

Hou, T. T., Lv, L., Shu, X. H, Tian, R. G. (2023). Spillover Effects of Land Port Economy: A Case Study of Huaihua International Land Port in Hunan, China. Journal of Applied Business and Economics, 25(5): 20-23

http: //www.news.cn/photo/2022-01/06/c_1128238328_3.htm.

https: //www.gov.cn/xinwen/2019-08/15/content_5421375.htm.

Hunan Provincial People' s Government. (2022). Implementation Plan on Deepening Integration into the "Belt and Road" and Supporting the Development of Huaihua International Inland Port. Changsha, China: Issued by the General Office of Hunan Provincial People' s Government.

Hunan Social Science Foundation Project: Research on Hunan' s Connection and Co-construction of the New International Land-Sea Trade Corridor in Western China, Grant No.: 23YBX004

Ilman, H. I., Chumaidiyah, E., Zulbetti, R. (2021). Designing Strategy of Indonesia Port Car Terminal Based on Analysis of Profitability Ratio Before And After the IPO. International Journal of Mechanical Engineering Technologies and Applications, 2(1), 33-39.

Jager, P., Schmidt, T. (2017). Demographic Change and House Prices: Headwind or Tailwind. Economics Letters, 160, 82-85.

Jeevan, J., Chen, S. L., Cahoon, S. (2019). The impact of dry port operations on container seaports competitiveness. Maritime Policy & Management, 46(1), 4 – 23.

Jeevan, J., Maskey, R., Chen, S. L., Sharma, R., Mohd Zaideen, I. M. (2022). A Comparative Analysis of Dry Port Operations in Coastal and Landlocked Countries. Transactions on Maritime Science, 11, 1-24. 10.7225/toms.v11.n02.w02.

Jeevan, J., Othman, R,, Harun, M., Selvaduray, M., Mohd Zain, R. (2023). Incorporation of Dry Ports into the National Transport Policy: A Proposal for International Trade Acceleration. Transactions on Maritime Science, 12. 10.7225/toms.v12.n01.w01.

Jia, G. L. (2017). Research on the Coordinated Logistics Operation between Xi' an International Inland Port and Air Port. Co-operative Economy & Science, 2: 9-11.

Jiang, J. L. (2023). Study on Competitiveness Evaluation and Enhancement Strategies of Qingdao International Inland Port. Shandong University of Finance and Economics.

Jiang, M. Y. (2022). Research on Competitiveness Evaluation and Countermeasures of Gansu (Lanzhou) International Inland Port. Lanzhou Jiaotong University.

Jiang, R., Guo, P. (2019). Building a Free Trade Inland Port in Xi' an under The Belt and Road. Special Zone Economy, (05): 69-72.

Lamsali, H., Salleh, M., Lazim, H., Osman, W., Iteng, R., Tio, M., Razak, M., Ja'afar, H. (2023). Developing a Sustainable Framework For Cross Border Inland Port. Compendium by PaperASIA, 39, 21-33. 10.59953/cpa.v39i6(b).30.

Lang, Y., Yan, J. T., Sun, Q., et al. (2022). Housing costs, population mobility and industrial clusters. Statistics & Decision, 38(22):

Langen, P. W. D. (2007). Port Competition and Selection in Contestable Hinterlands: the Case of Austria. European Journal of Transport and Infrastructure, 7(1), 1-14.

Li, H. Y. (2020). Forecast of consumer price index in Henan Province. Modern Business Trade Industry, 41(25): 97-98.

Li, J., Zhong, P., Lv, J. (2020). Sustainable development of an inland port economy based on system dynamics. Systems Engineering, 38(05):

Li, K. H. (1985). How to understand the developing economy of the Shenzhen Special Administrative

Li, K. H. (1985). Several issues in the transformation of Shenzhen’ s economy into an export-oriented economy. South China Journal of Economics, 6: 24-30.

Li, K. Y. (2012). Research on Strategic Planning of Kunming International Inland Port. Kunming University of Science and Technology.

Li, W. J., Bai, X. W., Yang, D., Hou, Y. (2023). Maritime connectivity, transport infrastructure expansion and economic growth: A global perspective. Transportation Research Part A: Policy and Practice, Elsevier, 170(C).

Li, Y. (2021). The New International Land-Sea Trade Corridor in Western China: A Discussion on the Construction of Strategic Gateway Cities--Taking Huaihua as an Example. China-Arab States Science and Technology Forum, (11): 8-10.

Li, Y. H., Dong, Q. L., Sun, S. W. (2015). Dry Port Development in China: Current Status and Future Strategic Directions. Journal of Coastal Research, (73 (10073): 641 – 646.

Lian, F. (2023). Huaihua International Inland Port is developing into a new growth pole in Hunan. Xinxiang Review, 3, 40

Liang, W. S. (1985). On the export-oriented economy of the special administrative region. Special Zone Economy, 1: 12-18.

Liang, Y. M. (2023). Classification of overcapacity and implications for governance. Journal of University of Science and Technology Beijing (Social Sciences Edition), 39(06).

Lin, Z. F., Lin, S. J., Zhang, Z. Q. (2020). Analysis of the Development Status Quo, Problems and Suggestions of Organic Tea Industry in Guzhang County. China Southern Agricultural Machinery, 51(15): 20-21.

Liu, J. (2023). Study the driving effect of the inland port economy on the financing of local state-owned enterprises: a case study of Huaihua

International Inland Port in Hunan Province. Trade Fair Economy, 12: 153-156.

Liu, J. (2023). The Driving Effect of Inland Port Economy on the Financing of Local State-owned Enterprises--A Case Study of Huaihua International Inland Port in Hunan Province. Trade Fair Economy, (12): 153-156. DOI: 10.19995/j.cnki.CN10-1617/F7.2023.12.153.

Liu, M., Niu, X. (2023). The impact of capital market opening on earnings management: Empirical evidence based on Land– Port Connection. Finance Research Letters, 55, 103864.

Liu, P. L., Qian, T., Huang, X. H., et al. (2021). Connotation, realization path and measurement method of commonwealth. Management World, 37(08):

Liu, Q., Hu, H. L. (2023). Modernization of large populations: Connotations, challenges and responses. Journal of China West Normal University (Philosophy & Social Sciences), 10.

Liu, X. B., Li, B. F., Yang, B., Zhang, Z. X., Guo, Y. (2021). Essentials of international inland port planning under the new economic development paradigm of "dual-circulation." Port and Waterway Engineering, (10):37-43.

Liu, Y. F., Lee, C. B., Qi, G. Q., Yuen, K. F., Su, M. (2021). Relationship Between Dry Ports and Regional Economy: Evidence from Yangtze River Economic Belt. The Journal of Asian Finance, Economics and Business, 8(5): 345 - 354. https: //doi.org/10.13106/JAFEB.2021.VOL8.NO5.0345

Liu, Y., Gao, H., Cai, J., et al. (2022). Urbanization path, housing price and inland finance: International experience and China's facts. Inland Use Policy.

Lu, H. (2022). Current situation of Xiangyang's export-oriented economic development and countermeasures analysis. Journal of Xiangyang Vocational and Technical Collage, 21(4): 11-16.

Lu, J.B., Lan, J., The Research Group of The People's Bank of China Honghe Central Sub-branch. (2023). The "Steel Camel Corps" along "The Belt and Road" --A Study on the Impact of the Opening of the China-Laos Railway on China's Economic Development. Times Finance, (07): 12-19.

Lu, Y.(ed.), Du, B. (annotated). (2020). The Classic of Tea: Chapter One Origin. Beijing: Zhonghua Book Company.

Lv, N. (2020). Optimization of planning methods for international inland ports based on spatial genetic theory. Chang' an University.

Miraj, P., Berawi, M. A., Zagloel, T. Y., Sari, M., Saroji, G. (2021). Research trend of dry port studies: a two-decade systematic review. Maritime Policy & Management, 48(4), 563 - 582.

Monios, J., Wilmsmeier, G. (2013). The role of intermodal transport in port regionalization. Transport Policy, 30 (2013): 161-172.

Mou, Y. F. (2016). A review of research on the relationship between employed population and industrial development in the context of industrial transformation. Population & Economics, 3.

Munford, C. (1980). Buenos Aires-congestion and the Dry Port Solution. Cargo Systems International: The Journal of ICHCA, 7(10): 26-27.

Ng, A. K. Y., Cetin, I. B. (2012). Locational Characteristics of Dry Ports in Developing Economies: Some Lessons from Northern India. Regional Studies, 46(6): 757 - 773. https: //doi.org/10.1080/00343404.2010.532117

Ng, A. K. Y., Ducruet, C., Jacobs, W., Monios, J., Notteboom, T., Rodrigue, J., …Wilmsmeier, G. (2014). Port geography at the crossroads with human geography: between flows and spaces. Journal of Transport Geography, 41, 84-96. https: //doi.org/10.1016/j.jtrangeo.2014.08.012

Ng, A. K. Y., Padilha, F., Pallis, A. A. (2013). Institutions, bureaucratic and logistical roles of dry ports: the Brazilian experiences. Journal of Transport Geography, 27, 46-55. https: //doi.org/10.1016/j.jtrangeo.2012.05.003.

Ng, A. K. Y., Tongzon, J. L. (2010). The Transportation Sector of India' s Economy: Dry Ports as Catalysts for Regional Development. Eurasian Geography and Economics, 51(5): 669 - 682. https: //doi.org/10.2747/1539-7216.51.5.669

Nguyen, C.L., Notteboom, T. (2016), Dry Ports As Extensions of Maritime Deep-Sea Ports: A Case Study of Vietnam. Journal of International Logistics and Trade, 14 (1): 65-88. https: //doi.org/10.24006/jilt.2016.14.1.65

Nguyen, L.C., Thai, V.V., Nguyen, D.M., Tran, M.D. (2021). Evaluating the Role of Dry Ports in the Port-hinterland Settings: Conceptual

Framework and the Case of Vietnam. Journal of Transport Geography, 37(4): 307-320.

Niemann, J., Schloesser, M., Fussenecker, C., et al. (2016). A Marketing Strategy for a Dry Port in Jakarta/ Indonesia as an Integral Part to Solve Local Logistic Bottlenecks//International Conference on Competitive Manufacturing.

Olk, D. C., Bloom, P. R., Perdue, E. M., McKnight, D. M., Chen, Y., Farenhorst, A., Senesi, N., Chin, Y. P., Schmitt-Kopplin, P., Hertkorn, N. and Harir, M. (2019). Environmental and Agricultural Relevance of Humic Fractions Extracted by Alkali from Soils and Natural Waters. J. Environ. Qual., 48: 217-232. https: //doi.org/10.2134/jeq2019.02.0041

Osman, W., Lamsali, H., Lazim, H., Salleh, M., Iteng, R., Yiaw, M. (2024). Opportunities and Challenges of Malaysia Cross Border Inland Port. Journal of Advanced Research in Business and Management Studies, 34. 35-41. 10.37934/arbms.34.1.3541.

Pablo, J. C., Ivan, S., Violeta, R., et al. (2023). Assessing the eco-efficiency benefits of empty container repositioning strategies via dry ports. Transportation Research Part D, 120. DOI: 10.1016/J.TRD.2023.103778

Pan, W. Q. (2012). Regional linkages and spatial spillovers of economic growth in China. Economic Research Journal, 1: 54-65

Per, W., Lokesh, K., Violeta, R. (2023). Efficiency effects of information on operational disruption management in port inter-inland freight transport: simulation of a Swedish dry port case. International Journal of Logistics Research and Applications, 26(5): 524-547.

Polat, M., ÇevrİmlI, M. B., Mat, B., Akin, A. C., Arikan, M. S., Tekİ ndal, M. A. (2023). Economic analysis of beekeeping enterprises producing chestnut honey in the Black Sea region in Türkiye. Cogent Food & Agriculture, 9(1): 1-13. DOI: 10.1080/23311932.2023.2237279

Pratiwi, F. I. (2020). China Belt and Road Initiatives (BRI) in Indonesia' s Socio-Economic Security Challenges: A Policy Recommendation.

Pu, Y. X. (2021). Exploring the Development of the Tea Culture Industry in Western Hunan. South China Agriculture, 15(35): 151-153.

Ran, H. H. (2022). Study on the impact of demographic change on housing demand in Chongqing. Shanxi University of Finance and Economics.

Region. Special Zone Economy, 1: 9-12.

Rodrigue, J. P., Debrie, J., Fremont, A., et al. (2010). Functions and actors of inland ports: European and North American dynamics. Journal of Transport Geography, 18(4):519-529.

Roso, V. (2008). Factors influencing implementation of a dry port. International Journal of Physical Distribution & Logistics Management, 38 (10): 782-798.

Roso, V., Lumsden, K. (2010). A review of dry ports. Maritime Economics & Logistics, 12 (2): 196-213.

Roso, V., Woxenius, J., Lumsden, K. (2009). The Dry Port Concept: Connecting Container Sea Ports with the Hinterland. Journal of Transport Geography, 17(5): 338-345.

Seguí, X., Puig, M., Quintieri, E. et al. (2016). New Environmental Performance Baseline for Inland Ports: A European Inland Port Sector Benchmark. Environmental Science & Policy, 58: 29-40.

Shu, H. F., Hu, J. W., Li, Y. H. (2021). Research on Countermeasures for Building "Pearl of Southwest China" in Huaihua-- A Case Study of Logistics Platform Construction of the New International Land-Sea Trade Corridor in Western China. Marketing Circles, (05): 63-64.

Shu, Y. T. (2022). Analysis of the development level of the export-oriented economy in Hubei Province. Economic Research Guide, 14: 24-27+31.

Sinan, M. Y. (2023). Quantifying the Operational Benefits of Dry Port Integrated Cooperation in Port Clusters: A Micro-simulation Study. Sustainability, 15(6): 4990-4990.

Sitthikone, S. (2023). A Study on the Trade Potential between China and Laos under The Belt and Road. Qingdao University of Science and Technology. DOI: 10.27264/d.cnki.gqdhc.2023.001235.

Song, X. L., Li, M. L., Zhan, Q. H., Lin, D. M., Yang, Y. M., Li, H. (2022). Demand forecasting of electric power materials based on the combination of SARIMA and ANFIS methods. Journal of Machine Design, 39(06): 66-72.

Sounvilevth, K. N. V. (2010). Lao Position and Role in CAFTA Cooperation. Crossroads: Southeast Asian Studies, (12): 39-43.

Sun, Q. R., Wu, Z. Y., Ma, X. H. (2022). Evaluation for the High-quality Development of Grain Industry in China: Based on the Standard

Deviation Revised G1 Method. Journal of Hebei Normal University for Nationalities, 42(04):96-104.

Sun, W. N., Yang, J., Yang, Y. Y., Liu, T. .T, Bai, X. D. (2018). Analysis and forecasting of China' s GDP based on the SARIMA model. China Collective Economy, (36): 78-80.

Syahchari, D. H., Kuncoro, E. A., Saroso, H., et al. (2021). Effect of Supply Chain Collaboration and Service Stakeholder Commitment on Dry Port Firm Performance//ICCMB 2021: 2021 The 4th International Conference on Computers in Management and Business. DOI: 10.1145/3450588.3450602.

Syahchari, D. H., Sudrajat, D., Saroso, H., Dwidienawati, D. (2021). Impact Of Supplier Innovation, Information Technology On Supply Chain Resilience In Dry Port. 2021 International Conference on Electrical, Computer and Energy Technologies (ICECET), Cape Town, South Africa, 1-5, doi: 10.1109/ICECET52533.2021.9698768.

Tang, S. Y., Zhang, J. B., Du, L. N. (2020). Research on Competitiveness Evaluation of Major Inland Ports in China. IOP Conference Series: Earth and Environmental Science, 526(1).

Teng, T. W., Chen, D. H., Hu, S. L. (2021). A study on housing prices, population size and innovation capacity of the Yangtze River Delta region cities. Journal of Tongji University (Social Science Section), 32(05).

The Central Committee of the Communist Party of China and the State Council. (2021). Working Guidance for Carbon Dioxide Peaking and Carbon Neutrality in Full and Faithful Implementation of the New Development Philosophy (September 22, 2021), Last updated on July 8, 2024: https: //www.mofcom.gov.cn/zcfb/zgdwjjmywg/art/2021/art_dee4aa25a54049d1bd69b6cfff7d195d.html.

The National Development and Reform Commission. (2019). Notice by the National Development and Reform Commission of Issuing the Framework Plan for New Land and Marine Routes for Western Regions (No. 1333 [2019] of the National Development and Reform Commission), Last updated on July 8, 2024,

Thenuwara, W., Siriwardana, M., Hoang, N. (2019). Will Population Ageing Cause a House Price Meltdown in Australia? The Journal of Developing Areas, 53(2):63-77.

Tian, S. D., Huang, Y. F., Zhang, C. (2021). Human capital and housing prices in urbanization. Journal of Technical Economics & Management, 7.

Udall, A. (1980). Urbanization and Rural Labor Supply: A Historical of Bogota, Colombia Since 1920. Studies in Comparative International Development, 15(3): 70-83.

Walter C. K., Poist P. F. (2003). Desired Attributes of An Inland Port-shipper vs. Carrier Perspectives. Transportation Journal, 42(5): 42-55.

Wang, C. R., Pang, X. Y. (2022).A study on the relationship between population aging, housing price volatility and banking stability. Journal of Hebei University of Economics and Trade, 43(4):23-33.

Wang, F. (2003). Comparison and Application of Principal Component Analysis & Factor Analysis. Statistical Education, (05):14-17.

Wang, G. (2009). Exploration of the construction and development models of inland dry ports. Port Economy, 3.

Wang, H. Z. (2018). Optimization of Logistics Node Layout of Shaanxi International Inland Ports under Belt and Road Initiative. Logistics Technology, 9: 66-69.

Wang, N. (2023). Mayang Miao Autonomous County, Huaihua City, Hunan Province: An Orange Adds Popularity to a City. China City News, 010.

Wang, Q., Guan, H. S. (2018). Empirical analysis of SARIMA model for time series of China’ s total imports and exports. Economy Forum, 12: 78-83.

Wang, S. R. (1985). Discussion on the export-oriented economy of the Shenzhen Special Administrative Region. Shenzhen University Journal (Humanities & Social Sciences), 4: 4-13.

Wang, X. L., Zhu, G. (2022). Research on demand forecasting of Chinese herbal medicine in Central Asia based on the SARIMA model. Asia-Pacific Traditional Medicine, 18(12): 6-10

Wang, Y. Q. (2022). On the Coupling and Coordinated Development of Logistics and Hinterland Economy in Xi’ an International Inland Port. Railway Purchase and Logistics, 17(12): 50-53.

Wei, X. X. (2017). Research on the Evaluation of the Development Level and Countermeasures of Xi’ an International Inland Port. Xi’ an University of Architecture and Technology.

Wickramasinghe, N. D., Samarutilake, N., Wettasinghe, M. C., et al. Public health programs to promote mental health in young people: a systematic integrative review protocol. BMJ Open. 10: e037241. doi: 10.1136/ bmjopen-2020-037241

Wiegmans, B., Witte, P., Spit, T. (2015). Characteristics of European inland ports: A statistical analysis of inland waterway port development in Dutch municipalities. Transportation Research Part A: Policy and Practice, Elsevier, 78(C): 566-577.

Witte, P., Wiegmans, B., Braun, C., et al. (2016). Weakest link or strongest node? Comparing governance strategies for inland ports in transnational European corridors. Research in Transportation Business Management, 19.

Witte, P., Wiegmans, B., Ng, A. K. (2019). A critical review on the evolution and development of inland port research. Journal of Transport Geography, 74 (2019): 53-61.

Witte, P., Wiegmans, B., van Oort, F., Spit, T. (2014). Governing inland ports: a multi-dimensional approach to addressing inland port - city challenges in European transport corridors. Journal of Transport Geography, Elsevier, 36(C): 42-52.

Wrobel, R. M. (2019). Chinese Geopolitics in Southeast Asia: A New Pattern of Economic Power within ASEAN. Asiatische Studien Études Asiatiques, 73(1): 149-191. DOI: 10.1515/asia-2017-0049.

Wu, C. Y. (2012). "Guzhang Maojian Tea" Won the First "China Famous Trademark" for Local Public Brands in China's Tea Sector. Shanghai Tea, 1: 42-43.

Wu, F. X. (2021). Comparison of export-oriented economic models of Shenzhen and Shanghai and their implications. People's Tribune, 27: 72-75.

Wu, K. Z. (2023). Living and working in peace: A study on the factors influencing the willingness of young talented immigrants to settle in large cities. Journal of East China Normal University (Humanities and Social Sciences), 55(04).

Wu, P. Y., Wu, S. Y. (2021). Comparative analysis of the economic effects of government consumption vouchers: empirical evidence based on SARIMA model. China Price, 11: 6-8.

Wu, X. W. (2020). Study on the Impact of China-Europe Freight Trains on Trade Costs between China and the Countries Along the Belt and Road. Beijing Forestry University. DOI: 10.26949/d.cnki.gblyu.2020.000703.

Xi, P., Yan, G. R., Cao, H. (2001). Building an international port in western China: the proposal of “Xi’ an Inland Port.” Tangdu Journal, 4: 12-14.

Xiang, G. F. (1992). Guzhang Maojian Tea. China’ s Ethnic Groups, 2: 41.

Xiao, S. D., Hou, T. T., Shu, X. H., Tian, R. G. (2023). Huaihua International Inland Port Development and Its Impact on Local Residents’ Housing Demand. Journal of Knowledge Management and Practice, 23(2): 31

Xiao, S. D., Tian, G. (2023). Migrant Worker’ Housing Effects on Their Urban Adaptation: An Empirical Case Study of the Wuling Mountains Area in China. Journal of Applied Business and Economics, 25(1).

Yan, R. (2021). Research Enhancing the Comprehensive Competitiveness of International Inland Ports Based on Cloud Modeling. Chang’ an University.

Yang, F., Dai, M. H., Hong, Y., et al. (2023). Exploration of the port industry in Huaihua. Cooperative Economy & Science, (19): 26-28. DOI: 10.13665/j.cnki.hzjjykj.2023.19.035.

Yang, H. T., Deng, Y. J. (2023). The China-Laos Railway Brings New Dynamics to China-Laos Economic and Trade Cooperation. Foreign Investment in China, (18): 82-84.

Yang, J. C., Zhao, C. (2019). Survey on K-Means Clustering Algorithm. Computer Engineering and Applications, 55 (23): 7-14+63.

Yang, Y., Li, L. S. (2019). Evaluation of coordination between logistics capacity and socio-economic development of international inland port cities: a case study of Kunming City. Journal of Beijing Jiaotong University(Social Sciences Edition), 18(3): 129-137.

Yao, Y. (2021). Study on the impact of population aging and housing affordability on housing demand. Chongqing University.

Yao, Y. L., Kou, J., Zhang, M. H. (2023). Risk assessment of one-ventilation and three-prevention in coal mine based on game theory combination weighting-TOPSIS. Mining Safety & Environmental Protection, 1-10.

Yi, X. D. (2023). GRA-TOPSIS Evaluation Model of Voltage Sag Risk Based on Game Theory Weighting. Electrical & Energy Management Technology, (08): 47-52.

Zhang, M. (2023). The Huaihua International Inland Port is across the mountains and the waters. Xinxiang Review, 13: 57.

Zhang, Q. H. (2024). Impact of the Opening of the China-Laos Railway on the Economic Development along the Border of Yunnan Province: A Study on the Development of the Mohan-Boten Economic Cooperation Zone. China Journal of Commerce, (02): 84-87. DOI: 10.19699/j.cnki.issn2096-0298.2024.02.084.

Zhang, S. (2023). The China-Laos Railway from the Perspective of Multi-Community Construction. Journal of World Peoples Studies, (04): 115-124.

Zhang, T. G. (2021). Economic and trade cooperation between China and Laos. Market Modernization, (12): 64-66. DOI: 10.14013/j.cnki.scxdh.2021.12.024.

Zhang, X. L. (2012). Does China’ s transportation infrastructure boost regional economic growth? - An overview of the spatial spillover effects of transportation infrastructure. Social Sciences in China, 3: 60-77+206

Zhang, X. S., Wang, T. L., Xue, Y. T. (2015). Further, the International Hub Function of Xi’ an is being performed as an Inland Port. Urban Development Studies, 22(11): 120-124.

Zhang, X., Luo, Z. H., Jiang, J. (2021). A comparative study of models for predicting weather derivatives and temperature. Computer Science, 48(S1): 169-177.

Zhang, Y. Y. (1985). Review of the export-oriented economy: some strategic issues on the economic development of the coastal areas of Guangdong. South China Journal of Economics, 6: 67-73.

Zhang, Y., Ding, Y. W., Zhu, M. J. (2021). Study on the Impact of China-Laos Railway Construction on the Regional Economy Along the Route. China Storage & Transport, (12): 108-109. DOI: 10.16301/j.cnki.cn12-1204/f.2021.12.056.

Zhao, W. X. (2022). The Impact of Transformation of Old and New Dynamic Forces on the Export-oriented Economy of Shandong Province. Jinan: Shandong University of Finance and Economics.

Zheng, X. G., Yang, J., Qian, T. T., Xu, Y. Y. (2020). SARIMA-based analysis and prediction of vegetable prices in Shanghai in the past ten years. Acta Agriculturae Shanghai, 36(06): 138-141.

Zhou, J. J., Wang, Y. J., Zhang, M. (2021). Research on the spatial spillover effects of economic accumulation, population mobility and residential prices. The Theory and Practice of Finance and Economics, 42(01).

Zhou, Y., Gan, L. J., Jin, L. (2020). Forecasting daily express business size based on the SARIMA sliding window model in R language. Logistics Technology, 39(10): 103-108.

Zhu, C. Z., Dong, Q. L. (2009). Research and discussion on the basic theory of international inland ports. Logistics Technology, 28(1): 17-19.

Zhu, Z. C., Zhang, Z. (2019). Modified G2 Weighting Method and Demonstration Based on Coefficient of Variation. Statistics & Decision, 35(02): 70-74.

Index

D

E

F

G

H

I

J

K

L

M

N

O

P

R

S

T

U

V

W

Afterword

Huaihua International Land Port is a vital hub standing on the land of Western Hunan, showing a unique and crucial position. It is a place full of infinite possibilities and vitality and a key node where various resources and elements converge, interact and merge. It has a strong capacity for logistics carrying and transfer, just like a vast and precise network that closely connects different regions and realizes the efficient distribution and circulation of goods. Its complete facilities and advanced operation mode complement each other, shaping a vibrant and efficient logistics ecological environment.

The development of the land port not only drives the activity and prosperity of trade but also provides a strong support and driving force for the development of the regional economy. It is like a power core, continuously injecting development momentum into the surrounding and even more expansive areas. It is expected that this monograph can become an essential reference for understanding and researching Huaihua International Land Port, promoting it to continue to release great potential in the future and make more outstanding contributions to the development of Huaihua and even a wider area.

Dr. Shu is a professor at the College of Business of Huaihua University. He is a "121" project talent, a leading disciplinarian of Hunan Province, a young backbone teacher of Hunan Province, a visiting scholar of Andrews King University (2013.7-8) and Bemidji State University (2017.8-2018.8) in the United States. He has presided over one research project funded by the National Social Science Foundation and three research projects funded by the government of Hunan Province.

Hou Tengteng is a faculty member at the College of Business of Huaihua University. He graduated from Jinan University with a master's degree. His research interests include economic statistics and cross-border trade. He has carried out empirical research projects in economic statistics and cross-border trade and has published several research papers in academic journals.

Tian Guang is a specially appointed professor at the School of Business, Huaihua University in China. He also serves as the Dean of the Advanced Research Institute for Applied Anthropology at Jishou University and the Doctoral Supervisor at Hebei University. His research interests are regional development, cross-cultural marketing management, and economic anthropology. He received his Ph.D. in social anthropology from York University in 1995 and an MBA from Wilfried Laurier University in 1999.

Made in United States
Orlando, FL
04 November 2026

90209479R00138

FSC
www.fsc.org
MIX
Papier | Fördert gute Waldnutzung
FSC® C083411

Kolibri 360 GmbH
Ferdinand-Jühlke-Straße 7
99095 Erfurt, Deutschland
produktsicherheit@kolibri360.de